Using Microsoft® FrontPage™ 98

que®

Using
Microsoft® FrontPage™ 98

que®

Steve Banick and
Ryan Sutter

Using Microsoft® FrontPage™ 98

Copyright© 1998 by Que® Corporation.

All rights reserved. Printed in the United States of America. No part of this book may be used or reproduced in any form or by any means, or stored in a database or retrieval system, without prior written permission of the publisher except in the case of brief quotations embodied in critical articles and reviews. Making copies of any part of this book for any purpose other than your own personal use is a violation of United States copyright laws. For information, address Que Corporation, 201 W. 103rd Street, Indianapolis, IN, 46290. You may reach Que's direct sales line by calling 1-800-428-5331.

Library of Congress Catalog No.: 97-69812

ISBN: 0-7897-1497-3

This book is sold *as is*, without warranty of any kind, either express or implied, respecting the contents of this book, including but not limited to implied warranties for the book's quality, performance, merchantability, or fitness for any particular purpose. Neither Que Corporation nor its dealers or distributors shall be liable to the purchaser or any other person or entity with respect to any liability, loss, or damage caused or alleged to have been caused directly or indirectly by this book.

00 99 98   6 5 4 3 2

Interpretation of the printing code: the rightmost double-digit number is the year of the book's printing; the rightmost single-digit number, the number of the book's printing. For example, a printing code of 98-1 shows that the first printing of the book occurred in 1998.

All terms mentioned in this book that are known to be trademarks or service marks have been appropriately capitalized. Que cannot attest to the accuracy of this information. Use of a term in this book should not be regarded as affecting the validity of any trademark or service mark.

Screen reproductions in this book were created using Collage Plus from Inner Media, Inc., Hollis, NH.

Contents at a Glance

I Getting Started with FrontPage 98

1 An Introduction to FrontPage 98   11
2 Installation and Setup   23
3 A Guided Tour to the FrontPage Components   37

II The FrontPage 98 Primer

4 Creating Your First Web Site   55
5 Working with the FrontPage Editor   67
6 Organizing Your First Web Site   81

III Creating Pages with the FrontPage Editor

7 Editor Basics   101
8 Enhancing Pages with Graphics and Multimedia   123
9 Activating Your Pages with Java, ActiveX Scripting, and More   147
10 Using Templates, FrontPage Components, and Wizards to Build Your Pages   165

IV Managing Your Web with the FrontPage Explorer

11 Basic Operations of FrontPage Explorer   187
12 Managing Your Web Site   205
13 Advanced Web Site Creation   223

V Creating and Adapting Graphics with Image Explorer

14 Getting Started with Image Composer   243
15 Working with Sprites   261
16 Using Effects for Maximum Impact   279
17 Tailoring Your Images for FrontPage Documents   295

VI Appendix

A FrontPage and Other Web Servers   311

Index   319

Table of Contents

Introduction 1

What Is FrontPage? 2

The Scope of This Book 2

Who Should Be Reading This Book? 3

How to Use This Book 4
    Part I—Getting Started with FrontPage 98 4
    Part II—The FrontPage 98 Primer 4
    Part III—Creating Pages with the FrontPage Editor 4
    Part IV—Managing Your Web with the FrontPage Explorer 4
    Part V—Creating and Adapting Graphics with Image Composer 4
    Part VI—Appendix 5

Information That's Easy to Understand 5
    Chapter Roadmaps 5
    Tips, Notes, Cautions, 5
    Keyboard Conventions 6
    Mouse Conventions 6
    Typeface Conventions 7
    On the Web References 7

Our Thanks to You 7

I Getting Started with FrontPage 98

1 An Introduction to FrontPage 98 11

Learning FrontPage Concepts and Terminology 12

Learning the Basics of Web Pages, Web Sites, and Web Servers 12

Using FrontPage Web Sites 13

Applying FrontPage Server Extensions 14

Familiarizing Yourself with FrontPage Documents 14

Exploring the Contents of the FrontPage 98 Package 15

Understanding The FrontPage Explorer 15

Using the FrontPage Editor 16

Bonus Utilities 18

Overview of Microsoft Image Composer 18

Overview of Microsoft Personal Web Server 19

Before You Start 20

2 Installation and Setup 23

Installing FrontPage 98 24

Choosing What to Install 24

Installing Microsoft Image Composer 27

Connecting with Your Web Server 29

Using Personal Web Server 29
    Administering Your WWW Service 30
    Using FrontPage Server Extensions 34

3 A Guided Tour to the FrontPage Components 37

Introducing the FrontPage Explorer 38
    What Does the FrontPage Explorer Look Like? 39
    When Will I Use the FrontPage Explorer? 39

Introducing the FrontPage Editor 40
    What Does the FrontPage Editor Look Like? 42
    When Will I Use the FrontPage Editor? 44

Introducing the Personal Web Server 44
    What Does the Personal Web Server Look Like? 45

When Will I Use the Personal Web Server? 45

Introducing Image Composer 46
What Does Image Composer Look Like? 47
When Will I Use Image Composer? 49

The Web Publishing Wizard 49
What Does the Web Publishing Wizard Look Like? 50
When Will I Use the Web Publishing Wizard? 51

II The FrontPage 98 Primer

4 Creating Your First Web Site 55

Determining the Content of Your Site 56
Rule #1: Content Is King 56
Rule #2: Style Is Queen 57
Rule #3: Change or Die 58

Picking an Effective Layout 59

Importing an Existing Web Site 59

Starting with Wizards or Templates 62

Building Your Site from Scratch 66

5 Working with the FrontPage Editor 67

Creating a New Page 68
Adding a Blank Page From Within the Explorer 68
Creating an Empty Page 69
Using a Template or Wizard 69

Working with an Existing Page 70

Adding and Editing Basic Text 71
Cutting and Deleting Text 71

Using Lists 72

Using Tables 73

Adding Hyperlinks 74

Inserting Images 76

Previewing and Saving 77

6 Organizing Your First Web Site 81

Loading the Web Into the Explorer 82

Working with FrontPage Views 83
Folders View 83
All Files View 85
Navigation View 86
Hyperlinks View 86

Adding Pages 89

Deleting Pages 91

Reorganizing Your Site's Structure 92

Checking Links and Spelling 93
Verifying and Recalculating Hyperlinks 94
Checking Spelling 95

Working with the Task List 96

Publishing Your Site to the Internet 97

III Creating Pages with the FrontPage Editor

7 Editor Basics 101

Page Design Considerations 102

Basic Text and Page Layout 105
Adding a Title to Your Page 105
Using the Format Menu to Add Headings 106
Adding Paragraphs of Normal Text 108
Enlarging and Shrinking Normal Text 110
Justification 111
Using Logical Styles 111
Horizontal Rules 112

Working with Tables 113
Adjusting Table Properties 114
Cell Properties 116

Creating Lists   117

Working with Fonts   119

Changing Backgrounds and Text Color   120

8 Enhancing Pages with Graphics and Multimedia   123

Using Images on Your Web Pages   124
   Putting an Image onto a Page   124
   Deleting an Image   125
   Inserting an Image from Your Hard Drive   125
   Getting Images from the Internet   126
   Adding a Clip Art Image   127
   Scanning an Image   127
   Modifying an Image   127
   Positioning Text Around an Image   129
   Spacing Between Text and Image   130
   Adjusting Image Size from the Appearance Sheet   130
   Adding Borders to an Image   132
   Providing Alternative Text   132
   Adding a Background Image Using a File   132
   Using Watermarked Background Images   133
   Using Images As Hyperlinks   133
   Making Navigational Controls   134
   Using Thumbnails   134

Working with JPG, GIF, and PNG Image Files   135
   Making the Most of Image File Formats   137
   Converting Image File Formats   137
   Using Interlaced GIFs for Speed   138
   Using Low Res for Speed   138
   Making Transparent Images   138

Setting Up Imagemaps   140
   Creating an Imagemap   140
   Deleting a Hotspot   142

Adding Sound to Your Page   142

Working with MIDI, RealAudio, WAV, and AU sound Files   142
   MIDI Files   142
   WAV Files   143
   AU Files   143
   RealAudio   143
   Adding Background Music   143
   Linking to Audio Files   144

Adding Video to Your Site   144

Working with AVI and RealVideo Files   144

Other Video Formats   145

9 Activating Your Pages with Java, ActiveX, Scripting and More   147

Scripting Your Pages   148
   Using JavaScript   149
   Learning More About JavaScript   152
   Using VBScript   152
   What Scripting Language Should You Use?   154
   Using FrontPage Editor's Script Wizard   154

Using Plug-Ins and ActiveX   155
   Inserting a Plug-In   156
   Inserting ActiveX Controls   157

Adding Java Applets   161
   Why Use Java?   161

Going 3-D: Adding VRML Worlds   163

10 Using Templates, FrontPage Components, and Wizards to Build Your Web Pages   165

Using the FrontPage Templates   166
   Frames Templates   168
   Creating Your Own Page Templates   172

Using the FrontPage Wizards   172
   The Discussion Web Wizard   172
   The Form Page Wizard   174

Working with FrontPage Components   176
   The Timestamp Component   177
   The Table of Contents Component   178

The Navigation Bar Component   179
The Comment Component   179
The Confirmation Field Component   180
The Hit Counter Component   180
The Include Page Component   181
The Insert HTML Component   181
The Page Banner Component   181
The Scheduled Image and Scheduled Include Page Components   182
The Substitution Component   183

IV Managing Your Web with the FrontPage Explorer

11 Basic Operations of FrontPage Explorer   187

Loading a Web Site   188

Publishing a Web Site   190

Using the View Panel   191

Using the Browser Panel   200

Reconfiguring Explorer   201

12 Managing Your Web Site   205

Using Tasks   206

Spell Checking   209

Checking Hyperlinks   213

Checking Internal Hyperlinks with Hyperlink View   213

Checking External Hyperlinks with Hyperlink Status View   215

Managing Structure with Navigation View   218

Creating Shared Borders   219

13 Advanced Web Site Creation   223

Using Cascading Style Sheets   224

Creating Styles   225

Linking to an External Style Sheet   229

Using Your Defined Styles   231

Using Inline Styles   231

Beyond HTML: Dynamic HTML   231

DHTML: Creating a Collapsible Outline   233

DHTML: Using Form Field Extensions   234

DHTML: Using Page Transitions and Text Animations   235

Pushing Your Site with the Channel Definition Format   236

V Creating and Adapting Graphics with Image Explorer

14 Getting Started with Image Composer   243

What does Image Composer Offer?   244

Associating Your Images with Image Composer   244

Using Image Composer with FrontPage   246

Using Tools, Toolbars & Palettes   247

Creating and Editing Your First Sprites   253

Changing and Copying Sprites   255

Using Composition Guides   256

Using Clip Art   256

15 Working with Sprites   261

Composing Graphical Text   262

Sizing and Rotating Your Graphical Text   267

Using Graphical Text in Your Web Pages   268

Working with Rectangles and Ovals   271

Using Curves in Images   273

Odd Shapes and Zigzag Lines   274

Moving Sprites Forward and Back   275

Aligning Sprites   275

Grouping Sprites Together   275

Flattening Sprites   277

Cropping, Resizing, and Rotating Sprites   277

Setting a Sprite's Home Position   278

16 Using Effects for Maximum Impact   279

Using Special Patterns   280

Changing Colors in Patterns and Fills   281

Applying Gradient Fills   282

Applying a Texture Transfer   283

Outlining Sprites   285

Filtering Sprites   286

Using Color Tuning to Enhance Your Sprites   289

Using Warp Transformations to Enhance Your Sprites   290

Using the Paintbrush, Airbrush, and Pencil   291

Using the Smear and Impression tools   292

Using the Eraser and Tinting Effects   292

Transferring and Using the Rubber Stamp   293

Creating Warp Effects   293

17 Tailoring Your Images for FrontPage Documents   295

Designing a Background Image   296

Using Custom Background Fills   296

What File Type Should I Use?   298

What Are Compression Levels?   299

Why Should I Change Compression?   299

Adjusting JPEG Compression   299

Why Use GIFs?   301

Creating Transparent GIFs   302

Creating Animated GIFs   303

Using the Sample Sprite Catalog   306

VI Appendix

A FrontPage and Other Web Servers   311

Server Basics   312

FrontPage Server Extensions: What Are They?   312

Using FrontPage with Windows 95 and Windows NT Web Servers   315

Using FrontPage with UNIX Web Servers   316

Getting Help   317

Index   319

Credits

SENIOR VICE PRESIDENT OF PUBLISHING
Richard K. Swadley

PUBLISHER
Jordan Gold

GENERAL MANAGER
Joe Muldoon

MANAGER OF PUBLISHING OPERATIONS
Linda H. Buehler

EXECUTIVE EDITOR
Beverly M. Eppink

DIRECTOR OF EDITORIAL SERVICES
Lisa Wilson

MANAGING EDITOR
Patrick Kanouse

SENIOR ACQUISITIONS EDITOR
Jeff Taylor

ACQUISITIONS EDITOR
David Mayhew

DEVELOPMENT EDITOR
Bob Correll

SENIOR EDITOR
Elizabeth A. Bruns

COPY EDITORS
Sean Dixon
Patricia Kinyon
Tonya Maddox
Sean Medlock
San Dee Philips

PRODUCT MARKETING MANAGER
Kourtnaye Sturgeon

TECHNICAL EDITOR
Pamela Rice Hahn

SOFTWARE RELATIONS COORDINATOR
Susan D. Gallahger

TEAM COORDINATOR
Lorraine E. Schaffer

EDITORIAL ASSISTANT
Rhonda Tinch-Mize

BOOK DESIGNER
Ruth Harvey

COVER DESIGNER
Sandra Schroeder

PRODUCTION TEAM
Marcia Deboy
Michael Dietsch
Cynthia Fields
Maureen West

INDEXER
Chris Wilcox

Composed in *Century Old Style* and *ITC Franklin Gothic* by Que Corporation.

This book is dedicated to all the little nobby people who said "Hey, you can write?" Nyah. SB

I would like to dedicate this book to the memory of Roger Kris. His faith in me started my career, his friendship will always be missed. RS

About the Authors

Steve Banick is still waiting for the adoration that all injured gelatin-powder wrestlers deserve. Steve has settled into a peaceful coexistence with his wife Christina, his two barky dogs (Spooky and Density, if you must know), and his never ending search to cure the plague that ails all modern man: cable television. Steve can be haggled with at his creative services and graphic design firm, Steven Banick and Associates. Believing you should practice what you preach he is available on the Web at **http://www.Banick.com**, and via email at **Steve@Banick.com**.

His published works as a contributing and lead author include: *Special Edition Using Microsoft Commercial Internet System*, *Special Edition Using Microsoft Visual InterDev*, *Web Management with Microsoft Visual SourceSafe 5.0*, *Special Edition Using Microsoft Internet Information Server 4.0*, and *FrontPage Unleashed*.

Ryan Sutter is a freelance writer, programmer analyst, Webmaster and founder of a small record company called Nuclear Gopher Productions. By day, he works for Performark Incorporated. By night, he writes techie books, plays with his 3-year-old son, Sydney, plots world-domination for Nuclear Gopher Productions and eats too much pizza. Ryan has been a computer nut since he purchased his first Commodore VIC20 for $40.00 at K-Mart in 1982. In the 15 years since, he has coded in BASIC, C, Clipper, Visual Basic, dBase, Powerbuilder, Java, HTML, JavaScript, C++, Objective-C, Perl and then some. He is a fanatic about cross-platform computing via Internet standards and Java. He is also a guitarist, a Minnesota Vikings fan and a terrible chess player. He can be reached at **rockboy@nucleargopher.com**.

Acknowledgments

Special thanks and recognition to Chris Denschikoff, for being more than a ghost (although, not a timely one), my editors at Macmillan (first Jeff Taylor, who then was spirited away to other projects and replaced with the capable Beverly Eppink, Bob Correll, and Elizabeth Bruns), and to my friends who have always reminded me it's a far better world when you don't have to commute. Love and thanks to my wife Christina who still thinks that the keyboard is attached to my fingers. SB

I would like to acknowledge the understanding and patience on the part of my wife, Tabithah, and my son, Sydney, while writing this book. Tab helped give me the time and Syd (although he didn't know what I was up to) behaved himself. RS

We'd Like to Hear from You!

QUE Corporation has a long-standing reputation for high-quality books and products. To ensure your continued satisfaction, we also understand the importance of customer service and support.

Tech Support

If you need assistance with the information in this book, please access Macmillan Computer Publishing's online Knowledge Base at **http://www.superlibrary.com/general/support**. If you do not find the answer to your questions on our Web site, you may contact Macmillan Technical Support by phone at **317-581-3833** or via e-mail at **support@mcp.com**.

Also be sure to visit QUE's Web resource center for all the latest information, enhancements, errata, downloads, and more. It's located at **http://www.quecorp.com/**.

Orders, Catalogs, and Customer Service

To order other QUE or Macmillan Computer Publishing books, catalogs, or products, please contact our Customer Service Department at **800-428-5331** or fax us at **800-835-3202** (International Fax: 317-228-4400). Or visit our online bookstore at **http://www.mcp.com/**.

Comments and Suggestions

We want you to let us know what you like or dislike most about this book or other QUE products. Your comments will help us to continue publishing the best books available on computer topics in today's market.

Fax: 317-581-4669

E-mail: **mset_mgr@sams.mcp.com**

Mail: Beverly M. Eppink
Comments Department
QUE
201 W. 103rd Street
Indianapolis, IN 46290

Please be sure to include the book's title and authors as well as your name, phone or fax number, and e-mail address. We will carefully review your comments and share them with the authors. Please note that due to the high volume of mail we receive, we may not be able to reply to every message.

Thank you for choosing QUE!

INTRODUCTION

Introduction

Welcome to *Using Microsoft FrontPage 98*, and thank you for choosing this book. Like its predecessors, this volume focuses on Microsoft FrontPage, the Web site creation and management suite. However, unlike previous Que publications on FrontPage, this book has a very specific focus in mind. Previous books, such as *Special Edition Using FrontPage 97*, focused on giving you as much information on FrontPage as possible. This included documenting virtually every aspect of the program and Web site creation. *Using FrontPage 98*, however, aims to give you a much more select batch of information so that you can get up to speed and down to work right away.

This book is not intended to be read cover to cover in one sitting. Instead, it's meant to sit beside your computer for quick reference while you're using FrontPage 98. This isn't to say that you *can't* read this book cover to cover. Rather, it has been designed to offer completely independent resources for particular aspects of FrontPage as well as tasks that you may have to complete. This introduction will give you an understanding of the history of FrontPage, how this book is organized, and how you can quickly get underway while getting the most out of this reference. ■

What Is FrontPage?

Since the advent of the World Wide Web, developers of Web sites have been seeking tools to make their jobs easier. This need has grown, feeding a rapidly expanding market for Web-oriented tools and packages. At the heart of these tools is the Web editor, somewhat akin to the specialized editor a programmer uses when creating software. Each editor on the market offers a variety of "unique" features, all aimed at convincing the developer that he is better off using that vendor's special program.

The first Web editors were essentially glorified text or programming editors, with a few features to please the early Web developers. Shortcuts for coding the pages and deploying them were the norm in early programs. As the Web became more advanced, the demand for "visual" editors rose, similar to What-You-See-Is-What-You-Get (WYSIWYG) word processors (such as Microsoft Word or Corel WordPerfect). What many were seeking was a truly WYSIWYG-oriented Web editor that let designers create their pages without the seemingly complex code at the heart of HTML.

When it was first introduced to the public, Vermeer Technologies' FrontPage captured the heart and imagination of many Web developers. Its visual nature and powerful organizational tools garnered rare praise from the media, but the hefty price tag put it out of the reach of most developers. FrontPage captured so much attention that it caught the eye of Microsoft. Recognizing a noticeable hole in their Web-authoring product options, Microsoft opted to wholly consume Vermeer and FrontPage by purchasing the entire company. Microsoft's evolution to the FrontPage product has brought us to FrontPage 98. FrontPage 98 is a complete Web site management and authoring suite, empowering you with the tools to create a complete Web site from the ground up as well as the tools to manage it on an ongoing basis.

FrontPage 98 transforms the product from a useful but overpriced package in the hands of Vermeer to a widespread commercial product obtainable by nearly anyone. The package now consists of tools that fulfill the requirements for many developers, without forcing them to rely on additional outside packages. It includes considerable leaps into advanced functionality and the support for the latest in Web technologies.

FrontPage 98 is Microsoft's latest effort to convince the designers on the Web (both professional and amateur) to adopt another feature-filled Microsoft product, and is a tempting offer to nearly anyone who uses it.

The Scope of This Book

This book does not aim to tell you everything there is to know about FrontPage 98. Instead, it gives you what you need to accomplish your tasks within the FrontPage environment without reading through a tome of information. From the outset, this book has been designed for page-flipping and task-oriented reading, rather than page-to-page reading. Primarily, it concentrates on a few important details:

- *You have a job to do, and FrontPage is the tool you have chosen.* This book is not intended to sell FrontPage or Microsoft products (or any products, for that matter). By holding this book, you have already expressed at least an interest in using FrontPage, if you aren't using it already.

If you want to explore facets of FrontPage that aren't covered in this book, please consider reading both the Microsoft online documentation for FrontPage and any FrontPage-related publications. Keep in mind that if you've already read a previous FrontPage book (such as *Special Edition Using FrontPage 97* from Que), a great deal of the information still applies. You don't need to throw out your old book. Just be sure to consider any changes in the program by reading this book and the online help.

Who Should Be Reading This Book?

Egghead, jarhead, or overworked manager? Have you been given the job of creating your company's Web site on top of your already demanding workload? Or perhaps you're new to the Web and want to create your own Web site without drowning in technical information. Either way, this book should help. The following list explains who can benefit most from this book:

- *Intranet managers.* So, you've been given the job of managing your company's Intranet and editing all of the content. You have a ream of documents and Microsoft Word files to import to the Web, and you're looking to FrontPage to ease your suffering. FrontPage 98 has the stunning capability to integrate with Microsoft Office, and can help you finish your job in time for an early dinner. This book can give you the information you need to create a functional Intranet site and organize your content in such a manner that your boss will think you're part of the tech crew.

- *Web toadies.* Sad but true, your boss has handed down the task of updating your company's Web site and making it "in tune" with your mission statement. Between all the mentions of "keeping in the paradigm" and "concentrating on our core team values," you're not sure how to get the job done. Rather than sit in a corner and stare blankly at your computer, put it to work by using this book with your copy of FrontPage 98. This book will give you everything you need to get that Web site into top form without melting your brain in the process.

- *The casual user.* Casual users like you are the backbone of the computer industry. You're eager to get your feet wet by making your own Web site, and you have the gumption to get it done. FrontPage is a great tool to introduce you to the world of Web development, without stifling you as you advance to expert levels.

It doesn't matter whether or not you fit one of these roles specifically. You may even be a combination of two or more of them. Regardless, this book is meant to help you get comfortable using FrontPage so you can explore on your own for more advanced features.

How to Use This Book

This book has been organized into six parts to take you step-by-step through FrontPage 98. You don't need to read each part, nor do you need to read the parts in order. If you feel you need to start out in part 5, do so. You may sometimes encounter references to other parts and chapters to help you understand particular concepts. Within each part are several chapters, organized to highlight specific tasks and ideas. Each chapter acts as a self-contained entity, giving you the information you need to complete the covered task.

NOTE Throughout this book, it's assumed that you have at least a passing familiarity with the Windows operating system and know how to use programs within it. We have tried to minimize the layers of confusion by giving you clear, concise instructions and information without duplicating redundant instructions on using Windows.

The six parts are as follows:

Part I—Getting Started with FrontPage 98
Part I gives you the information you need to get started. This includes an introduction to FrontPage, the installation and setup process, and a brief guided tour of the components of FrontPage 98. If you're new to FrontPage in general, you'd best start off here and learn the fundamentals.

Part II—The FrontPage 98 Primer
Just like Cliff's Notes, this section acts as your study guide to FrontPage. You're taken through the process of creating your first Web site from start to finish so that you can begin working on your own. If you don't have much experience in Web development, this section is a must-read.

Part III—Creating Pages with the FrontPage Editor
Part II was your introduction to the two most important aspects of FrontPage: the Editor and the Explorer. Part III continues in that vein by giving you a more comprehensive look at using the FrontPage Editor to create your beautiful Web sites. If you're familiar with FrontPage and have worked with it in the past, this is an ideal section to start with.

Part IV—Managing your Web with the FrontPage Explorer
When you're done creating your Web site, you need a way to manage it. The FrontPage Explorer, first discussed in Part II, is a powerful tool for administering and maintaining your Web site. The Explorer is more than a pretty file manager—it lets you quality-control your site and keep track of important tasks to be done.

Part V—Creating and Adapting Graphics with Image Composer
If you've ever felt that you could be the Web van Gogh, Microsoft's Image Composer might just be the tool for you. This section focuses on the graphic editing and creation program that's part of the FrontPage package. Even if you aren't building Web sites, this section may interest you if you want to create masterful works of art for the World Wide Web.

Part VI—Appendix

The appendix provided in this book gives more information on how to make the most of FrontPage 98 once you've gone beyond the basics in Parts I through V.

Beyond these six sections, you should explore the documentation provided with FrontPage. You can use both the printed documentation and the useful online material. Beyond this, you may want to refer to additional resources from Que and on the World Wide Web, including:

- *Special Edition Using FrontPage 98*. This large volume gives you a great deal of information about FrontPage 98. It includes much more detailed coverage of each FrontPage component.
- *The FrontPage Web Site*. Microsoft's own FrontPage Web site offers tips and tricks, additional downloads, and upgrade information. Be sure to point your Web browser to **http://www.microsoft.com/frontpage** for the latest.

Information That's Easy to Understand

This book contains a variety of special features to help you find the information you need. For example, it uses formatting conventions to make important keywords or special text obvious and it uses specific language to make keyboard and mouse actions clear.

Chapter Roadmaps

Each chapter begins with a brief introduction and a list of the topics you'll find covered in that chapter. You know what you'll be reading about before you start.

Tips, Notes, Cautions,

You'll find a number of special elements and conventions in this book that will jump right off of the page. These elements will provide just-in-time information.

TIP Tips point out things that you can do to get the most out of the Internet. Often, these come from my personal experience.

NOTE Notes are extra chunks of information that don't necessarily fit into the surrounding text but could be valuable nonetheless. ■

> **CAUTION**
> Cautions warn you about things that you should avoid or things that you need to do to protect yourself or your computer.

> **Sidebars are oh-by-the-ways**
> Sidebars provide useful and interesting information that doesn't really fit the subject matter. You'll also find more technical information.

Cross references point you to specific sections within other chapters so that you can get more information that's related to the topic you're reading about. Here is what a cross reference looks like:

▶ **See** "Section Title," **p.xx**, (ch. #)

Keyboard Conventions

This book uses some special text conventions that make information easier to understand:

Element	Convention
Hot keys	Hot keys are underlined in this book, just as they appear in Windows menus and dialog boxes. To use a hot key, press Alt and the underlined letter. The F in File is a hot key that represents the File menu, for example.
Key combinations	Key combinations that you must press together are separated by plus signs. For example, "Press Ctrl+Alt+D" means that you press and hold down the Ctrl key, then press and hold down the Alt key, and then press and release the D key. Always press and release, rather than hold, the last key in a key combination.
Menu commands	A comma is used to separate the parts of a pull-down menu command. For example, "Choose File, New" means to open the File menu and select the New option.

In most cases, special-purpose keys are referred to by the text that actually appears on them on a standard 101-key keyboard. For example, press "Esc" or press "F1" or press "Enter." Some of the keys on your keyboard don't actually have words on them. So here are the conventions used in this book for those keys:

- The Backspace key, which is labeled with a left arrow, usually is located directly above the Enter key. The Tab key usually is labeled with two arrows pointing to lines, with one arrow pointing right and the other arrow pointing left.
- The cursor keys, labeled on most keyboards with arrows pointing up, down, right, and left, are called the up-arrow key, down-arrow key, right-arrow key, and left-arrow key.
- Case is not important unless explicitly stated. So "Press A" and "Press a" mean the same thing. This book always uses the uppercase version, though.

Mouse Conventions

In this book, the following phrases tell you how to operate your mouse within Windows:

- **Click**—Move the mouse pointer so that it is in the area of the screen specified and press the left mouse button. (If you've reversed these buttons—as many left-handed people like to do—whenever the instructions say to press the left button, press the right button instead.)

- **Double-Click**—Press the left mouse button twice rapidly without moving the mouse between clicks.
- **Drag**—Press and hold down the left mouse button while you're moving the mouse pointer. You'll see an outline of the object as you drag the mouse pointer.
- **Drop**—Release the mouse button after a drag operation.

On the Web References

Similar to a cross-reference, these references point to information on the World Wide Web. By entering the URL provided in your Web browser, you'll be taken to a page of relevant information. For example:

For more information on other Que *Using* titles, refer to the Que Web site at **http://www.mcp.com/que**.

Our Thanks to You

We, the authors of this book, extend our appreciation and thanks to you for purchasing this book and for your continued support of Que. It's our sincere hope that you find this book a valuable addition to your reference library, and that you'll look to Que for timely and useful information in the future. Best of luck with FrontPage and your Web site.

Sincerely,

Steve Banick and Ryan Sutter

PART I

Getting Started with FrontPage 98

1 An Introduction to FrontPage 98   11

2 Installation and Setup   23

3 A Guided Tour to the FrontPage Components   37

CHAPTER 1

An Introduction to FrontPage 98

FrontPage 98 is a World Wide Web development environment that was designed to be both powerful and easy to use. This ease of use extends even to the actual creation of the Web site; no esoteric codes or pseudo-programming is required. This doesn't mean that experienced Web designers can't use this software. FrontPage 98 can serve both the novice and expert audiences. However, before you can leap into the world of Web design with both feet, you need to know some basic concepts that'll help you formulate ideas and use FrontPage 98. Logically, you should read this chapter before installing FrontPage 98, so you have a basis to work from when you create your first projects.

Walk before you run
Learn the underlying concepts behind the World Wide Web and FrontPage 98 before you tackle the technical aspects of creating a Web site.

Ingredients
Find out exactly what you get with your FrontPage 98 package, so you can double-check everything as you remove it from the box.

Preliminary preparation
Before reading the next chapter about installation, make sure you meet the minimum requirements.

Learning FrontPage Concepts and Terminology

You may be wondering, "What sets FrontPage 98 apart from the vast array of Web editing/creation software out there?" The competition in this market is fierce, with several differing products clamoring for attention. What makes FrontPage 98 different is that it works on both your computer and your remote server. What makes FrontPage 98 so powerful is that it is intended as a *remote*-editing tool. This means that you can make changes to a Web site that is stored locally, on another computer, or another continent. All you need is a connection to the server and appropriate security clearance on the host machine. This is a tremendous step forward compared to other systems, which pretended to let you work remotely, but were essentially glorified clients that used the age-old Internet FTP standard for transfers. FrontPage 98 lets you make changes to files, Web site structures—just about anything that influences your Web project. The amount of freedom and control this grants is tremendous, especially for users that are relative novices when it comes to the World Wide Web and networks in general.

Secondly, everything you'll need comes in the FrontPage 98 package. A graphical editor, a layout tool, a site and server manager, essentially all of the important ingredients to a complete Web solution are included. Normally you'd have to scour the Web to find all of the utilities and programs that add up to a usable package, but in this case Microsoft provides all the solutions.

Learning the Basics of Web Pages, Web Sites, and Web Servers

FrontPage 98 is primarily a Web tool, and it shows in the conceptual framework the program is based on. Many of the concepts and terms are similar to those of the World Wide Web at large, except they are applied specifically to the FrontPage 98 mind-set. This isn't to say that the World Wide Web terminology and FrontPage parlance are considerably different, rather the semantics are.

Before you can properly understand what FrontPage can do, you need to understand the media that the program manipulates: The World Wide Web. You probably already know that the Web is a series of linked computers joined by data connections and the *Hypertext Transfer Protocol* (HTTP). However, there are some terms and ideas unique to the Web that you might not be familiar with.

> **CAUTION**
> The following is intended for Web neophytes only. If you think you already know it all and need no further prompting, then skip ahead to the FrontPage Webs section for more specific information. If not, don't be ashamed. It's far better to read on than it is to skip ahead and possibly miss useful information.

FTP—An acronym for File Transfer Protocol. FTP was (and still is) the basic file system of the Internet. It's mentioned here because a lot of FrontPage's transfer options make the traditional

FTP method of Web site management obsolete. FTP is slowly being supplanted by the World Wide Web.

HTML—An acronym for HyperText Markup Language. Essentially the language of the Web, as it controls how Web pages are laid out and perceived. You don't actually need a comprehensive knowledge of HTML to use FrontPage; part of the power of FrontPage is that it writes the HTML for you. Sometimes, the act of writing HTML for a page is referred to as "marking up."

Web Page—The most basic unit of the Web. A Web page is a single document, formatted using HTML, to create a linkable resource for visitors to view. The FrontPage Editor is used to create individual Web pages that comprise a Web site.

Web Server—A computer that acts as a host for World Wide Web content, which can also refer to any software that resides on such a computer and doles out Web content. Often shortened to "server."

Web Site—A collection of files and graphics that make up an entire Web project. Another common usage is "Web page," although a Web site can be made up of several Web pages but not vice versa. The FrontPage Explorer is used to manage and organize all of the Web pages that make up a Web site.

WYSIWYG—A mouthful of an acronym that stands for What-You-See-Is-What-You-Get, a particular method of software design that lets users design pages as they would be visible under normal conditions. This was a big step forward at the time, since most layout packages only let you see the finished product in a cumbersome "preview" mode, if at all. FrontPage's inclusion of this feature allows you to design Web pages by dragging-and-dropping objects directly onto a page, instead of painful second-hand layout.

Using FrontPage Web Sites

The most important concept you need to understand within FrontPage 98 is that of a Web. This is not to be confused with the (World Wide) Web. A FrontPage Web refers to an aggregate sum of files and folders that can be manipulated within FrontPage itself. It's mostly a convenient method of organization and allows for several Web sites to be gathered under and umbrella label. The Web is the largest unit of organization within the FrontPage 98 system.

The advantages to a Web are many, but the most important is that it allows the FrontPage server extensions to reduce the amount of traffic between you and your server. Being able to control your Web content remotely using FrontPage is an incredible tool, but imagine if it were implemented poorly or uncontrolled. Every time you tried to do something, the program would download the contents of the server's entire Web directory. Because projects as a whole can be divided into Webs, you can reduce the amount of information that has to be transferred from the server to you. You also have a simple means of dividing content into more coherent sections.

If you have a Web server that is home to three distinctly different Web sites, you should want three different Webs to represent them. Otherwise, every time you want to work on one of the sites you have to download and process the other two as well. Separate Webs are especially handy for organization if the sites are unique to each other and don't really share that many resources in the first place.

Applying FrontPage Server Extensions

There are two main areas where activity takes place when using FrontPage 98. The first is on the client or local side. This refers to the FrontPage Explorer and other local tools to help you design and implement a Web site. The other focal point is the server or remote side, which refers to your remote Web server and the software that runs it.

Webs may be a valuable authoring tool locally, but FrontPage server extensions are important in their own right, too. "FrontPage" refers to more than just some editing software for Web sites. It also includes a method of interacting with your Web server; this method is more a protocol than a piece of software. The protocol grants you the power to influence events on your server remotely, all through the FrontPage graphical user interface.

These extensions are powerful in their own right, as they are responsible for the majority of the interaction that takes place between you and your remote server. Without the FrontPage server extensions, the utility of FrontPage is curtailed somewhat. You can still edit and manipulate your Web as a whole, just not as efficiently. Instead of using the specialized extensions, the FrontPage software uses a Web-publishing wizard to copy over your new work after you've finished creating it. This is a less elegant and seamless operation than using the server extensions.

Familiarizing Yourself with FrontPage Documents

You are likely familiar with Microsoft Word's association with the .doc file. This file is Microsoft Word's means of storing your Word documents. FrontPage also uses files to store your Web, in the form of Web content files. Web content files can be several different kinds of files, ranging from the actual Web page (an HTML file, with a .htm or .html extension) to the graphics that are included on the page. FrontPage supports the standard file types associated with a Web site, including:

- **HTML pages**—Whether it is a client side Web page (.html, .htm), or a server side page (.asp, .shtml), you can edit and manage it from within FrontPage.
- **Graphics**—FrontPage supports the standard Web graphic formats, JPEG (.jpg), GIF (.gif), as well as other graphic formats such as Windows Bitmaps (.bmp).
- **Multimedia files**—If you want to organize your multimedia files for your Web site, fear not. FrontPage directly supports the traditional Windows multimedia formats, including Video for Windows (.avi) and Wave sound files (.wav).

You can manipulate virtually any type of file into your Web site. If FrontPage does not directly know how to read your file when you ask it to, it may prompt you to locate a program that does.

For example, if you want to include a diagram from your art department in a different file format, you can include it within your Web site. Unfortunately, if you want to open and change that file, you are forced to use the program that originally created it. Additionally, your file type may not be supported by your Web site visitor's browser. The good thing is that FrontPage doesn't see these files as necessarily different, because they're all simply considered documents, and documents can be handled universally by the FrontPage Editor.

Exploring the Contents of the FrontPage 98 Package

Getting a new piece of software is a lot like getting a birthday present. You never know what's inside, and you're scared to shake it in case you break something. Fortunately, the people at Microsoft are forthright about what's in their software packages. The FrontPage package includes two flexible pieces of software: the FrontPage Explorer and the FrontPage Editor. Both are an integral part of the overall FrontPage solution.

Understanding The FrontPage Explorer

The FrontPage Explorer is your primary administrative tool, which is invaluable to managing Web projects from remote. Before FrontPage, if you wanted to change your Web site's configuration, or just add or remove files, you usually had to use an FTP client to transfer your changes. The FrontPage Explorer has all the options for moving, renaming, and deleting files that the old FTP solution did, all contained within an easy-to-use graphical user interface (see Figure 1.1).

FIG. 1.1
The FrontPage Explorer is a powerful interface for managing Web sites.

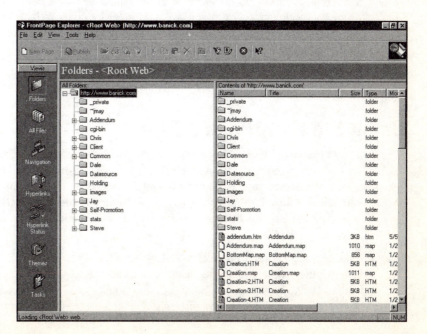

However, the FrontPage Explorer is more than just a glorified means of transferring your Web site. Because of the graphical user interface, you get as much information as you give out. Directory structures and file locations are easily determined by reviewing the appropriate pane. The Explorer also includes a Navigator pane that mimics your traditional Windows 95 folder interface almost exactly. The best part is, this entire window dressing interface has some real power underneath. It's all drag-and-drop, which means you can duplicate sites or make much-needed changes with the click, drag, and release of a mouse. This is invaluable when compared to the traditional method of creating a new directory, copying all the files to that directory, all of this involving laborious typed commands.

Another useful aspect of the FrontPage Explorer is the implementation of a To Do List. This is essentially a shared task manager within the Web management software. The To Do List can be viewed by anyone who is authorized to work on a particular site, and you can create lists for each different FrontPage Web. This list functionality lets you schedule, assign, and mark complete tasks on-the-fly. These tasks are updated immediately, allowing you to interact with other designers and administrators for the project when you normally would be unable to.

The To Do Lists are an incredible asset to planning as well, as they allow you to make a coherent outline early and assign the appropriate work to the appropriate person. This approach eliminates a lot of the confusion associated with new projects and encapsulates all the relevant information in one easily accessible place. A list also provides you with a general indicator of progress, as you can easily discern which tasks are finished and unfinished. Because they are accessible by all the staff who would be working on the project, and because they're updated quickly and easily, To Do Lists can be vital to any speedy development project.

The FrontPage Explorer is capable of far more than file handling and creating prioritized lists. There's an option for theme-based layout schemes for quick Web pages. You can also diagnose and repair broken hyperlinks between documents. Most of all, you can control your Web and its operations on a day-to-day basis. The FrontPage Explorer is an invaluable tool.

▶ **See** "A Guided Tour to the FrontPage Components," **p. 37**
▶ **See** "Part IV—Managing your Web with the FrontPage Explorer," **p. 185**

Using the FrontPage Editor

If the FrontPage Explorer is the administrative tool, then the FrontPage Editor is the creative tool. The most powerful aspect of the FrontPage Editor is its WYSIWYG aspect, shown in Figure 1.2. Because of this feature, even total World Wide Web neophytes can create an entire site, because they don't have to do any HTML coding whatsoever. You drag an element into place, and the editor writes the requisite HTML code in the background to make your design work on the Web.

The FrontPage Editor's control is absolute. Even font size and type changes are all integrated into the menu system. The interface is once again a simple and direct graphical user interface, with the menu bars and icons you've become familiar with. The advantages don't just stop at the interface, though. You have three different options to view a potential page.

- Normal, which represents your WYSIWYG view combined with a powerful drag-and-drop editing interface.
- HTML, which displays all the underlying source code that makes up the formatting found in the Normal view. In the HTML view, you can make certain your directives are being carried out accurately, or learn the basics of coding by loading up some existing pages.
- Preview, which takes your page and views it as a browser would. This is almost identical to the Normal view, except it includes things such as animated GIFs and other display functionality that would interfere with the editing process.

FIG. 1.2
The FrontPage Editor allows you to create complex layouts as if you were creating a graphic design using a desktop publishing program.

N O T E Using the FrontPage Editor, you can easily incorporate your existing Java applets and ActiveX components into your Web site without relying on additional tools. ■

The FrontPage Editor supports most of the latest Web authoring standards and lets you work with new technologies such as Java, ActiveX, and multimedia tools. Using the FrontPage Editor, you can easily incorporate your existing Java applets and ActiveX components into your Web site without relying on additional tools. Although FrontPage does not let you create these applets or components, there is plenty of support for using them within your site.

▶ **See** "A Guided Tour to the FrontPage Components," **p. 37**
▶ **See** "Part III – Creating Pages with the FrontPage Editor," **p. 99**

A powerful feature of the FrontPage Editor are the FrontPage components. The FrontPage components are time-and-energy savers that allow you to automate certain procedures when you save your page, or when a visitor views your page on the Web site. Say for example that you have an advertising banner you want to insert in a certain number of pages. Instead of typing out the instructions, or even dragging the image into the page, you can simply insert a FrontPage component responsible for creating that banner. The power of FrontPage components includes instant hit counters, page banners, comment fields, form handlers, and more.

The FrontPage components are modifiable to an amazing degree. In fact, using the information given in the FrontPage Software Development Kit (SDK), you can create your own specific FrontPage components, limited only by the current World Wide Web technologies. You can also modify existing FrontPage components to suit your needs. The FrontPage Editor, when combined with its attractive interface and interactive features such as FrontPage components, makes an incredible Web development tool that no designer should be without.

Bonus Utilities

There is also an assortment of additional software that contributes to the overall functionality of FrontPage but isn't an essential part of the core package. Mostly, it's a batch of supplemental Microsoft technology already available elsewhere, bundled together in this handy package. These programs are still a good value, though, and the various parts and ingredients interoperate seamlessly, which is better than most third party add-on products can claim. The additional utilities consist primarily of three programs: Microsoft Image Composer, the Microsoft Personal Web Server, and the Web Publishing Wizard. They also include a variety of clip-art samples and additional themes for use within FrontPage.

Overview of Microsoft Image Composer

Ever since the inclusion of GIFs in the HTML format, the Web has been all about graphics. However, for most people, there hasn't really been a good, affordable graphic development tool that geared toward the World Wide Web. Now there is, with the release of Microsoft's Image Composer version 1.5. Image Composer gives you the power to create attractive graphics for your Web site without relying on more costly or complicated software packages (see Figure 1.3).

Image Composer 1.5 is a good compromise between power and usability, as well as being specifically designed to produce Web graphics. Image Composer is based around a system of *sprites*, as opposed to the more traditional object- or raster-based programs. This innovative approach allows more freedom in placing objects and controlling things such as transparency and filtered effects. It also makes it easier to include things such as clip art and other source graphics into an already existing picture.

Image Composer includes a powerful filtering feature based around plug-ins. The software comes with the powerful "Impressionist" plug-in that can create all sorts of artful effects on your masterpiece. Not only can you choose from one of several default settings from the Impressionist plug-in, but you can also create your own effects using the flexible slider controls provided. This lets you create unique effects for your pictures, save those effects, and re-use them. Image Composer also supports the industry standard Adobe PhotoShop plug-in format, allowing you to tap the large market of plug-ins for your own use.

One of the most difficult aspects of preparing graphics for the Web is making certain that color depths are properly set. One of the more valuable and intuitive features of Image Composer is a simple, on-the-fly control that shows you what your picture looks like in various GIF dithering modes, as well as the JPG "true-color" mode. With this feature, you easily can make decisions about what color depths to use, and eventually save, in your file. The on-the-fly switching lets you see what your graphic's color looks like in various stages of its production, allowing you to make changes as the image grows more complex.

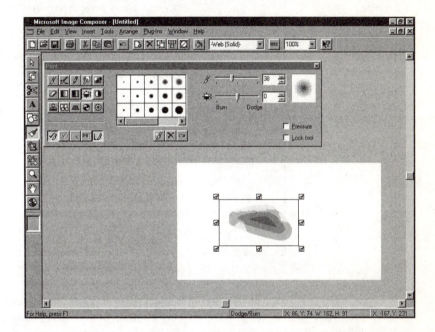

FIG. 1.3
Image Composer is a powerful graphic manipulation program in the tradition of Adobe Photoshop or Fractal Painter, but with a few unique tricks of its own.

Another feature of Image Composer that makes creating graphics easier is the built-in support for scanners. Many programs require a clumsy work-around method to incorporate scanner support, but in Image Composer the ability to import scanned images is an intrinsic one.

As an added bonus to the additional utilities packaged with FrontPage, Image Composer comes with several Sample Sprites and other royalty-free images. The program is designed to help implement that particular "cut-and-paste" feel common to the Web, with simple tools to aid inserting and manipulating other graphics. The library of images is diverse and valuable, and added to the Sprite handling methods make Image Composer a useful program in any Web designer's repertoire.

▶ **See** "Getting Started with Image Composer," on **p. 243**

Overview of Microsoft Personal Web Server

The Microsoft Personal Web Server (Figure 1.4) is the ideal solution for a beginner who won't be doing a lot of high-end Web publishing. It's easy to install, easy to configure, and easy to administer. Most of the administration and configuration duties are actually done through your browser, so there's no fiddling with control panels and properties. This also lets you administrate the server remotely, granting you much more freedom when deciding where to locate your Web server.

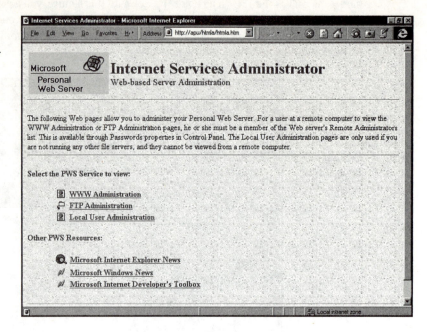

FIG. 1.4
Microsoft Personal Web Server truly brings power to the people with its combination of user-friendliness and flexibility.

Personal Web server replaces the previous inline server that shipped with the previous version of FrontPage. Personal Web Server is much more dependable and portable than the old FrontPage Web Server, as it is a direct descendant of Microsoft's powerful Internet Information Server for Windows NT. You can expand the Personal Web Server with programmable extensions and server side scripting with Microsoft Active Server Pages.

Overview of Microsoft Web Publishing Wizard When you are publishing to a Web server that does not support the FrontPage server extensions, you still can take advantage of FrontPage's features. The Microsoft Web Publishing Wizard is a small tool that helps you transfer your Web site contents using a step by step "wizard." Using this tool, you may update your Web site using the standard FTP or Windows Networking methods (depending on your server), rather than using a cumbersome FTP client or other software. The Web Publishing Wizard is a simple program meant for a simple task: making it easier to upload your Web site when you aren't using the FrontPage server extensions.

Before You Start

Before starting any ambitious enterprise, there are a few things you should be thinking about. The first is determining if you have the proper components to run FrontPage, and how to get them if you don't. The second is making sure your procedures can take advantage of the services FrontPage 98 offers, within a secure framework. FrontPage 98 is a relatively low-powered solution, with system demands only in the 486 range. Obviously though, you'll want the best system you can get. The minimum requirements for running FrontPage 98 are:

- 486 or better processor
- Windows 95 or Windows NT 3.51 with Service Pack 5 in place
- 8 megabytes of RAM for Windows 95 installations, 16 megabytes for NT
- At least 30 megabytes of hard disk space
- A CD-ROM drive
- A VGA-compatible display
- A mouse or other pointing device
- For the remote functionality, an Internet connection of some kind

However, minimum requirements are exactly that, a minimum. As you will be using this software to create your pride-and-joy Web site, you may want to consider a more powerful system. The most important addition you can give your computer is more RAM, but this is true of just about any computer improvement. The following is a list of recommendations from Microsoft for improved use of FrontPage:

- At least 16 megabytes of RAM, 32 megabytes for a NT installation
- A SVGA-compatible display
- At least 60 megabytes of hard drive space if you want to include all of the Bonus Pack components
- A fast Internet connection, 28.8 or greater

Before pressing that final install button, there are a few points to consider within your own organization. If you plan ahead to integrate FrontPage into your Web development plan, you can save yourself a lot of heartache and confusion later. FrontPage 98 can be an incredible boon to Webmasters and designers everywhere; it can also be an atrocious security risk. Before installing, you need to determine who should have access to the FrontPage client and who should not. This is especially important because of FrontPage's ease of use—literally anyone can make changes and possibly destroy your Web site because it's so easy.

> **NOTE** Before installing, you need to determine who should have access to the FrontPage client and who should not.

However, it's also quite easy for you to restrict access, as the FrontPage server extensions also include some security provisions. Each FrontPage Web has a user account and password attached to it. To keep out undesirables, you simply don't share the password. If you want people to have access to one Web site but not necessarily another, remember that you can use FrontPage Webs to organize content into the different sections that FrontPage can control. If you put the "sensitive" Web sites into their own Web, you can easily control access to them.

Once again though, it's important to determine who will have the power to make these changes within your organization. If people are operating at cross-purposes, it's quite easy for their work to cancel out, or even overwrite existing material. When planning to implement FrontPage 98, make sure to have the right procedures in place. For example, the quick turn-around and development that FrontPage encourages can actually end up getting you in trouble. You should insert (if you haven't already) a more rigorous proofreading and checking process to make sure that inaccurate or damaging material doesn't get published on the Web.

The process of publishing Web information has changed from a convoluted process to a simple click of a button. You need to ensure that the same amount of care goes into selecting which information is published as is used to go into getting that information out to the server. Be steadfast, wary, and most of all, thorough. ●

CHAPTER 2

Installation and Setup

That installation thing
The FrontPage 98 Setup Program handles the process of copying FrontPage 98 to your machine and getting it ready to work.

Web servers and FrontPage 98
If you use an existing Web server for your development, FrontPage 98 uses the FrontPage server extensions to communicate. If you don't have a server on your machine, you can use the Microsoft Personal Web Server for your development.

Composing an image
To create graphics for your Web site, you need to install Microsoft Image Composer. This useful program integrates smoothly with FrontPage 98 and is easy to setup.

FrontPage 98 can become a powerful part of your Web site creation routine, but in order to use it properly, you need to install and configure the software. Setting your workstation up for FrontPage 98 is a painless process thanks to Microsoft's Setup program. Your only fear is how much hard disk drive space you may be losing to your productivity gain. If you have never installed FrontPage, read through this chapter to become familiar with the easy process. This chapter also provides you with information on setting up and using the Microsoft Personal Web Server for your development, and Microsoft Image Composer for creating your pixel masterpieces. ■

Installing FrontPage 98

In the past, the installation and configuration of new software could bring tears to the eyes of even the most experienced of computer users. Fortunately, installing FrontPage 98 is a painless process, made easier by the simple Setup program that takes you through the process. An important point to remember is that you can always go back and modify your installation at a later time by re-opening the FrontPage 98 Setup program, or by visiting the Add/Remove Programs control panel on your workstation.

Before you can start using FrontPage, you need to run the FrontPage Setup application. This is done automatically by inserting the CD-ROM into the applicable drive. If you have disabled auto-start on your CD-ROM, or if your CD-ROM drive doesn't support this, you can choose to view the disc's contents by choosing to explore the disc. To do so, you must:

1. Open the My Computer window from your desktop.
2. Right-click on the CD-ROM drive icon (usually D:).
3. Choose Explore from the pop-up menu that appears.
4. Locate the Setup program icon and launch the program.
5. Continue installation from the ensuing Setup Window (Figure 2.1).

FIG. 2.1
From the Setup window, you may choose to install FrontPage 98 components, Microsoft Image Composer, and Microsoft Internet Explorer.

Choosing What to Install

Installing and configuring are two different things. The first you stand by and watch happen, the second you control to your advantage. There aren't many pre-installation options available, but you do have control over which FrontPage components are installed and which are left to linger on the distribution CD-ROM. To begin installation, highlight the Install FrontPage 98 option and click once. The FrontPage 98 Install Wizard begins by asking you to fill out some brief registration information and to read the licensing agreement. When the installation process begins, you are welcomed by the screen shown in Figure 2.2.

To install the default FrontPage 98 Components and options, choose the Typical installation. In choosing this, you are telling Setup to install the most common components and features of FrontPage 98 including:

- The FrontPage 98 Explorer and Editor.
- The Personal Web Server and/or FrontPage Server Extensions, depending on your machine's current setup.
- The FrontPage 98 Themes and supplementary programs.
- The Microsoft Web Publishing Wizard.

FIG. 2.2
You have two choices for installation: a typical installation or a custom. If you are not sure exactly what you'll need, choose the Typical installation option.

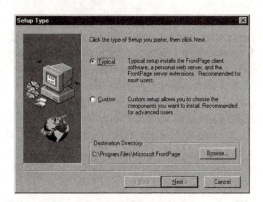

For users more experienced with FrontPage and familiar with what they need, Microsoft also provides a Custom option for installation. The Custom installation lets you select the particular components to install on your workstation, rather than relying on the default options. Using a Custom installation, you can control the size and flexibility of your FrontPage setup and avoid installing features you won't likely use. When you choose the Custom setup option, the FrontPage Setup Wizard provides you with a number of choices for installation, shown in Figure 2.3.

FIG. 2.3
Custom installations let you trim your FrontPage installation's size and control the components you want installed. This is ideal if you know exactly what you want to use.

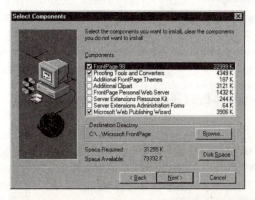

This screen provides you with eight options for installation. Click in the check boxes to select options for installation. Deselected check boxes indicate components that will not be installed. Note at the bottom of the wizard is an updated detail for the amount of space that your selected installation requires on your hard disk drive. As you select and deselect options, this number changes. You can use this to keep track of exactly how much disk space you will be using with FrontPage 98's programs, and to make sure that you have the prerequisite room. The eight different components that you can install are:

- **FrontPage 98**—These are the FrontPage executables (programs) and resource files. This is the backbone of FrontPage 98 and includes the versatile FrontPage Explorer and FrontPage Editor. Without these options installed, you would not have a functioning FrontPage 98 setup.
- **Proofing Tools and Converters**—With FrontPage's links to the Microsoft Office suite, it has inherited both a powerful spell checking utility and document importing powers. With the Proofing Tools and Converters installed, you can check your Web page's spelling and import existing Microsoft Office documents into your Web site. If you do not install this option, you cannot import documents other than Web pages and graphics.
- **Additional FrontPage Themes**—The FrontPage Explorer and Editor already come with a variety of professionally designed themes for Web sites. If you are looking for more predesigned templates for use in your Web development, select this option. This option installs the required image files and code to use these themes with your Web sites.
- **Additional Clipart**—If you are looking to add more spice to your Web site without creating your own graphics, you can use Microsoft's own clip art gallery. This option chooses to install more of the Microsoft clip art that you may already be familiar with.
- **FrontPage Personal Web Server**—An alternative to the more powerful Microsoft Personal Web Server, the FrontPage Personal Web Server is a small Web server that is installed locally onto your computer for development. Microsoft recommends using the more robust MPWS but provides you with a choice.
- **Server Extensions Resource Kit**—If you use an existing Web server and the FrontPage server extensions, the Server Extensions Resource Kit is a valuable option. This kit contains information on installing and using the FrontPage server extensions, as well as important information on maintaining and securing your Web server with them.
- **Server Extensions Administration Forms**—In previous releases of FrontPage 98, administration of the FrontPage server extensions relied on a set of command line and obscure window tools. Recognizing this deficiency, Microsoft included a set of Web pages and forms that let you administer your server extensions from a standard Web browser.
- **Microsoft Web Publishing Wizard**—When using the FrontPage server extensions is not an option, the Microsoft Web Publishing Wizard is the easiest choice for deployment of your Web site. Using a friendly wizard approach, this tool manages the updates for your Web site without complication. If you are using the FrontPage server extensions, this component is purely optional.

▶ **See** "An Introduction to FrontPage 98," **p. 11**

N O T E Remember! You can always go back and add or remove components to your installation. You are not permanently locked into your first choices. To add or remove components, simply launch the FrontPage 98 Setup program again. ■

Once you have made your choices, you are ready to begin the installation by clicking the Next button. Follow the on-screen instructions for the Setup Wizard to complete the process.

Installing Microsoft Image Composer

Microsoft Image Composer is a powerful, yet simple, graphic manipulation package designed expressly for creating Web graphics. Image Composer is a valuable addition to the FrontPage suite, and fortunately, the simplicity of use extends to its installation process.

You can access the Setup by simply inserting the FrontPage 98 CD-ROM into your drive. If you have disabled auto-start on your CD-ROM, or if your CD-ROM drive doesn't support this, you can choose to view the disc's contents by choosing to explore the disc. To do so, open the My Computer window from your desktop and right-click the CD-ROM drive icon. Choose to Explore the drive so that the Windows Explorer appears. Locate the Setup program icon and launch the program. Once you launch the Setup program, the Setup Window appears (as shown in Figure 2.1 earlier in this chapter). To begin the installation of Image Composer, highlight Install Image Composer and click once. The Image Composer Setup Wizard launches and begins the installation.

Like most graphic manipulation programs, Image Composer has a variety of add-ons to choose from. You need to decide what installation suits your needs, and what type of work you'll be doing within Image Composer. You also need to decide which options are worth using hard drive space on and which are not. Figure 2.4 shows your first list of choices.

FIG. 2.4
Choose the Typical installation option if you are pressed for time or simply aren't concerned about hard disk drive space. This gives you the standard Microsoft components.

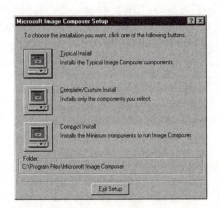

One aspect of graphics programs that never seems to change is that they need a lot of hard disk drive space to store their images and sample art. Image Composer is no exception, with a staggering 21 megabytes of sample photos and Web art. If you want to circumvent that hard drive bite, choose the Compact installation option, which will install the bare minimum needed to run the program. If you're not choosy about what's included in the installation or how much hard drive space you have, pick the Typical install. If you want to see it all, pick the Complete/Custom install. For these instructions, choose the Custom install to view even more options, as shown in Figure 2.5.

FIG. 2.5
Remember to keep an eye on your hard disk drive space as you choose components to install. Ideally, you should be able to install everything and still have a lot of space left.

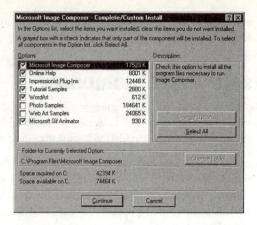

The Setup program options are:

- **Microsoft Image Composer**—The heart of Image Composer is the executable and resources required to run the program. Without installing this option, you might as well return to Paintbrush.

- **Online Help**—Online reference material is always useful. When you select this option, you are choosing to install the Microsoft Help files for Image Composer. Without this option, no online help is available.

- **Impressionist Plug-Ins**—For livening up your digital works of art, you can use this powerful add-in to Image Composer. The Impressionist Plug-ins let you create a variety of effects when applied to nearly any graphic. Use of the plug-ins is optional.

- **Tutorial Samples**—If you are new to Image Composer, the Tutorial Samples can help you adjust to the new program. These images teach you the fundamentals of using Image Composer, step by step.

- **Word Art**—For exciting text effects, Word Art is a fun and friendly addition to Image Composer. Similar to Word Art in Microsoft Office, this tool lets you create stylish text instead of using the bland defaults.

- **Photo Samples and Web Art Samples**—If you want to add free images to your Web site or discover ideas for your own images, try these samples. These images, created by professional artists and photographers, can make your image creation job easier. This is a sizable option and will take considerable space on your hard disk drive. You can still access the images from the CD-ROM if you choose not to install them here.

- **Microsoft GIF Animator**—Anyone who has visited a Web site with an animated GIF has surely said, "Wow, how did they do that?" Now you can also create animated works of art using the Microsoft GIF Animator. If you install this option, the GIF Animator is installed as a closely integrated add-in for Image Composer. If you do not plan on making Animated GIFs, you don't need to install this option.

NOTE Much like any other Microsoft setup program, you can use this one to delete the software as well. More importantly though, you can go back later and add components you don't necessarily want right away.

Connecting with Your Web Server

The primary appeal of FrontPage over many of the other Web-authoring suites is its capability to tie directly into your Web server. Accessing your Web server to update Web contents, FrontPage is a valuable development tool that eases the complexity of developing your Web site. Regardless of what kind of installation you have chosen, it makes little difference if you can't access your remote server. This is the main reason that FrontPage 98 exists as a development tool, to ease transactions between your remote server and you.

How you communicate with your Web server depends on your installation. If you do not have an existing Web server to develop on, the Microsoft Personal Web Server is an ideal local solution. However, if you already have an existing Web server on your workstation (such as Microsoft Internet Information Server), you only need to install the FrontPage server extensions on your machine.

▶ **See** "FrontPage and Other Web Servers," **p. 311**

Using Personal Web Server

Personal Web Server is the default local server to work with FrontPage 98. If you want to view or test your own work before publishing it then Personal Web Server is an ideal solution. Microsoft offers Personal Web Server as a part of FrontPage 98. You can also obtain it from their Web site as a Windows 95 upgrade, or on the CD-ROM of some releases of Windows 95 (Version B or OSR2 to be precise). Installation of the MPWS depends on how you have obtained the package (in FrontPage, online, or as part of Windows 95) but is a very simple process of one installation program. No intervention is required on your part for the installation. Administration however, is a bit different.

The Personal Web Server is administered through a series of easy-to-use Web pages. The entire process is simple, yet powerful, especially for people who don't necessarily know much about the World Wide Web. Keep in mind that the MPWS is the direct descendant of the powerful Microsoft Internet Information Server family of Web servers, which prides itself on power and ease of administration. When the MPWS is installed, a new icon is added to your icon tray. This icon, resembling a globe, is for the Personal Web Server and acts as a shortcut for administration. To access the administrative functions of the Personal Web Server, follow these quick steps:

1. Locate the MPWS icon in the icon tray. If the icon is not present, open the Personal Web Server control panel and click the Administer button.

2. Right-click the MPWS icon and choose <u>A</u>dminister. This launches your Web browser to display the administrative functions page, shown in Figure 2.6.

FIG. 2.6
Almost every aspect of your Personal Web Server can be controlled from the Internet Services Administrator. You can do so from any Web-enabled workstation on your network.

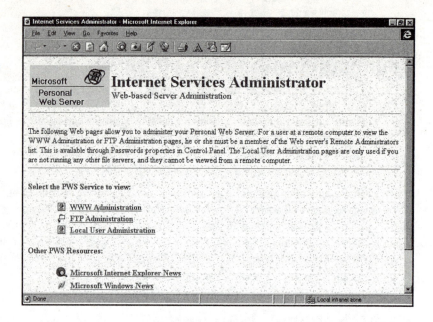

The first page of the Internet Services Administrator site provides you with links to the three different aspects of administration.

- The WWW Administration, which leads to three tributary pages that let you assign directory permissions, control logging behavior, and set general attributes for your Personal Web Server.
- The FTP Administration page, which lets you set server messages, directory permissions, and logging behavior, much the same as the WWW Administration.
- The Local User Administrator, which allows you to control user accounts and access if you don't have any other means of security in place.

Administering Your WWW Service

The WWW Administration pages let you control how your Web server reacts on the Web; most of the controls within the pages deal with granting permissions in one way or another. Three pages comprise the WWW Administration section and are selectable by clicking the named tabs along the top of the page. These three pages are:

- **Service**—The Service page is used to control the service-specific aspects of the Personal Web Server. This includes connection limitations and security.
- **Directories**—Web sites are filled with directories and virtual directories. All management of these resources is handled on the Directories page.

■ **Logging**—If you want to keep track of who has been visiting your Web server, the Personal Web Server provides you with a series of options for logging. The Logging page lets you determine the frequency of log files and the size.

By default, you'll be sent to the Service Administration page when entering the WWW Administration section, as shown in Figure 2.7.

FIG. 2.7
The Service administration page lets you control connection limits and security authentication for your Personal Web Server.

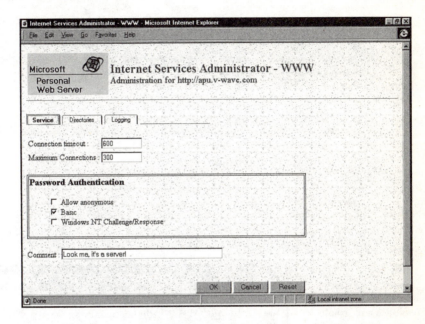

This page provides you with three basic regions for configuration:

■ **Connection limitations**—The Connection Timeout and Maximum Connections fields let you control just how busy your Web server can get. Used in conjunction, you can effectively limit the amount of strain the Personal Web Server can enact on your workstation. The Connection Timeout field is used to determine how long a connection between the Web server and a browser should remain open before lapsing due to lack of response. The higher the value, the longer the delay, thus the longer a connection remains open.

Closely tied to the Timeout value is the Maximum Connections field. Using this field, you can effectively limit the total number of simultaneous connections to your Web server. Once the maximum is reached, your server declines to serve any new requests until the server is less busy. Keep in mind for your calculations that each object on your Web page (graphics, multimedia files, the page itself) count as a connection.

■ **Password authentication**—How visitors credentials are identified is an important aspect of security. When you deal with a public site (such as an Internet Web server for your home page), the option to Allow Anonymous should be selected. However, when you deal with more sensitive data (perhaps on an intranet), you have two tighter methods for how password and account information is transmitted. Using Basic Authentication, all passwords and user names are transmitted in a clear text burst without any encoding or encryption. Challenge/Response, however, requires authentication from an Internet Explorer browser and passes the user's name and password to the server in an encrypted exchange.

> **CAUTION**
> Basic authentication calls can be easily intercepted and decoded. This means more than just access to a particular Web site, since the account information could be applicable to any aspect of your server, depending on your configuration.

- **Comment**—The final text box is a simple item. You can enter a comment about your server in this space. This is used for your own reference when you manage more than one Web server. Your comment should be a descriptive entry, such as "Bob's Web server for serving the accounting data."

The next administrative section is the Directories page. This page controls how directories are referred to, and what basic operations are allowable within those directories. When you enter the Directories page, you'll be presented with a listing of all of your Web directories, as shown in Figure 2.8.

FIG. 2.8
From the Directories page, you can create, edit, and even remove the virtual directories of your Web site.

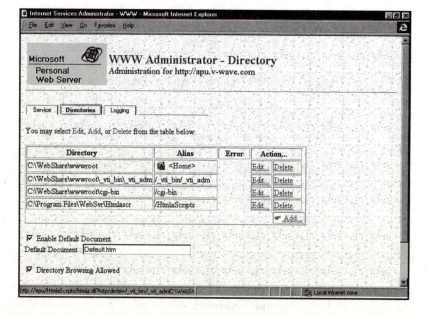

Virtual Directory—What is it?
A virtual directory acts like a place holder on your Web site for a physical directory somewhere on your computer (or network). Virtual directory structures aren't forced to duplicate the physical directory structure in any way. You can use virtual directories to pool different directories into one common structure. For example, consider that your Web server's document root (**http://www.yourserver.dom/**) is located at C:\WebShare. You have a directory full of Web content located at D:\Projects\Web. Using a virtual directory, you can leave your Web content directory where it is and map it to your Web server as **http://www.yourserver.dom/project/**.

The Directories page gives you five essential functions:

- **Adding virtual directories**—Creating a new virtual directory is an easy task. When you click the Add button below the directory list, you are prompted for the location of the physical directory and the name for the new virtual directory. You also can control if this new virtual directory will act as the "home," or root, directory for your Web server. Finally, you can control the Read and Execute permissions for this directory. If you select the Read check box, the contents of the directory are available to your visitors. However, if you do not want visitors to read the content, you can deselect this check box. The Execute check box is used to indicate that the directory contains server side programs, such as a CGI application or an Active Server Pages script. Without this check box selected, these programs will not run for visitors. Keep in mind that you do not need Read permissions for Execute permissions to function.

> **CAUTION**
> Grant execute access sparingly. If you give a user the ability to execute programs within a certain directory, there's nothing stopping that user from creating an application that damages or crashes your computer.

- **Deleting virtual directories**—If you have an existing virtual directory that you are ready to retire, it is a simple job to remove it. Beside each virtual directory in the directory list is a Delete action button. By clicking this button, you can remove the virtual directory from the Web server. The physical directory that this virtual directory referred to is left untouched.

- **Editing virtual directories**—There are times that changes must be made. When you have an existing virtual directory that you want to modify, click the Edit action button beside the directory name. This allows you to reopen the directory options page, identical to adding a new virtual directory, to alter the directory's configuration.

- **Setting the default document**—When a visitor enters your Web server's URL into their Web browser, your server returns with the appropriate document. If that URL ends with a virtual directory name (for example, **http://www.yourserver.dom/**) rather than a specific file (for example, **http://www.yourserver.dom/default.htm**), the Personal

Web Server searches the directory for a document matching the name of the default document. This document is the first document displayed when a visitor visits your site without specifying a file. You can choose to disable the default document, or to change the name of the default document to suit your needs. The default is default.htm.

- **Allowing directory browsing**—When your visitor enters a URL for a directory that does not have a default document, or if you have disabled the default document for your server, the Personal Web Server displays the contents of the directory to the visitor. If you do not want visitors to see the full contents of your directories, disable this option.

The final administrative page is the Logging page. The page is very simple, but you should always know ahead of time what sorts of arrangements are being made for user access logs. Logs are a contingency measure; you don't think of reading them until you actually need them. The Logging page can enable whether logging is actually turned, from the Enable Logging check box.

You can also choose to automatically open a new log depending on certain timed intervals. The possible increments are daily, weekly, monthly, or when the log reaches a certain size. Weekly logs are a nice digestible size and only require weekly readings to keep current. A monthly log can be quite a burden to read through in its entirety.

Which logging type you decide upon depends mostly on the amount of traffic you foresee visiting your site. If you have a lot of traffic going through, you may want to consider a smaller log in the weekly or daily scale. Sparse or erratic traffic can be tracked on a monthly basis. You can also decide exactly where the logs should be stored, which can makes things easier for remote administration, although downloading 500 megabytes of log file could take a long time.

Using FrontPage Server Extensions

If you run Microsoft Personal Web Server, Personal Web Services (under Windows NT Workstation), or Internet Information Server (under Windows NT Server), then your FrontPage server extensions are automatically installed. However, if you use another vendor's Web server, you must install the server extensions on your own. Microsoft offers a stand-alone server extension package that you can install into most existing Windows Web servers, as well as separate server extension packages for several UNIX environments.

▶ **See** "FrontPage and Other Servers," **p. 311**

The server extensions will integrate smoothly with most existing Windows 32-bit server packages. For example, you can install FrontPage functionality on all of Netscape's server suites and the O'Reilly Web Site. Support for several UNIX platforms (ranging from Linux to Solaris) and Web servers (such as Netscape, Apache, NCSA, and CERN) is also provided. You can find your copy of the stand-alone server extensions on the FrontPage CD-ROM in the \ServExt directory. There are several different files to be found there, organized based on processor type and language. For example, the traditional Intel processor, English language file name would be "FP98EXT_X86_ENU.EXE". To install the extensions, you need simply to launch the self-extracting installation program and follow the wizard's instructions. If you run a non-Microsoft server package, you will be prompted for an Administrator account and password to control the FrontPage Server Extensions. You can later utilize this account using the FrontPage Explorer.

You can also find the most recent FrontPage server extensions and the FrontPage Server Extensions Resource Kit on Microsoft's Web site, at **http://www.microsoft.com/frontpage/wpp/**.

The server extensions are vital for you to fully utilize FrontPage, as an aid in developing Web content and as a powerful site management tool. The server extensions can make remote administration simple and can also be integrated into other Microsoft products, such as Visual InterDev. Without the server extensions, you are forced to upload content using the Microsoft Web Publishing Wizard, having no remote control over directory structure and permissions aside from what your current server package grants you. ●

CHAPTER 3

A Guided Tour to the FrontPage Components

As the previous chapter introduced, FrontPage is comprised of several different components. These different programs each offer you a flexible tool for accomplishing a specific task. This chapter concentrates on the five different components of FrontPage 98, making your transition to using them easy. Each component is briefly discussed, with highlights of the component's features listed in an easy-to-read format. Helpful screenshots have also been included to help you quickly identify each program. To round out each component's description is a brief summary on when and why you would use each particular component. If you are new to FrontPage, carefully read through this chapter, as it will introduce each program you will be using in the rest of this book. ■

Web site exploration
The FrontPage Explorer gives you a useful management tool for maintaining and organizing your Web site.

Masterful Web page editing
If the FrontPage Explorer was your eyes, the FrontPage Editor would be your hands. This powerful WYSIWYG editor lets you quickly create extravagant Web pages for your site.

Web service with a smile
When you're looking for a home for your Web site, the Microsoft Personal Web Server is a surprisingly robust server for low-demand hosting and local testing.

Be a digital Monet
Whether or not you are an accomplished artist, Microsoft Image Composer is a friendly and powerful image creation tool that can enhance your Web site with vibrant graphics.

Publishing straight to the server
When you deploy your Web site to a server that doesn't support FrontPage Server Extensions, the Microsoft Web Publishing Wizard takes over and handles the messy task of updating your site for you.

Introducing the FrontPage Explorer

If you think of FrontPage 98 as a complete system, the FrontPage Explorer (shown in Figure 3.1) is the hub of activity. Almost everything you do in FrontPage in some way involves the FrontPage Explorer. This important program comprises the backbone of the FrontPage environment and empowers you to successfully manage your Web site.

FIG. 3.1
The FrontPage Explorer is your infallible hand in managing and manipulating your Web site to your satisfaction.

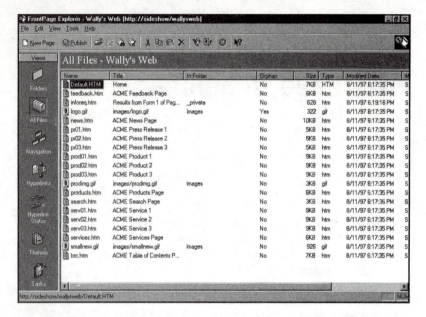

The singular task of the FrontPage Explorer is to provide you with a management tool for your Web site. Using the Explorer, you can manipulate your existing FrontPage Webs (independent Web sites) and create new ones. You can also maintain your site using the Explorer's "quality-assurance" features, such as link checking. The Explorer was created to give you one tool to organize and control your Web site without relying on complicated third-party programs. You can easily move, delete, and rename your Web site contents, add new files, and even apply a *theme* to your entire site. The Explorer in FrontPage 98 has been enhanced from previous versions and offers you many compelling features, some of which are:

- *Creation of professional-quality Web sites of many different types using FrontPage wizards and templates.* You don't need to be a professional Web developer to create a vibrant and effective site. Microsoft has included an array of predesigned sites that you can customize to fit your needs.
- *Comprehensive support for multiple contributor environments.* As an administrator, you can limit the abilities of contributing authors and even restrict end-users.
- *Graphical viewing of your Web site and its contents.* Rather than sift through an endless directory listing for your Web site, you can use FrontPage Explorer's powerful views to display your site. You can view and track each hyperlink in your site to insure its quality.

- *Automatic hyperlink reference updates.* If you use the FrontPage Explorer to move or rename a content file, the Explorer can then go back and fix any hyperlinks to the affected documents—all this without any intervention required on your part.
- *Easy import of new and existing content.* If you already have a ream of content ready for your Web site, you don't need to recreate it in FrontPage. You can easily use the FrontPage Explorer to import your files and add them to your Web site.
- *Easier editing through associations.* FrontPage Explorer associates your content files with the program you used to create them. You can modify a file by double-clicking its icon, instead of opening it separately. You can also change the program associations to suit your needs.
- *Comprehensive to-do lists.* Maintaining a Web site can be a headache involving scraps of paper reminding you of what has to be done. The Explorer gives you an integrated Tasks List for your Web site that makes it easy to name, track, and complete all unfinished tasks. You can use the Tasks List to assign jobs to other authors, and even have some tasks automatically added and removed as needed.

What Does the FrontPage Explorer Look Like?

The FrontPage Explorer resembles a modified Windows Explorer interface. Using the new Microsoft Office 97 style toolbars (where the icons change to a highlighted box on a mouseover), Explorer also inherits some of the new interface conventions from Internet Explorer 4.0/Windows 98. This includes underline selection on a mouseover and single-click functionality in file lists. The Explorer interface has a standard toolbar along the top of the window, and a vertical icon bar that you can use to switch "views" within the larger screen region of the Explorer window. Using the view buttons, you can change the Explorer view to suit your particular task at the moment. Samples of three different views are shown in Figure 3.2, Figure 3.3, and Figure 3.4.

When Will I Use the FrontPage Explorer?

If you are using FrontPage 98 as your primary Web development environment, you will practically live inside the FrontPage Explorer. The Explorer is used as a launching pad for all other work for your Web site. The creation of new sites and pages is all done from the Explorer, with supplementary programs (such as the FrontPage Editor and Image Composer) being launched from within the Explorer. Even if you are not using FrontPage exclusively in your Web development, you likely will be using the Explorer to manage and organize your content for upload to your Web server. The FrontPage Explorer also handles the task of updating your Web server automatically using the FrontPage server extensions, or the Web Publishing Wizard if the extensions are not available.

FIG. 3.2
The Folder view is the default view in the Explorer. Using this view, you can manipulate your site contents as you do your hard drive with the Windows Explorer.

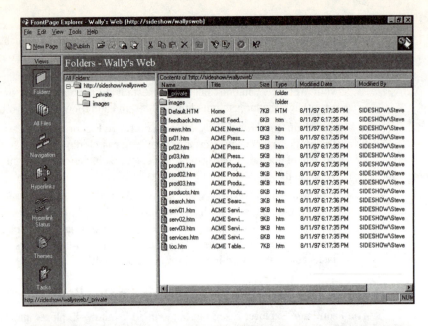

FIG. 3.3
Navigation view is new to FrontPage 98. Using this view, you can easily manipulate your site, as well as create comprehensive site maps.

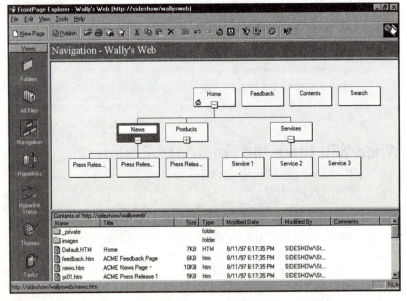

Introducing the FrontPage Editor

The FrontPage Editor (Figure 3.5) is to the World Wide Web what Microsoft Word is to the print world. The Editor is Microsoft's attempt at creating the end-all and be-all of What-You-See-Is-What-You-Get (WYSIWYG) Web page creation tools, while retaining close integration with the FrontPage Explorer. The Editor in FrontPage 98 has been updated to provide even easier page creation for beginners and more advanced features for expert developers. While previous versions of the Editor were geared more toward neophytes and intermediates, this release appeals to nearly anyone creating Web content. You can compare the FrontPage Editor with the early desktop publishing software, such as Adobe PageMaker. In this context, the FrontPage Editor is to the Web what the early DTP programs were to print documents.

FIG. 3.4
Use the HyperLink view to monitor the links that exist within your site. You can also track broken links to other pages or even images.

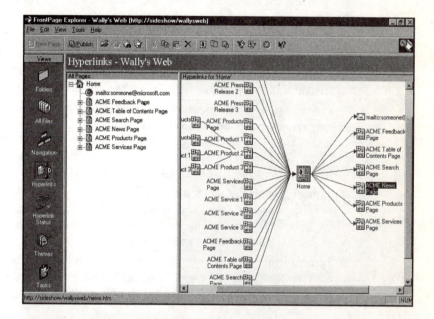

FIG. 3.5
Creating great pages no longer requires knowledge of HTML.

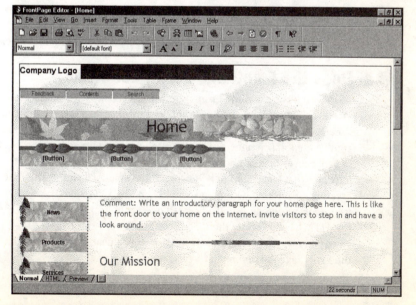

While you use the FrontPage Explorer to create and organize your Web site, it is actually the job of the FrontPage Editor to create the individual Web pages. Using the Editor like you would a word processor, you can create attractive and full-featured Web pages without needing to enter a single line of HTML code (although you can, if you want). The Editor also keeps in mind the recent efforts of Microsoft to make document creation easier with drag-and-drop and a simple, friendly interface. All editing in the Editor takes place in a view that displays how your page will look to the visitor. You can also preview all of your work in an external browser to make sure everything works just as you planned it. Although the Editor is a powerful tool, it remains easy to use and offers you a great deal of features, such as:

- **Create beautiful pages using templates and wizards.** Just as the FrontPage Explorer gives you site level templates and wizards, the Editor lets you take advantage of templates and wizards created by Web development professionals.

- **Import existing documents of many differing formats.** Not only can you import existing Web pages and retain all information, you can also use the FrontPage Editor to import almost any Microsoft Office document and retain most formatting. FrontPage Editor also takes advantage of Office 97's Web integration features by retaining all hyperlinks you may have placed in your document.

- **Import graphics of many different types.** You can insert almost any graphic by dragging it into the FrontPage Editor. The Editor will then deal with translating the image into a GIF or JPEG file usable on your Web site. You can also manipulate these images, including cropping and resizing, to fit your Web site's style.

- **Insert forms, components, and controls in an instant.** The FrontPage Editor's interface lets you enhance your Web page with forms, FrontPage components, ActiveX controls and Java applets. The friendly interface lets you double-click any item and change its properties without effort.

- **View and manipulate your frames and tables.** The WYSIWYG interface of the FrontPage Editor lets you visualize your pages exactly as they will appear. Manipulating your frames and tables is a point-and-click effort, without any extra coding.

What Does the FrontPage Editor Look Like?

It isn't surprising that the FrontPage Editor has inherited some similarities with Microsoft Word. The most dominant region of the Editor screen is the editing area. This area behaves exactly how you would expect a WYSIWYG editor to; as you enter text and elements, you can control their appearance and position. Above the editing area are two toolbars that provide instant access to commonly used Editor features. At the bottom of the screen area is a tabbed interface that lets you switch between three standard views. The first, Normal view, is used for creating and editing your pages with the WYSIWYG interface. The second view, HTML, is useful for intermediate and advanced users who want to take charge and manually control the raw HTML code behind the Web page. Finally, the third view is the Preview. Using Preview view, you can see exactly how your page will appear in the end user's browser and outside of the FrontPage environment.

Figure 3.6 shows the FrontPage Editor in the Normal view, creating a new Web page using a provided theme.

FIG. 3.6.
FrontPage Editor's Normal view is where you will spend most of your time. It differs only slightly from the Preview, giving you visual indications for editing.

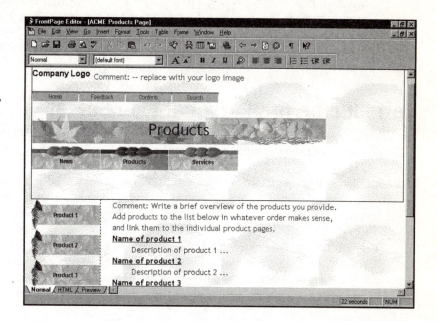

If you are ready to move beyond a WYSIWYG view and manually control the HTML code of your Web page, the HTML view will be useful. The HTML view is shown in Figure 3.7:

FIG. 3.7
HTML view lets you create and edit your pages using a text-editing environment. Raw HTML code appears and can be edited freely.

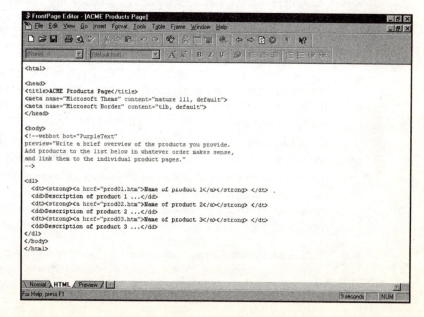

When Will I Use the FrontPage Editor?

The FrontPage Editor is used any time you want to edit the contents of an existing Web page or create a new one. You *can* use a different editor and still use the FrontPage Explorer to organize your site, but this is unlikely considering the power of the FrontPage Editor. In the hands of a novice or an expert, masterfully created Web pages take minimal effort when using the creative features of the program.

Introducing the Personal Web Server

Accurate Web development relies on using a real-time connection with a Web server. When it is unrealistic to be constantly connected to your public Web server, or when you don't even have one, the Microsoft Personal Web Server gives you a small and effectual Web server that runs on your Windows 95 workstation. The MPWS gives you a solid and speedy local Web server that is ideal for your own development or serving content to a low traffic intranet. You can even use the MPWS to share your message on the Internet if you have a dedicated connection.

NOTE Why not include a Personal Web Server for Windows NT Workstation 4.0? Simple: because you already have one! Windows NT Workstation 4.0 includes the powerful Peer Web Services Web and FTP server. The PWS is a user-limited version of the enterprise Internet Information Server included with Windows NT Server 4.0.

For your Web content to be viewable by the public, you need a Web server. You can use the Microsoft Personal Web Server either to publish your material in a low traffic environment, or to carry out your own development on a local Web server. Without the presence of a Web server, many of FrontPage's features are limited or completely unavailable. You can use the MPWS as a local Web server on your workstation to develop and test your Web site, and then deploy the final product to your production Web server. The Personal Web Server gives you many features, including:

- *High performance local Web hosting.* The MPWS is based on the powerful Microsoft Internet Information Server architecture, part of Microsoft Windows NT Server. This gives you a reliable and robust little Web server that is ideal for serving content to a small local area network or to a few visitors on the Internet.
- *Extensibility with server side applications.* You can also extend your Web site with server side activation in the form of ISAPI applications, CGI programs, and Active Server Pages.
- *Ease of use and maintenance.* Running the Microsoft Personal Web Server couldn't be easier. A new control panel is added to your Windows 95 configuration that lets you choose the MPWS startup options and control the Web server. Administration of the server is all done using your Web browser, such as Internet Explorer.

NOTE ISAPI and CGI Active Server Pages. What are they? ISAPI stands for *Internet Server Application Programming Interface*. ISAPI is a high-level feature for programmers to create powerful Web-based applications. You can create ISAPI programs using C++, Borland Delphi, or

Microsoft Visual BASIC. CGI, or *Common Gateway Interface*, is the industry-wide standard for server programs. You can use the CGI standard to run server side programs and scripts from almost any platform. Active Server Pages, or *ASP*, is a Microsoft solution for server side activity without complex programming. ASP lets you embed scripting code into your Web pages and have it completed on the server before it is sent to your visitor's Web browser. ■

What Does the Personal Web Server Look Like?

Unlike the other FrontPage 98 components, the MPWS runs primarily in the background of your computer. You have little visual interaction with the Personal Web Server, except when you start and stop the service or configure it. The fact that you can see your Web pages is testament to the Personal Web Server's functionality. What little interaction you *will* have with the Microsoft Personal Web Server will be through the Web Server control panel (shown in Figure 3.8). Any configuration changes that you may want to make to the server are done through your Web browser and a series of administrative Web pages, shown in Figure 3.9.

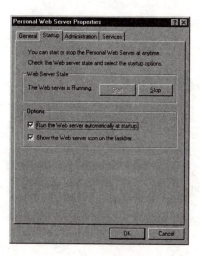

FIG. 3.8
The Web Services control panel lets you start and stop the Web service, as well as control the Web server's startup behavior.

When Will I Use the Personal Web Server?

If you do not have an existing Web server to work on, you will need to use the Personal Web Server. If you work on a local area network, you may be able to connect to your LAN Web server and use it with the FrontPage server extensions. You can also connect to the Internet and Web servers if your machine is set up to do so. However, if you have no other Web server to work on for your development, you will want to use the MPWS as your construction platform.

FIG. 3.9
When you want to change an aspect of your Personal Web Services setup, you can use your Web browser and the administrative Web pages.

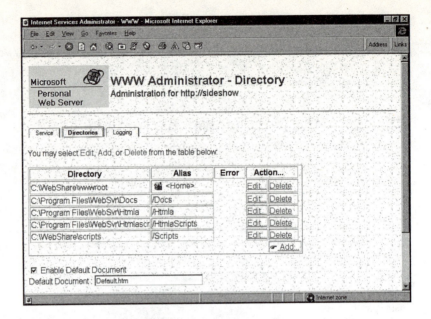

Introducing Image Composer

Web pages aren't just reams of text, at least not anymore. Web pages now are filled with rich and colorful graphics and images to enhance our experiences. In the past, creating graphics usable for the Web was complicated and often relied on expensive and/or confusing software. Thankfully, Microsoft recognized the need for an inexpensive and easy-to-use package and introduced Microsoft Image Composer (shown in Figure 3.10). Image Composer acts as a virtual canvas for your imagination, letting you create imagery for your Web site without needing to be an accomplished artist. Moreover, although Image Composer is cheap and easy, it certainly isn't limited. Image Composer offers you a variety of tools and features to let you create your Web-based masterpiece.

If you have ever opened Microsoft Paintbrush in aspiration of creating the next great digital masterpiece, you've undoubtedly learned how difficult it is to translate your mind's eye into a beautiful image. Image Composer tries to help you out by making image creation an easier, if not more fun, endeavor. Using a series of helpful tools and features, Image Composer lets you create graphics that are ideal for your Web site. Image Composer also includes a powerful array of "shortcuts" called *filters*, that you can use to enhance your picture and make it that piece of art you've wanted all along. The features of Image Composer are many, such as:

- *Powerful sprite-based technology.* Rather than using simple bitmaps like most Web image creation packages, Image Composer uses *sprites*. A sprite is an image object with shape and transparency, and when combined with other sprites, it creates a *composition* (the final image).

- *Industry standard formats.* Image Composer doesn't reinvent the wheel. Instead, Image Composer uses the industry-standard graphic file formats created by leading vendors, such as TIFF, GIF, PNG, JPEG, PhotoShop, and more. Image Composer also takes advantage of the industry standard for image importing, TWAIN, when dealing with scanners and digital cameras.
- *Simple wizards for creation.* You can use Image Composer's friendly button wizard to create the ideal button and image for your Web site, even if you are new to graphic creation.
- *Popular plug-in support.* Image Composer supports the industry-standard PhotoShop plug-in interface. These plug-ins let you extend Image Composer's feature set and enhance your images.

FIG. 3.10
Microsoft Image Composer has the power and features to make even novice artists come across as professionals.

What Does Image Composer Look Like?

Whether you have used a competing program or not, Image Composer is easy to learn. The Image Composer interface is comprised of two toolbars: one vertical and one horizontal.
The horizontal (top) toolbar gives you quick access to commonly used features of the program. The second toolbar, positioned vertically on the left of the screen, provides you with buttons for each "tool" in the Image Composer tool set. As you select a tool from the toolbar, a tool window appears to provide you with options as you work. The largest region of the screen is the composition area that acts as your digital canvas; this is where you manipulate and modify sprites to create your images (see Figure 3.11).

FIG. 3.11
The Image Composer interface is a clearly organized one. As you select a tool from the toolbar, a tools option window appears.

When you manipulate sprites, you use the mouse to move them anywhere in the composition area, as shown in Figure 3.12.

FIG. 3.12
Selected sprites have a large black bounding box with handles around them. You use this bounding box to manipulate and move sprites around your virtual canvas.

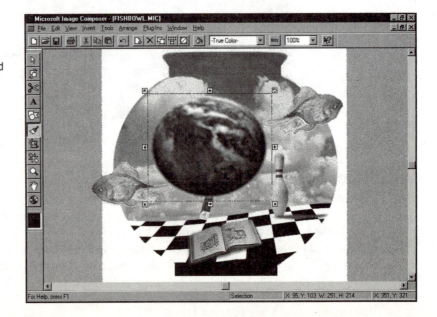

When Will I Use Image Composer?

If you want to liven up your Web site with original graphics, or if you want to customize existing graphics, Image Composer is likely the tool for you. Although you may be using an existing image manipulation program (such as Adobe PhotoShop), Image Composer can give you quick-and-easy access to creating and editing your graphics.

The Web Publishing Wizard

When using the FrontPage Server Extensions isn't an option, the Web Publishing Wizard is the means to your publishing ends. Deploying your Web site to a Web server traditionally involved the FTP protocol. Using a less-than-friendly FTP client, you would upload your content files each time you changed them. You were forced to navigate through your server's directory structure and create new directories, as you needed them. To solve the problems this caused, Microsoft has included a useful utility with FrontPage 98 called the Web Publishing Wizard. You can use the WPW (shown in Figure 3.13) to update your Web site using a simple Wizard-style approach, without relying on an FTP client.

FIG. 3.13
The Web Publishing Wizard is a welcome tool for those who have relied on FTP clients in the past.

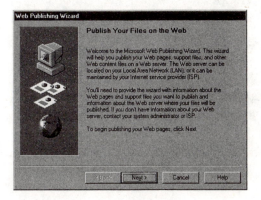

The Web Publishing Wizard acts by stepping you through a series of questions about your Web server. It supports both servers on the Internet or an intranet (using FTP), or on a local area network using Windows Networking. After you have decided how you want to upload your content and provided your credentials (a username and a password), the Web Publishing Wizard does the legwork of connecting to the server and uploading your content. The WPW offers you a few useful features:

- *Easy deployment without complication.* The Web Publishing Wizard uses a friendly, question-oriented Wizard to upload your Web site. You only need to provide your Web server's address, the method for transfer, and your credentials. The WPW handles the actual connection and upload without bothering you.

- *Stored server profiles.* You don't need to enter your server information each time you update your Web site. The Web Publishing Wizard remembers your servers and lets you choose them from a list rather than re-entering the information each time.
- *Support for FTP and Windows Networking.* If you are working over the Internet, FTP is the standard means for updating your site. However, on a local area network, you can take advantage of Windows Networking. Using the same means that you access a network printer, the WPW can update your site contents without issue.

What Does the Web Publishing Wizard Look Like?

You have used, no doubt, a wizard in other Microsoft programs, such as Microsoft Word or even FrontPage. The Web Publishing Wizard remains with the tried-and-true, step-by-step process of asking a question and letting you answer. You can use THE WPW from within the FrontPage Explorer or externally, straight from your Start Menu. Figure 3.14 shows how easy the Web Publishing Wizard is to use, by demonstrating how the wizard asks about your server.

FIG. 3.14
The Web Publishing Wizard remembers each server you connect to, so that you can quickly connect to it again in the future. Note how easy it is to set up a new connection.

In Figure 3.15, the Web Publishing Wizard begins the actual deployment of your Web site to the Web server.

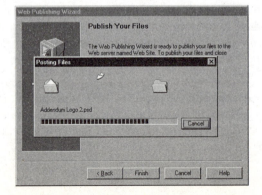

FIG. 3.15
Uploading your Web site with the Web Publishing Wizard is the best option if you aren't using the FrontPage Server Extensions.

When Will I Use the Web Publishing Wizard?

For environments that cannot (or will not) use the FrontPage server extensions on their Web server, the Web Publishing Wizard is the only convenient choice. If you cannot use the server extensions to update your Web site, use the convenient Web Publishing Wizard to put your site onto the network. ●

PART II

The FrontPage 98 Primer

4   Creating Your First Web Site   55

5   Working with the FrontPage Editor   67

6   Organizing Your First Web Site   81

CHAPTER 4

Creating Your First Web Site

The next three chapters are a FrontPage 98 Primer. We start with concepts and information you need to build an effective site, and then we take you through the process of using FrontPage to do it. Much of this chapter will focus on design principles rather than on working with the FrontPage software, but this is some of the most important information in the book. Web sites that fail usually do so because of bad planning in the initial design phase.

Determining the content of your site

Step one in creating any Web site is to plan it out. We'll talk about determining content, targeting the correct audience, and whether or not to use advanced technologies like Java and ActiveX.

Picking an effective layout

We'll discuss the impact that site layout has on your visitors. Look and feel are very important, as is navigation.

Importing an existing web

If you've already started building a Web site with other tools, you can use that as a starting point for your new FrontPage Web site.

Starting with a wizard or template

We'll discuss how you can jumpstart the creation of a new site with some of the Wizards and Templates that FrontPage provides.

Building your web site from scratch

We'll show you how to start your site with nothing more than a blank page.

Determining the Content of Your Site

The first step in building a Web site has nothing to do with software. This book is designed to help you get things done quickly, to look up a topic and find out how to accomplish something. This next section of the book is not as procedural as much of the rest of the material. This is because I cannot tell you exactly how to design an effective Web site. I can, however, tell you things you need to be thinking about when designing one. The fact that you are reading this means that you would like to know where to start. Start planning. I recommend that you plan your site out the old fashioned way, with a pencil and paper. Write down ideas for content, presentation and future growth. The information in this section will hopefully guide you.

The vast majority of Web sites that fail do so because of poor planning at the outset. Building a Web site is a deceptively easy task, especially with a powerful WYSIWYG editing tool like FrontPage. However, the one thing that will make or break your site is its content. It doesn't matter if you have the coolest, whiz-bang, animated, high-tech, gizmo-laden site in the world if the content isn't there. The three cardinal rules of Web site design I have developed for myself over the last three years are as follows:

1. Content is King.
2. Style is Queen.
3. Change or die.

(I know that Change could have been a prince or something, but I just like the sound of "Change or die." Humor me.) Let's take a look at each one of these rules.

Rule #1: Content Is King

The single most important thing you need to consider about your site is the content, because without compelling content your site is not going to attract anybody. It will be a Web-based ghost town.

The type of content you want on your site is going to vary depending on the target audience. Here are the most common audiences you're likely to have:

- The general Web-surfing public.
- Employees within your own company.
- Your existing clients and customers.

Your project might involve creating a corporate or personal Web presence, designing a corporate intranet, or creating a site to provide services to your current clients and customers. These differing types of sites are going to have radically different content requirements, but they'll all benefit from some careful design consideration. For example, a corporate site usually begins life by putting a bunch of corporate history and product information up on the Web. This is known as "brochure-ware" and isn't a bad start for getting your company up on the Web fast. However, shortly after the site goes up, the thrill of being on the Web wears off and you start to wonder, "Now what?" This happens all the time. Companies build Web sites with very little depth and then wonder why nobody ever visits. To avoid spending a lot of time and money producing a Web site that doesn't give you a return on your investment, ask yourself the following questions:

- Who is my target audience? How will they benefit from coming to my site?
- What am I trying to accomplish by putting up a Web site?
- How will I make my site stand out amid the millions of other sites on the Web?
- What will make people come back to my site?

Once you have some ideas, divide up your content logically. It often makes sense to write down your content ideas in an outline format as this may then also help you determine the physical layout of your site.

If you don't provide some sort of added value, you'll accomplish little by putting up a Web site. Some common ways to add value are:

- Providing forms to request information on products or services via e-mail.
- Setting up an online product catalog to sell your products.
- Providing links to other sites that contain information relevant to your area of expertise.

Sit down, grab a pencil and a notepad, and give these things some serious thought before you proceed. I recommend that you take the content ideas you just wrote down and think about how best to present those ideas to add value to your site.

Rule #2: Style Is Queen

Style is nearly as important as content. Good content presented in an unreadable or boring manner will hold the viewer's attention for less time than it took you to read this sentence. Many sites suffer from the following style mistakes:

- **Not enough flash.** You've seen the sites that are all plain text, with no graphics at all. Boring.
- **Too much flash.** Animations, music, Java applets, scrolling banners, dancing bears—and not one valuable idea. These sites take about a year to download and have 30 seconds' worth of valuable information.
- **Hard to read.** It seems like an obvious point, but some sites use confusing background patterns and badly chosen text colors that make the pages hard to read or give you a headache.
- **Difficult to navigate.** Many sites skip simple niceties, like having a link back to the main page located in a standard place on each page. Finding information on a site should be fast and easy.

Here are some things to keep in mind as you determine the style and layout of your site:

- Make your pages visually interesting but not distracting.

- Don't use technology for it's own sake. Make sure that everything on your site contributes to the goals of the site.
- Pay attention to the amount of time it takes to load each page. Large graphics, unnecessary controls, and other flashy extras will deter more people than they attract.
- Make sure your site is accessible to everybody in your target audience. If you design a site that can only be viewed by people with a certain browser, for example, you're only hurting yourself by keeping those people away from your site.

I have a sketch book that I use for designing the layout of my site. Pencil and paper allow you to work as you think and to quickly correct mistakes. Draw screen layouts for every screen you are going to have in your site. This will make it much easier to actually construct the site later and to visualize the results in advance. Plan a color scheme and use it consistently.

A Good Example of a Bad Example

Before we leave this topic, here's a great example of a badly planned site that I ran into recently. I was given a call by the president of the company I work for. He was trying to load up the Web page of a company that he was interested in doing business with. When he tried to load up their page, a box popped up from Internet Explorer informing him that a potential security threat had been avoided. When he clicked the OK button, he was left staring at an empty page. Why? The designers of the site had included an ActiveX control on the front page of their site that wasn't digitally signed, and therefore could not be downloaded by Internet Explorer at its strictest security setting. This control also couldn't be downloaded by 70% of the people surfing the Web, as the majority of Web browsers do not support ActiveX. Without installing that control, there was no way to get to the site because they didn't even include a simple link to their main page from the front page. Basically, the only people in the world who could view this Web site were people running Internet Explorer 3 or newer with a low security level set.

So, what did this incredibly limiting control do? It displayed a quick little animation that you had to click to get into the main site. If this had been accomplished with an animated GIF graphic, it would have set off no security warnings and would have allowed even users of text-based browsers to browse the site. Instead of enhancing the site, this ActiveX control made it impossible to use for all but a small percentage of the Web-surfing public. Needless to say, the company president wasn't too impressed by their Web site.

Rule #3: Change or Die

Finally, change is not only good, it's essential to the long-term survival of your site. Building a Web site isn't a one-time project; it's a continual process. You'll always be adding to it, revamping it, and enhancing it. When I talk about change, I don't mean just restructuring the information on your site to look better. Visual facelifts are somewhat important to your site, but some of the most popular sites on the Web have had the same general look for years. A good example is **http://www.yahoo.com**, possibly the most popular site on the Web.

No, the kind of change I'm referring to is content change. If you don't add anything new or interesting to your site on a regular basis, there will be very little reason for anybody to come back to your site after they've read it once. But if you provide a monthly column about the state of your industry, for example, you might get people to bookmark your site and come back next month to read the latest column.

There are plenty of different ways to keep your site interesting, and how you do it is up to you. Just make sure that you have a plan for the future of your site. It will affect your initial design.

Picking an Effective Layout

So you've figured out the kind of content you want to present on your site, and you know how you're going to keep it interesting over time. Now you need to figure out how it's going to be organized. A well laid out site will be easy to read and easy to navigate, and will make it easy to find the most important information.

Before you determine the look of your site, analyze your content from the standpoint of your target audience. Ask yourself the following questions:

- Can I divide this information into logical groups?
- What's the first thing I want my audience to see?
- What will my audience most likely be interested in seeing first?
- How can I make this information as easily accessible as possible?
- Are there ways that advanced technology, like Java, can present this material more effectively?

By planning not only the content but also the structure of the content, you'll be better equipped to determine a visual look for your site, as well as to determine if you need to add some of the cool interactivity and multimedia that many Web designers have fallen in love with.

If you've thoroughly planned out your site, from your goals and target audience all the way down to your structure, content, and layout, you're ready to begin creating your Web site. So, let's get to it!

Importing an Existing Web Site

There are several ways to start a Web site in FrontPage, and we'll go through each way in the next few sections of this chapter. This section will discuss the process you go through when you're starting with a site that's already in place. If you're starting from scratch, I recommend that you skip this section and move on to the next section, which is about starting your Web site with the FrontPage wizards and templates.

This section assumes that you want to start your Web site by bringing in an existing site. This could be the case if you're taking over an existing corporate Web site, or even if you've already started a Web site using a different authoring tool and would now like to work with it in FrontPage.

> **CAUTION**
> It can be tempting to save yourself some work by importing a Web site you really like and modifying it to suit your needs. However, some people who've done this have found themselves facing copyright suits. If you want to use an existing site as a starting point, make sure that you have permission from the creator of the site.

Importing an existing Web site into FrontPage is fairly simple. First, you'll need to create a new FrontPage Web. You can do this either by selecting "Create a New FrontPage Web" when you first open up FrontPage, or by selecting the File menu item, choosing New, and clicking FrontPage Web. You'll be presented with the screen shown in Figure 4.1.

FIG. 4.1
You can create a new Web site by importing an existing site, by using a wizard or template, or by starting with a single blank page.

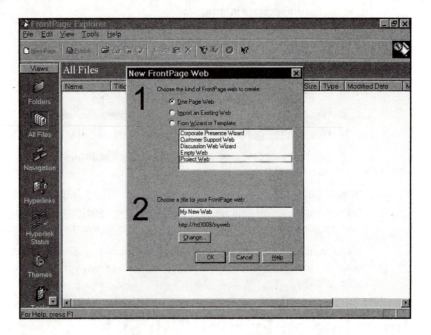

In order to import an existing site, select Import an Existing Web and then click the OK button. This will start up the Import Wizard.

Make sure to give your Web a unique name. If there's already a Web with the name you give, you'll get an error.

The Import Wizard will take you step by step through the process of importing an existing Web site, either from the Internet or from files stored on your own hard drive. The first step in the wizard is shown in Figure 4.2.

FIG. 4.2
The Import Web Wizard allows you to bring a Web site into FrontPage from either the Internet or your hard drive.

If you choose to import your site from your hard drive, you should put a drive letter and subdirectory into the Location box. Otherwise, you should put in the URL of a Web site. When you've chosen one or the other, click Next.

 If You're Importing From Your Hard Drive: You'll see a list of files to choose from. By default, all of the files in the directory you chose will be imported. If there are any files you don't want to import, you should select them and click the Exclude button. The file selection box is shown in Figure 4.3.

FIG. 4.3
Choose the files you want to import into your new Web site from your hard drive. Pick those you want to exclude and click the Exclude button.

After clicking Next one more time, you'll see the final dialog box of the Import Wizard. Click Finish and FrontPage will create your new site.

 If You're Importing Your Site From the Internet: After entering the URL of the site you want to import and clicking Next, you will see the dialog box shown in Figure 4.4. You can limit the number of levels imported from the site and the number of kilobytes' worth of data to import, or limit the imported files to text and image files. You might do so if the site you're importing is really large and you don't want to import the entire site. Go ahead and limit the download if you want. If you don't check any of the boxes, every file that's linked to on the entire site will be imported into your new Web site. Click Next and then click Finish to import your site from the Internet.

FIG. 4.4
The Import from the Internet dialog box lets you limit the amount of information imported from the Internet Web site.

Once the Web site is imported, you can start working with it. In fact, you can even skip to the next chapter to start learning how to work with your pages in the FrontPage Editor.

Starting with Wizards or Templates

FrontPage provides several different Wizards and Templates to help you get a head start on your site. We won't cover each and every one of them here. If you want to know more about what they can do for you, check out Chapter 10. For the purposes of this chapter, we're going to take you through the most commonly used Wizard: the Corporate Presence Wizard.

First, you'll need to create a new FrontPage Web. You can do this either by selecting "Create a New FrontPage Web" when you first open up FrontPage, or by selecting the File menu item, then choosing New, and finally clicking FrontPage Web. When you get a dialog box asking you how you want to start your new FrontPage Web (shown in Figure 4.1), you should choose From Wizard or Template and then click Corporate Presence Wizard in the box that lists the available Wizards and Templates. Enter a unique name for your new site, and click OK to have FrontPage create your new site and load up the Corporate Presence Wizard.

The Wizard will take you a step at a time through the process of creating a new site by asking you various questions about your company and about the kind of site you want. The types of pages you can add to your site in the first dialog box include:

- What's New
- Products/Services
- Table of Contents
- Feedback Form
- Search Form

The second dialog box asks for the information you would like to display on the front page of your site. This box is pictured in Figure 4.5.

FIG. 4.5
You can choose which topics to show on your home page by checking the boxes in the Corporate Presence Wizard.

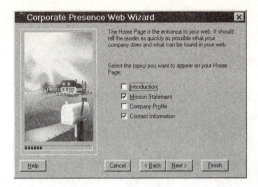

Depending on the pages you choose to show on your Web site, you'll be prompted for different information as you go through the Wizard. Read each of the dialog boxes and answer the questions. You'll be asked to provide detailed information on your company, products, and contact information so that FrontPage can create your corporate Web site for you.

One of the more interesting features of the Corporate Presence Wizard is the Feedback Form section. You can choose which pieces of information you want to gather about visitors when they provide you with comments, as illustrated in Figure 4.6.

FIG. 4.6
By selecting the pieces of information you want to gather from your visitors, you can build a database of contacts.

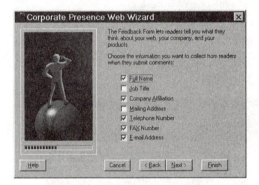

When soliciting feedback from your Web site, you have your choice of formats in which to store the information. As shown in Figure 4.7, you can either store the data in a Tab-Delimited format or in a Web Page format. If you choose the Tab-Delimited Format, you'll be able to import your feedback into a database, contact manager, or spreadsheet (such as Microsoft Excel).

Another important feature of the Corporate Presence Wizard is the capability to define header and footer information that will show up on every page of your Web site. You can show the any of the following at the top of each page:

Chapter 4 Creating Your First Web Site

- Your Company's Logo
- The Page Title
- Links to Your Main Pages

FIG. 4.7
You have your choice of a format that can be read into a database, or that can be displayed in a Web browser for the feedback you collect on your site.

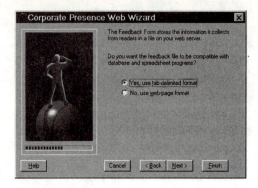

You can choose to show any of the following in your footer:

- Links to Your Main Pages
- The e-mail address of your Webmaster
- A copyright notice
- Last modified date

This dialog box is illustrated in Figure 4.8.

FIG. 4.8
Select the header and footer information you would like to have automatically displayed on all of your pages in this dialog box of the Corporate Presence Wizard.

Eventually you'll come to a dialog box that will ask you to choose a Web Theme. You don't need to choose it at this point if you don't want to, but FrontPage offers you quite a selection of graphics, buttons, and colors. You can always choose a theme later, but it's sort of fun to go through them here and pick a style you like. In Figure 4.9, you see the Web Theme dialog box, where you can preview the looks of various Themes.

Starting with Wizards or Templates 65

FIG. 4.9
FrontPage comes with a variety of Web Themes, including the cool LaVerne & Shirley style shown here. Selecting Active Graphics will give you buttons that visually react to mouse movements.

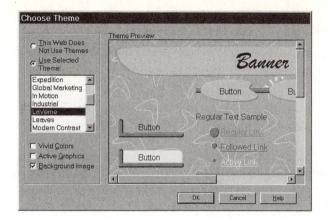

The final question you'll be asked by the Wizard is whether or not you want to show the tasks view after the Web is loaded. Checking this box will tell FrontPage to show you the Tasks screen when the Web has been generated. The Tasks screen is basically a "to do" list, preloaded with the things you'll probably want to modify on your newly generated Web site.

FIG. 4.10
The Tasks list is a valuable tool that helps you get your site in shape before publishing it.

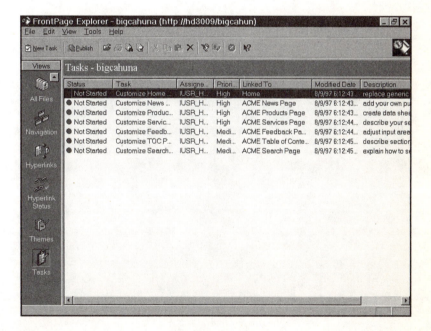

There are several different Wizards, and they all work essentially the same way as the Corporate Presence Wizard. Templates are similar to Wizards, except they don't take you step-by-step through a process. Instead, templates simply create the site and leave it to you to do the customizing. When you're creating a new site, the Wizards and Templates are listed together in the list box. If the choice ends with Web instead of Wizard, it's a template.

Building Your Site from Scratch

Finally, you can create a new Web site with nothing more than a single empty page. This does leave you with significantly more work to do, but if none of the Wizards or Templates suits your needs and there's no site to import, it's the way to go.

First, you'll need to create a new FrontPage Web. You can do this either by selecting "Create a New FrontPage Web" when you first open up FrontPage, or by selecting the File menu item, choosing New, and finally clicking FrontPage Web. When you get a dialog box asking you how you want to start your new FrontPage Web, you should choose Empty Web from the Wizards and Templates box and select the From Wizard or Template, or you should select the One Page Web option. Enter a unique name for your new site and click OK to have FrontPage create your new site, containing either one or no pages.

We will delve further into adding pages, modifying pages, and organizing your Web site in the next few chapters. Until then, congratulations! You have all the information you need to create your first Web. ●

CHAPTER 5

Working with the FrontPage Editor

The FrontPage Editor is a powerful WYSIWYG (What You See Is What You Get) HTML editor that allows you to create advanced Web pages with no knowledge of the underlying technical details. This chapter equips you with all the basic knowledge you need to create and modify your pages in the FrontPage Editor—it only covers the absolute basics. Chapter 7, "Editor Basics," goes farther in-depth on using the Editor. This chapter assumes that you have already created a Web site using FrontPage. If that is not the case you should go back a chapter and take a look at Chapter 4, "Creating Your First Web Site." ■

- **Creating new pages**
  Learn to create new pages with the FrontPage Editor either from scratch or by using Wizards and Templates.

- **Working with existing pages**
  Loading up, modifying and saving your current pages.

- **Working with text**
  How to add text, change fonts, colors and more.

- **Working with lists**
  How to create and format bulleted, numbered and other lists

- **Working with tables**
  Creating, modifying and formatting tables.

- **Working with hyperlinks**
  How to connect your files to each other, as well as connecting your pages to other resources on the Internet.

- **Saving and publishing your pages**
  How to save the pages when you are done and publish them to the Internet.

Creating a New Page

There are several ways to create new pages using FrontPage. Pages can be added to your site in either the Explorer or the Editor. Although this chapter deals with the Editor, you are also taught how to create a new page in the Explorer (in case you have nothing but an empty Web site created so far).

Adding a Blank Page From Within the Explorer

Adding pages to your site from within the Explorer is easy. First, open an existing Web site or create a new one. As you can see in Figure 5.1, there are two panes in the Explorer, the View Pane on the left and a pane on the right; that pane changes depending on the icon chosen in the View pane. When adding new pages to a Web site from within the Explorer, you need to select either the Folders, All Files, or Navigation icon in the view pane. You can then click the New Page button on the left side of the toolbar and a new blank page will be added to your page. The page's title is highlighted. You can change it while it is highlighted simply be typing. If it is the first page added to the Web site, it will be given the title *default.htm*. You probably don't want to change this title, but subsequent pages will all be titled *newpage.htm* and you definitely want to change those. Once you have added the page, you can double-click its title to open the page in the Editor.

> **NOTE** The default page title you use will depend on the web server the pages are going to be published to. Microsoft web servers are usually configured to look for files named default.htm as the default file to display in a directory. On Netscape and most other servers, the default file name is index.htm or index.html. Find out which web server you are working with in order to determine what default file name you should use.

FIG. 5.1
You have to select either the Folders, All Files, or Navigation icon from the View pane in the Explorer in order to add a page.

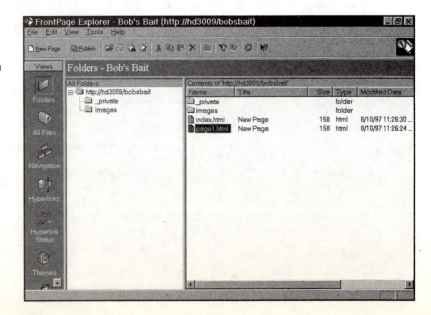

Creating an Empty Page

Creating a new page with the FrontPage Editor is fairly simple. First launch the Editor by clicking the Editor icon, which is located on the Explorer toolbar. The Editor icon is the one with the scroll and the red feather.

The Editor initially loads up with a new blank document and it looks like Figure 5.2.

FIG. 5.2
The FrontPage Editor initially opens up with a new blank document.

If you simply want to create a new blank page quickly and easily, just click the New Page icon on the toolbar. It is the icon that looks like a blank sheet of paper with the corner folded over.

Using a Template or Wizard

Templates and wizards are FrontPage features that give you a head start on typical pages. They can save you a significant amount of work. If you choose File, New you are confronted with the New File dialog box shown in Figure 5.3.

Note there is a Preview window on the right where you can see the kind of page each template creates. You can differentiate between the templates and the wizards just by reading the names—if it doesn't say wizard, then it is a template.

Notice also that there is a second tab called Frames. Frames are covered more thoroughly discussed in Chapter 10, but in short frames are a way to divide a page into separate, scrollable regions. You can create frames pages almost as easily as you can create regular pages in FrontPage.

After you select a template, the Editor creates a page in the style selected. If you choose a wizard, FrontPage prompts you for information with a series of dialog boxes.

FIG. 5.3
The New File dialog box in the Editor lets you create frames documents, normal documents, and more.

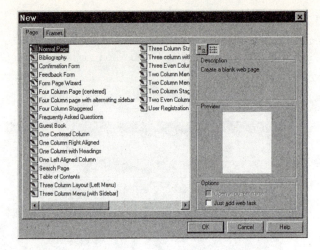

In Figure 5.4, the Three Column Layout Template has been chosen and FrontPage has created a file that is preformatted with a three-column newspaper style layout.

FIG. 5.4
The various templates, such as this Three Column Layout, create pages preformatted with popular layouts.

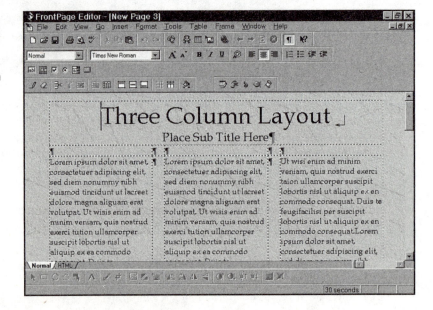

Working with an Existing Page

To open an existing page in the FrontPage Editor, choose File, Open. When opening files in the FrontPage Editor, you are not confronted with the usual Windows File Open dialog box you might be used to. Instead, you see the Open dialog box shown in Figure 5.5. This box prompts you for an URL instead of a drive and directory. By default it browses within the current Web site you have open in the FrontPage Explorer. If you are connected to the Internet, you can enter any Web site's URL into the URL box.

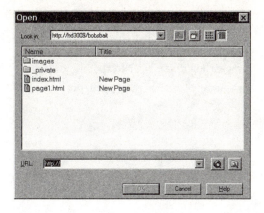

FIG. 5.5
The dialog box for opening files in the Editor is not the same as the File Open dialog box in most applications. This one lets you load files up from the Web.

You may be wondering how you can open a file located somewhere else on your hard drive or network, or even how you could load a file from the Internet if you were unsure of its location. There are two buttons located to the right of the URL box, one with a small globe and another with a file folder. Clicking the globe launches your Web browser and allows you to surf to whatever file you would like to open. The file folder button opens a typical File Open dialog box that enables you to view your entire hard drive's contents and any network drives to which you happen to be attached.

Adding and Editing Basic Text

If you have ever worked with HTML, the first thing you notice about a page opened in FrontPage is that you don't need HTML. All you have to do is type—just as in any word processor.

Although typing text isn't that complicated, the real power comes in when you can edit that text. FrontPage gives you full-featured word processing power by using a combination of the mouse, keyboard, and toolbars for editing functions like cutting, copying, and pasting.

To copy text:

1. In the FrontPage Editor, select the text to copy.
2. From the Edit menu, select Copy.
3. To paste the text, place the insertion point where you want to insert the copy.
4. From the Edit menu select Paste.

Cutting and Deleting Text

When you cut text it is removed from the page and copied to the clipboard. When you delete text, it is removed from the page, but it is not copied to the clipboard. It's just gone.

In the FrontPage Editor, do one of the following:

1. Select Edit, Cut.
2. To paste that text elsewhere, place the insertion point where you want to place the text. Select Edit, Paste.
3. To delete the selected text, press DELETE.
4. To delete the character before the insertion point, press BACKSPACE.
5. To delete the character after the insertion point, press the DELETE key.

Using Lists

Sometimes it is useful to organize information in lists and you can just create lists by typing them like this:

* Item 1
* Item 2

You can also do the following:

1. Item 1
2. Item 2

However, the asterisks aren't that attractive and if you need to insert another item into a numbered list you are forced to renumber the entire list. So, what do you do? FrontPage supports five types of lists that can be used to format text:

1. **Bulleted**—Presents an unordered list of items. Bulleted lists are generally rendered as paragraphs separated by white space and prefixed by bullets.
2. **Numbered**—Presents an ordered list of items, such as steps in a procedure. Generally, numbered lists are rendered as paragraphs separated by white space and prefixed by numbers.
3. **Directory**—Lists a sequence of short terms.
4. **Menu**—Presents an unordered list of short entries.
5. **Definition**—Presents terms and their definitions. Generally, a term is rendered flush left, and its definition is indented.

> **CAUTION**
> A list's exact formatting depends on the Web browser that will be used to view the list. Certain Web browsers do not display Directory and Menu list styles as intended. Always test your pages in several Web browsers. Don't assume that all pages will look exactly as they look in FrontPage.

The procedure for creating bulleted and numbered lists is similar. To create a numbered list, simply click the numbered list button. It is the button with the numbers 1, 2, and 3 and three lines on it. Right next to that button is another with three small squares and three lines on it. Clicking that button creates a bulleted list. Figure 5.6 shows a bulleted list and a numbered list.

FIG. 5.6
Lists are a valuable way to organize information on your Web pages.

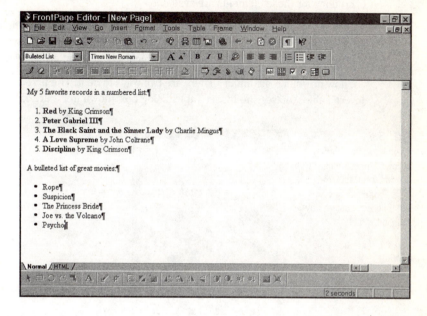

While editing a list, FrontPage assists by providing sequentially numbered line items, bullets, and indents as applicable to the style of list being created. You can also create nested lists by inserting a list within a list, or you can insert a paragraph in a list. To end any list, press the Enter key twice or Ctrl+Enter.

There is significantly more that can be done with lists, including quite a bit of formatting and customization that you can do. That information is not covered here. For more advanced information on using lists, take a look at Chapter 7, "Editor Basics," later in this book.

Using Tables

One of the most powerful early additions to HTML was when tables showed up. Tables are a powerful way to organize and display information in a grid format. Think of spreadsheets or the listings in your local television guide. Many people never think to use tables any other way, but tables can be used to produce complicated page layouts that are otherwise impossible.

Tables are made up of rows and columns of cells that can contain text, images, forms, or FrontPage Components. They can even contain other tables. A table allows you to display text in side-by-side paragraphs or arrange text beside graphics. In the previously-used Three Column Layout Template, FrontPage actually used a table to simulate columns of text. After you create a table, you can customize it by adding rows and columns, changing the size of cells, and adding a caption.

When you insert text, images, forms, or FrontPage Components into a cell, the cell expands horizontally and vertically to accommodate the added elements. All editing and formatting operations for those elements are available.

Tables can also be made invisible by setting the border width to 0. When used this way, they can provide layout control and formatting without it being apparent that a table is being used. Many of the sites on the Web use tables extensively and you probably don't even know it.

So, how do you create tables? There are two ways to do it. The first way is to select Table, Insert Table. You see the Insert Table dialog box shown in Figure 5.7.

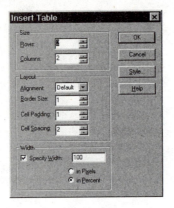

FIG. 5.7
If you know the number of rows and columns you want in your table, the Insert Table dialog box is the quickest, easiest way to insert a table.

Enter the number of rows and columns you would like to have in your table and FrontPage will create it. There are several more advanced options such as the table width, border line width, alignment, cell padding, cell spacing, and style. Those options are covered in Chapter 7, "Editor Basics," later in the book. For now, if you enter five rows and three columns, you end up with the table pictured in Figure 5.8.

The other method of table creation is also a method of table modification. If you move the mouse cursor over the table you notice it change into a small pencil. This pencil indicates the table-drawing tool. You can click and draw lines to split cells and rows freeform. When you select Table, Draw Table you can get the same tool to draw a new table at any place in your document. Figure 5.9 shows the drawing tool in action.

Once you have created your table, you can access a large number of the tables properties by right-clicking the table and choosing Table Properties from the pop-up menu.

Adding Hyperlinks

Hyperlinks are what make the World Wide Web a web. They are the connections between one document and another on the Internet. Hyperlinks are simply ways to tie an URL, or Universal Resource Locator, to text, an image, or some other item on a Web page. When that item is clicked, the Internet resource is loaded by the Web browser. The resource could be an image, another document, an audio file, or an e-mail address.

FIG. 5.8
You can create tables any size you like and in a variety of styles.

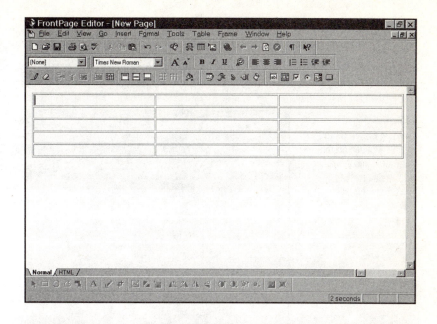

FIG. 5.9
The table-drawing tool lets you split cells and rows easily, as well as drawing new tables within your current table.

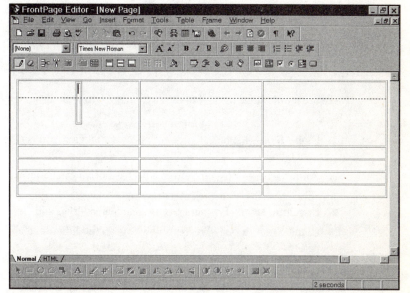

A quick review of URL's would be appropriate here. URL's are structured as *Protocol:// domain_address/directory/filename*.

The more common protocols are ftp, http, telnet, wais, gopher, mailto, or https. The *domain_address* portion is usually something like http://www.nucleargopher.com/ for a WWW address or ftp://ftp.citilink.com/ for an FTP address. A link to an e-mail address, rockboy@nucleargopher.com would read mailto:rockboy@nucleargopher.com.

How do you create hyperlinks in your documents? First type your text. Select that text and choose Insert, Hyperlink. You see the Create Hyperlink dialog box pictured in Figure 5.10.

FIG. 5.10
Creating hyperlinks to various sources on the Internet is accomplished by entering the URL in the Create Hyperlink box.

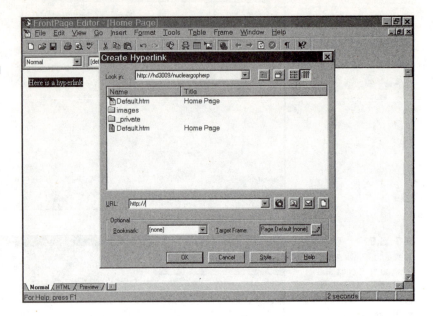

There are four buttons located to the right of the URL box. From left to right, they do the following:

- **Globe Icon**—Launches your Web browser and lets you surf to the URL to which you want to link.
- **Folder Icon**—Lets you browse your hard drive and choose a file on it to which you can link.
- **Envelope Icon**—Prompts you for an e-mail address and creates a mailto link.
- **Blank Sheet Icon**—Creates a new page in the Editor and also creates a link to the new page.

Hyperlinks are the main mechanism of the Internet. Linking various information resources to each other and following those links is what Web surfing is all about, so you are likely to be creating hyperlinks early and often.

Inserting Images

Images are a major part of the Web and also are a deep subject all their own. All the cool things you can do with images will be discussed later, but for now the basics are covered, after all it is a primer. How do you insert an image into your page?

As with almost everything in FrontPage, it is fairly simple. Select Insert, Image. You see the Insert Image dialog box shown in Figure 5.11.

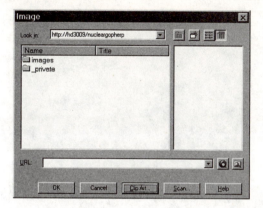

FIG. 5.11
You can scan images, get them from the Web or just load them from your hard drive from within the Insert Image dialog box.

The Insert Image dialog has two of the four buttons—the Globe and Folder icons—that were found on the Insert Hyperlink dialog box. They operate the same way here as they did there, providing you with access to the Internet or your hard drive, respectively. Images that you would like to insert need to be in either the JPG or GIF formats. If you are used to working with BMP files, you need to start converting them because BMP files are not supported on the Internet. Figure 5.12 shows a picture of yours truly taken with a digital camera and inserted into a Web page. Notice in the lower right hand corner of the page that the status bar says 67 seconds. That is estimated download time for this page using a 28.8 modem. When working with graphics it is a good idea to keep on eye on that time to make sure that the page doesn't take more time to download than it is worth. (Of course, this page would be worth the download time!)

Previewing and Saving

Once you have completed your new digital masterpiece and would like to save it and place it on the Internet, there is something else you ought to do first. Preview your work. You may be wondering, "Why would I need to preview it? I can see exactly what I have created on the screen in front of me." Well, you're right and you're wrong. HTML is subject to interpretation and different browsers display pages slightly differently. For this reason, the view of the page you see in FrontPage is usually the same as what the page will look like in a browser, but you should always check.

There are multiple ways to preview your new page in FrontPage. If you look closely at the Editor screen, you will see three tabs along the bottom of the page. One is labeled Normal, the second HTML, and the third Preview. So far you have been working with the Normal view but things are significantly different in the other two views. To illustrate, Figures 5.13 through 5.15 show the same page in the Normal Editor view, the HTML view, and the Preview view.

Chapter 5 Working with the FrontPage Editor

FIG. 5.12
Inserting your picture on your home page is fun and easy. Scanned images, drawn images, photos, and more can be inserted into any Web page.

FIG. 5.13
Note how the table lines show up in the Normal view. This assists you in creating the page, although they are not supposed to be seen in the final document.

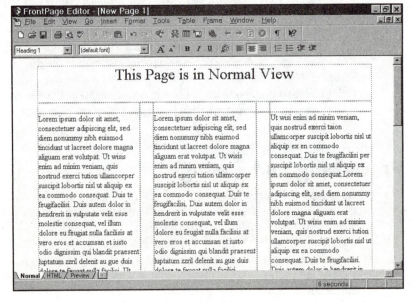

Previewing and Saving 79

FIG. 5.14
In HTML view, you can see your page's underlying structure—basically, all the stuff FrontPage was designed to keep you from needing to learn, but you can tweak it here.

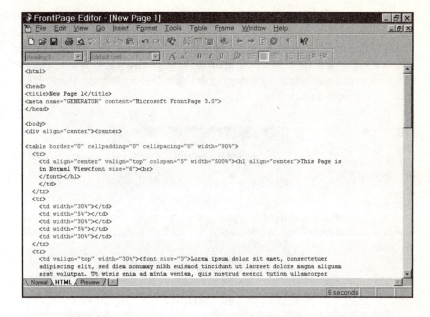

FIG. 5.15
Finally, the Preview view shows you what this page will look like in a browser. Note how the background is a different color and the lines are gone from the text.

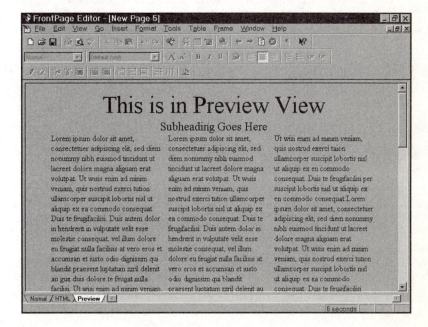

Part **II**
Ch **5**

For added assurance that your pages will look correct in the Web browser of your choice, you should also preview your pages in the browser itself. You do this by selecting File, Preview in Browser. You get a listing of all the browsers you have installed on your system and the option to preview the page in any of them. You can also see what your page will look like at various screen resolutions by changing the Window Size setting. The Preview In Browser dialog box is shown in Figure 5.16.

FIG. 5.16
Select the browser of your choice along with the window size in which to preview it. This gives you a more accurate picture of what your page will look like to a visitor.

Once you are happy with your previewed results, you need to save your file. Select File, Save and you are prompted with a dialog box. Enter the document title and the name you want it saved as and click OK. This will not put your document on the Web, however. You learn to actually publish your site in the Chapter 6, "Organizing Your First Web Site." ●

CHAPTER 6

Organizing Your First Web Site

When your site consists of nothing more than a page or two it is easy to keep up with the changes you make. However, as your site grows and you link to more Internet resources, you may find yourself getting overwhelmed with the sheer number of things.

Going through these chapters it is unlikely that you have reached that point, but this chapter takes you on a quick FrontPage Explorer tour and shows you how to perform basic organizational tasks on your site. ■

- **Deleting pages**
  In this section, you will learn how to remove pages from your site.

- **Adding pages**
  You will learn how to get a site built quickly by populating your site with empty pages quickly so you can fill the pages in later.

- **Reorganizing pages**
  Get your site into shape by adjusting links and moving pages around in the structure of your site.

- **Checking links**
  Nothing is worse than links that don't link. Learn how to make sure that the links all over your site are actually linking to something.

Loading the Web Into the Explorer

Once you have one or more Web sites created with FrontPage 98, you can load them into FrontPage Explorer by choosing File, Open FrontPage Web or by clicking the Open icon on Explorer's toolbar. If you've just loaded FrontPage itself, you can also open a Web site by selecting it from the list in the Getting Started with Microsoft FrontPage beginning screen. This method takes you right into the Explorer with that site opened. Choosing Open FrontPage Web from the File menu brings you to the same box, which is shown in Figure 6.1.

NOTE Note that this command is useful only for loading Webs created with FrontPage itself. If you are opening a web site created with another authoring tool, you will need to import it into FrontPage first.

FIG. 6.1
Selecting the More Webs button lets you open sites that are located on other Web servers.

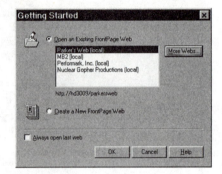

To load a site from another server, click the More Webs button. At this stage, the Open Web dialog box shown in Figure 6.2 pops up with no Webs to load unless you have already created a Web Site in FrontPage. In that case, all of the Sites you have created will be shown.

FIG. 6.2
It is possible to open Web sites from other servers running the FrontPage Extensions from the Open FrontPage Web dialog box.

Your first task is to choose the Web server where the Web resides. First, click the down arrow beside the Select a Web Server or Disk Location field to open the drop-down list. This reveals all servers you've worked with so far; if you've dealt only with the localhost IP number, that is the only IP that appears in this field.

With the desired Web server showing in the Web Server drop-down list box, determine whether you want to connect to the server using Secure Sockets Layer (SSL). This is the case only if your server supports SSL and if you have the necessary authorization on that server to make this kind of connection. Most full-featured servers do support SSL, but you must establish authentication keys before this feature can be used. Check with your server's documentation to determine how to do this (it's beyond this book's intended scope). If you want to establish a secure connection in this manner, click the Secure Connection Required (SSL) check box on the Open FrontPage Web dialog box.

Now, click the List Webs button. You see the names of the Webs you have created on the selected server in the Webs list box. If you're opening a Web from a server on a remote computer—especially if you're using a modem connection (even 28.8Kbps)—getting a list of the Webs can take several minutes. Eventually, however, it appears.

> **N O T E** In most cases, you won't actually click the List Webs button. Sometimes the list in the Web server or File Location field contains more than one entry. If you click the down-arrow to choose an entry different from the entry that appears when the dialog box first opens, the List Webs button is selected automatically by FrontPage Explorer and is thus grayed out. You'll actively select List Webs only if you want to see the pages on the default entry in the dialog box. ■

Working with FrontPage Views

By now you should be fairly familiar with the FrontPage Explorer. Therefore, you should realize that there are several different views of your site available by clicking the icons located in the View Pane on the left of your screen. Let's take a look at how to work with each of the available views.

Folders View

The first top icon in the View pane is the Folders icon. The Folders view provides a more technically-oriented perspective of your site. Folders view exists for Webmasters who want to see the Web as a series of individual files in various folders. It presents your site in much the same way you would see it if looking from within the Windows Explorer.

 The term "*folder*" is instantly recognizable to Windows 95 and Macintosh users. If you're more familiar with UNIX, MS-DOS, or Windows 3.x, think of folders as "*directories*" instead. Also, in the Contents frame of Folder view, "Name" really means "file name."

You can access the Folders view either by clicking the Folders icon or by selecting View, Folders View.

As Figure 6.3 shows, Folder view offers two separate panes: All Folders and Contents. The latter is called "*Folder Contents*" to make its function more apparent. Essentially, the All Folders pane shows the folders for that web, and these are the folders that FrontPage created when it built the Web you're working with. The Folder Contents page shows the files and subfolders within the folder selected in the All Folders pane.

FIG. 6.3
The Folders view shows your site in a manner similar to the Windows Explorer.

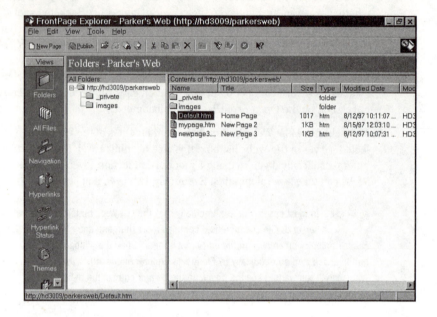

Windows Explorer's view of the Web is practically identical to Explorer's view. The only difference is that Windows Explorer shows all hidden directories, while FrontPage Explorer shows only the _private hidden directory.

The All Folders pane is primarily a navigation aid. When you click a folder, the subfolders and files contained within appear in the Folder Contents pane. If you right-click a folder, you can Cut, Copy, Rename, or Delete the folder, or you can view its Properties. The difference between Cut and Delete is that Cut moves the folder to the Clipboard, while Delete simply erases it. Use Cut when you want to move the folder, and Delete only when you no longer need it. Deleted folders cannot be retrieved.

> **NOTE** FrontPage keeps track of renamed folders and automatically changes the links for you. It is still a good idea to occasionally check all your links. Checking links is covered later in this chapter under the heading Checking Links and Spelling. ∎

In the Folder Contents pane, right-clicking a file name offers additional options. You can load the page into FrontPage Editor or another editing program, and you can cut, copy, rename, or delete it, view its properties, or add a task to the task list related to that page.

All Files View

The All Files view is exactly like the Folder Contents pane in the Folders view, except the All Files view shows you every single file in the site without separating them into their folders. This can be useful for finding a particular file in your site even if you are not sure in which folder it is located.

You can access the All Files view either by clicking the All Files View icon or by selecting View, All Files View.

All the menu options that applied when in the Folders view are applicable here, as well. All of the files in the site are shown in this view, but that does not mean you cannot tell which files belong in which folders. The All Files view contains a couple of columns that differ from the Folders View.

The first is the In Folder column. As its name suggests, this column displays the name of the folder that the file resides in so that you can keep files with the same name separate from each other based on location.

The second column is the Orphan column. This column is FrontPage's way of letting you know about files in your site that are not linked to any other files. Sometimes there are graphics you aren't using anymore, broken links you don't know about, or some other reason that a file might be *"orphaned."* If that is the case, you see a Yes in the Orphan column.

FIG. 6.4
The All Files view adds some useful information not included in the Folders view.

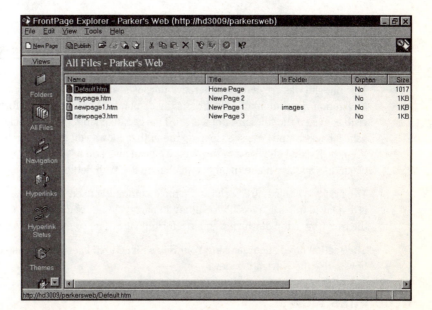

 Clicking the column headings in the All Files or Folders view sorts the file list by that column. This can very useful for seeing all of the default.htm files—for example, despite the fact that they are all located in separate directories.

Navigation View

When you create a new Web site with FrontPage the default view the site is shown in is the Navigation view. You can also get to this view be either clicking the Navigation Icon in the View Pane or by selecting View, Navigation. The usefulness of the Navigation view can easily be illustrated by Figure 6.5.

FIG. 6.5
Really huge sites are easy to handle in the Navigation View.

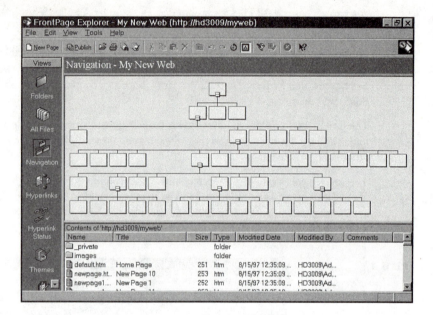

This big site was created for illustrative purposes and opened in Navigation view. By default the Navigation view automatically shrinks the display size of your site so that the entire site is visible, even if the titles are not shown. This can be changed by right-clicking the Navigation pane's background. You see a pop-up menu that allows you to deselect Size to Fit, Rotate the View, or Expand all Levels of the Tree. You can also add a New Top Page to the site, Apply Changes you have made (if any), and change the Web Settings.

The first two choices are perhaps the most commonly used. If you deselect Size to Fit, the tree is displayed full size, possibly resulting in parts of it not being visible. Choosing Rotate turns the tree from a top-down view into a left-right view. The rotated view is shown in Figure 6.6.

The section titled "Reorganizing Your Site's Structure" later in this chapter gets further into how to use the Navigation view.

Hyperlinks View

Finally, look at the Hyperlinks view. It has two parts: All Hyperlinks on the left, and hyperlinks for the currently selected page on the right. The latter view will be called the *Individual Hyperlinks* pane. Hyperlink view's purpose is to provide both an outline-like perspective and a visual-style perspective of your Web site.

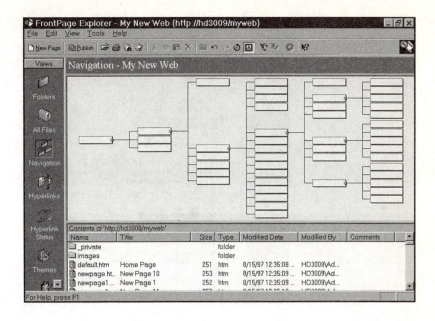

FIG. 6.6
The Navigation view can be turned on its side to show you your site in a left-to-right view, rather than a top-to-bottom view.

Hyperlink view is accessible by selecting View, Hyperlinks. You can also click the Hyperlink view icon in Explorer's toolbar.

All Hyperlinks Figure 6.7 shows the All Hyperlinks pane expanded by sliding the vertical separator fully to the right edge of the screen. This figure demonstrates how All Hyperlinks functions: It's very similar to the outline feature of word processors or personal information managers, showing the various headings and subheadings distinguished from one another by indentation. In this figure, some of the visible headings are fully expanded, as indicated by the minus signs (-) beside the main topic headings. By contrast, other topic headings remain unexpanded (closed), as indicated by the plus signs (+) beside them.

If you click the minus sign beside an expanded topic, you also close all the subordinate topics of that topic. Therefore, if you want to close all topics in the All Hyperlinks pane, close the highest topic in the hierarchy—in this case, Home. If you do, you see only one topic with a plus sign beside it. Again, those familiar with a word processor outliner or with the Windows Explorer interface will find all of this quite intuitive.

Actually, the division is not topic and subtopic. Instead, the All Hyperlinks pane shows links among pages. Main links lead to sublinks, sublinks to further sublinks, and so forth.

Figure 6.7 also shows that as you move the pointer up and down the All Hyperlinks view, the topic you're currently pointing at is highlighted to show where you are in the view. This helps orient your way through the hierarchy of topics.

By studying your pages' All Hyperlinks view, you can maintain a good sense of how the Web is constructed. Combining this view with the Individual Hyperlinks pane gives you two different perspectives, and together they make a powerful tool.

FIG. 6.7
The All Hyperlinks pane allows you to navigate through all the links in your site from one easy-to-use interface.

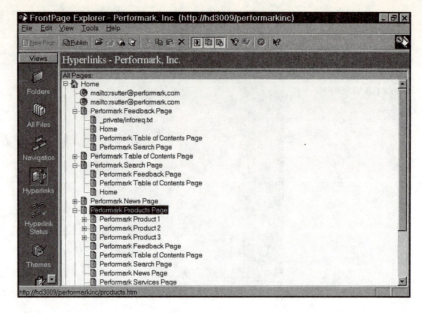

The main purpose of the All Hyperlinks pane is to help you easily find your way around your Web. You can locate everything in the Individual Hyperlink pane or in Folder view, but it's more cumbersome to do so. Again, there's a similarity here with a word processing outline; a well-outlined word processing document is an extremely easy document in which to locate specific headings and sections. This is exactly the case of the All Hyperlinks pane in FrontPage Explorer.

You can't actually manipulate the Web from the All Hyperlinks pane. Instead, it puts you in the position of being able to do so. Clicking any page in the All Hyperlinks pane immediately shows that page in the center of the Individual Hyperlinks pane, complete with all the links that stem from the page you clicked on. Clicking from subtopic to subtopic changes the display immediately and lets you jump back and forth from one perspective of the Web to the next.

Some icons in Hyperlink view display a plus sign at their top left corner. This indicates that additional documents in the Web are linked to the page represented by the icon. Clicking the plus sign displays the icons for the linked pages, and simultaneously changes the plus sign to a minus sign. Clicking the minus sign hides the icons for the linked pages.

Using the Individual Hyperlinks Pane   The Individual Hyperlinks pane shows the Web from the perspective of the currently-selected page in the All Hyperlinks pane, but you can maneuver around the Web by using the Individual Hyperlinks pane alone. Like the All Hyperlinks pane, the Individual Hyperlinks pane shows the Web as a series of pages with or without additional links leading from them, and you can expand or contract the links to see a larger portion of that particular part of the Web. Figure 6.8 shows how the Individual Hyperlinks Pane looks relative to the All Hyperlinks pane.

FIG. 6.8
The Individual Hyperlinks pane lets you follow the links in your site relative to each other. It is a great tool for navigating and viewing your site.

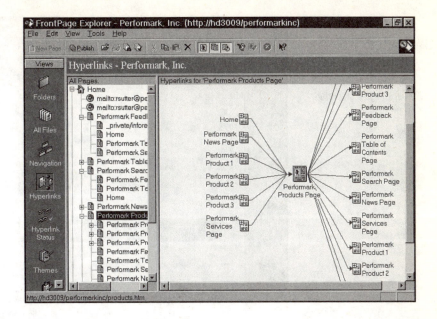

In FrontPage 97, one could find themselves working with their site primarily from this view, but with FrontPage 98 you may find that the Navigation view gives a truer picture of the site layout and is easier to work with.

Adding Pages

You may have created a site already and maybe created a new page or two with the FrontPage Editor. However, you may be asking yourself whether or not it is possible to add several pages quickly and make them all relate to each other. Using the Explorer is the best way to do this.

Start with an example. Say that you have sketched out your Web site structure in advance. You have figured out that there will be one main page that will link to three separate pages. Each of these pages, in turn, will link to two pages each. A little quick math will tell you that you are going to need ten pages in your site.

Creating this structure with the Explorer would be done as follows. First, click the Navigation Icon in the Views Pane. This gives you a view of your site similar to the one shown in Figure 6.9.

The site shown in Figure 6.9 currently has only one page—the Home Page. To create the site structure described previously in this site, click the box labeled Home Page in the Navigation pane on the right. Do not double-click it, as that launches the Editor and loads the page you double-clicked. With the page selected, click the New Page toolbar button. The first time this is done, a dialog box pops up, asking if you would like to add links to a menu bar at the top of all the pages in your site. If you click Yes, the Explorer adds a new page and connects it to the previous page with a line. With the site shown in Figure 6.9, new pages and pages under those new pages were added until the structure shown in Figure 6.10 was achieved.

FIG. 6.9
The Navigation view of your Web site provides you with a flowchart-like view of how the pages in your site relate to one another.

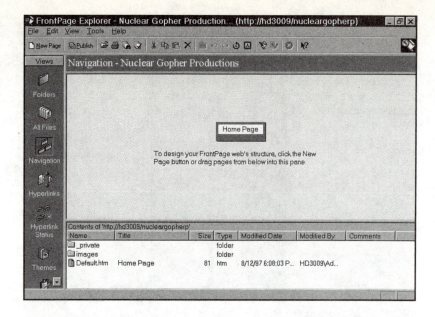

FIG. 6.10
By adding new pages and new pages relative the pages added you can create entire site structures in a flowchart layout.

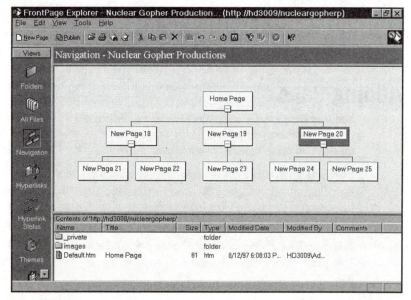

You may have noticed the file listing being shown in the pane directly below the Navigation pane. This listing shows all the files in your site in a familiar directory listing format. One of the nice things about this arrangement is the fact that you can drag files from the lower pane and drop them up on to the Navigation pane to create links to existing files.

The added links look different depending on the theme you have chosen for your site. However, look at Figure 6.11. Notice that directly underneath the page title caption are three buttons for the home page and the two documents that are directly underneath the home page in the hierarchy of pages. At the bottom of the page text links to the pages beneath that page in the hierarchy. FrontPage organizes your site for you in this manner when pages are added via the Navigation pane.

FIG. 6.11
Although the style may vary, the automatic creation of menu bars at the top and links at the bottom by FrontPage is a very useful feature.

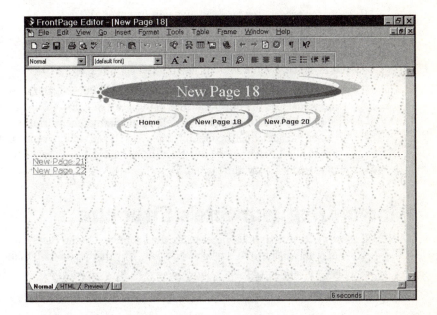

Although you can add new files to your site as long as any of the first three icons (Folders, All Files, and Navigation) is selected, the Navigation view is the only one with which you can add files relative to one another and graphically browse your site's layout.

Deleting Pages

Occasionally you find you really don't like a particular page or group of pages and you want to get rid of them. Deleting pages is very easy, but there are a few things to be aware of:

- When you delete a page in either the All Files or Folders view, the page is deleted from the disk.
- In the Navigator view, the default behavior is to remove the page from the menu bars on the other pages, not to delete the page.

> **CAUTION**
> Files deleted from your site via FrontPage are *not* placed into the Windows Recycle Bin. They are permanently removed from your hard drive. Make sure you really want the file to be blown away before you click Yes.

Here are the procedures for deleting pages from your Web:

If browsing the site in the All Files or Folders views—To delete a page, click the file you want to delete and then hit the Delete key. A box prompts you for confirmation. If you are sure you want to delete the file, click Yes.

If browsing the site in the Navigator view—In Navigator view you can either delete individual files or entire branches of the site's tree. By default, selecting a page and hitting the Delete key in this view deletes menu references from other pages (if any exist) rather than deleting the file(s) themselves. If you want to remove the files from your site permanently, make sure you select the second option. It asks if you want to delete, rather than remove, from the menu bars.

Reorganizing Your Site's Structure

If your site has been put together using the FrontPage Menu Bar system, you have great flexibility in reorganizing your site's information. Why might you want to do that? Well, suppose you have a product page that is linked to a customer support page, which in turn is linked to your main home page as illustrated in Figure 6.12.

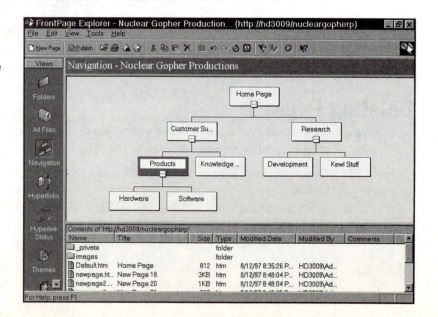

FIG. 6.12
This Web site has its product information buried too deeply in the hierarchy and doesn't get enough hits. It is easy to rearrange the site with Navigator.

Moving the Product section up so that it links to the main page of the site would be a big job if it had to be done manually. You would have to change links and buttons and one mistake could make your product page inaccessible. With the Explorer it is possible to simply click the Products page, drag it up to the Home Page, and drop it there. This automatically adjusts all the menu bar links in the site to point to the correct place for the Product page. Figure 6.13 shows the modified site layout.

FIG. 6.13
By simply dragging and dropping the section of the site that needs to be moved, all links are automatically readjusted.

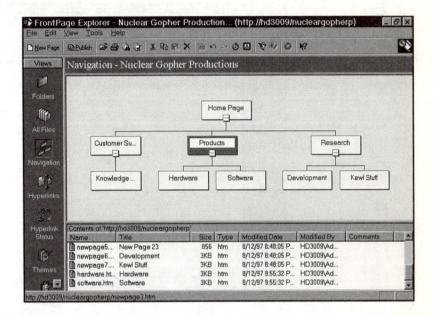

What if you are not using the FrontPage Menu Bar system on your site? How would you reorganize all of your pages and links then? Even without actual links between the pages, FrontPage lets you arrange a logical order to your site in the Navigation page by dragging and dropping pages onto the pane and connecting them. This can be tremendously valuable for keeping your site organized and navigable, even if you do not want to use FrontPage's predefined menus and themes.

Checking Links and Spelling

Spell checking an entire Web site one page at a time would be an incredibly tedious task. Another incredibly tedious task is making sure all the files on your Web site link correctly to each other, as well as to other pages and resources on the Internet.

There are third-party programs available that do nothing but perform these two functions, but fortunately for you FrontPage 98 includes these capabilities in the Explorer.

Verifying and Recalculating Hyperlinks

This brings you to the fourth icon in the Views Pane, the Hyperlink Status icon. Selecting this icon shows you the Hyperlink Status screen. Two links have been added to the example Web site. One of the links is real and the other isn't. The hyperlink status screen is shown in Figure 6.14 prior to running the Link Verification tool.

FIG. 6.14
Links in your site to sites on the Internet can be checked for accuracy in the Hyperlink Status screen.

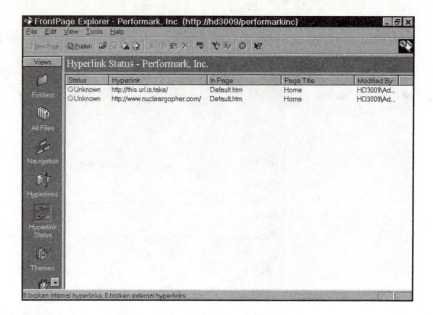

In order to verify the links in your site you need to be connected to the Internet or an intranet. In order to verify your links, FrontPage attempts to connect to the URL and get a response from it. If the hostname does not exist, the file is missing, or something similar, the URL will be reported broken. The example has two URL's: http://this.site.is.fake/ and **http://www.nucleargopher.com/**. The first is fake, the second isn't.

Checking the validity of the links is done by choosing Tools, Verify Hyperlinks. There are three options in the Verify Hyperlinks dialog box. The first verifies all links in the site, the second resumes verification if it has been interrupted, and the final option verifies only a selected link. Select Start when you have decided what you would like to verify.

Figure 6.15 shows the result of running the link verification tool. Notice how the fake URL is listed as Broken and the real URL is listed as OK. Sites on the Internet change rapidly. Regularly verifying all the links in your site is a good idea.

You may be wondering now what Link Recalculation is, as opposed to Verification. Recalculate Hyperlinks performs several important updating functions. First, it updates the views of the site in FrontPage Explorer, which is extremely important if you've edited hyperlinks or added or deleted pages. Next, it updates the text indexes produced by any FrontPage Components you have in your site. FrontPage Components create indexes of all searchable pages, and as you add or delete pages these indexes become incomplete. Finally, Recalculate Hyperlinks regenerates all the Include FrontPage components in your Web. These components are, in a sense, empty containers with pointers to fields in your pages containing specific information; when a visitor calls up the page, the components retrieve the most current version of that information. Recalculate Hyperlinks updates all the Web content that depends on these components. To run Recalculate Hyperlinks, simply select Tools, Recalculate Hyperlinks.

FIG. 6.15
After running the Link Verification tool, it is obvious that there is a bad URL linked to this site.

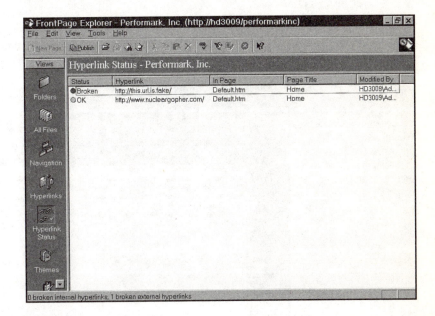

You should run the Recalculate and Verify Hyperlinks commands frequently, certainly after any significant changes to your Web.

Checking Spelling

One problem every Webmaster encounters is the difficulty of ensuring accurate spelling across the entire site. Authors can check their work on individual documents in FrontPage Editor, but when all the documents are linked in a Web, it's essential that spelling be checked for errors and for lack of standardization. Almost nothing can reduce the professional appearance of a site more quickly than a measly little spelling mistake. It simply looks bad.

To invoke global spell checking, choose Tools, Spelling. You are asked if you want to check All Pages or only the pages you've Selected, and whether you want to add pages that contain misspellings automatically to the Task List. Since FrontPage's spelling tool cannot actually correct the spelling (as can a word processor's), adding to the Task list is a good idea. You can choose to edit pages directly from the results of the spell check, so the Task list addition might not be necessary—especially in the case of a relatively small Web site. Should you decide to add items to the Task list however, you should read the following section.

Working with the Task List

If you have never worked with a large Web site, you may not have any idea how many details there are to take care of—miss one and you can publish a site with incorrect text, out-of-date links, or incorrect spelling. It isn't really all that different from those papers you probably have on and in your desk. The more documents there are, the more details you need to take care of. The FrontPage Task list is the solution to this problem, and it is likely that you will find yourself using it often.

To get to the Task list you can either click the Tasks icon in the Views pane or choose View, Tasks. If you created your site using one of the templates or wizards it is likely that there are tasks filled in on the list, just as is shown in Figure 6.16.

FIG. 6.16
After creating a site with the Corporate Presence Wizard, the Task list is populated with items that need to be done in order to finish personalizing the site.

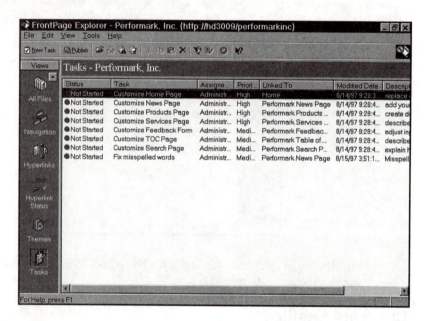

Double-clicking any task in the list brings up the Task Details dialog box (shown in Figure 6.17). From there you can assign the task to a particular user, change the description of a task, and prioritize your task as either High, Medium, or Low. Most importantly, however, tasks on your site can be related to pages on your site. This means that by clicking the Do Task button, FrontPage launches the Editor and loads the page being referenced. Tasks that are not associated with a page do not have a Do Task button.

Adding tasks to the Task list can be accomplished in many ways. When looking at the Task list, you can right-click the list itself and choose New Task from the pop-up menu. Alternately, in any of the other site views such as Folders, All Files, or Navigation, you can right-click any page in your site and select Add Task from the pop-up menu there. Either way, you see the New Task dialog box shown in Figure 6.17. Just fill it in and click OK.

FIG. 6.17
You can assign tasks to other users, describe them in detail, and prioritize tasks in the New Task dialog box.

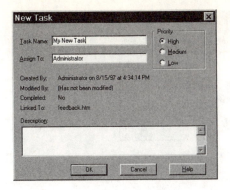

Finally, you may be wondering how you complete a task that is not associated with anything in the site. After completion of the task, simply right-click the task in the list and choose Mark Complete. This changes the status of your task to Completed.

Publishing Your Site to the Internet

Okay, you have created a site, browsed your pages, spell-checked every thing, verified your links, organized and fiddled to your heart's content. Now you want to put your site on the Internet.

There are a couple of things that are assumed here. First, it is assumed that you are publishing this site to a Web server that is running the FrontPage Server Extensions. Publishing to a non-FrontPage-enabled server. Second, it is assumed that you have all the information you need to publish the site, including user name, URL, and password.

1. After making sure all of your files are saved, you simply need to select File, Publish FrontPage Web.
2. If this is the first time you have published the site, you see a dialog box asking a desired publication site.
3. Enter the URL. Click the Secure Connection Required box only if you are absolutely sure you need to use SSL.

The Globe button on the left in this box launches your Web browser and takes you to the Microsoft FrontPage Web site if you want to find an Internet service provider who is running a FrontPage-enabled server. Otherwise, you should be able to click OK and FrontPage will publish your site. Yes, it is that easy.

You cannot do any work on your site until it is done publishing, and if your site is big that can take a while. The first time you publish your site you need not wait as long other times. When you publish your site again you see a different dialog box. Looking at Figure 6.18, notice that there is a Publish Changed Pages Only check box. As long as that is checked, your subsequent site uploads take significantly less time.

FIG. 6.18
Publishing only the pages that have changed saves you a lot of time on uploads.

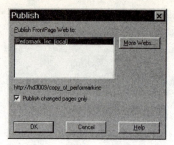

PART III

Creating Pages with the FrontPage Editor

- **7** Editor Basics   101
- **8** Enhancing Pages with Graphics and Multimedia   123
- **9** Activating Your Pages with Java, Active X, Scripting, and More   147
- **10** Using Templates, FrontPage Components, and Wizards to Build Your Pages   165

CHAPTER 7

Editor Basics

T he FrontPage Primer section of this book got you up and running with the FrontPage Editor and the Explorer. This chapter is going to take it further. It is going to cover all of the major areas of web page creation with the FrontPage Editor. This chapter will not, however, cover any of the advanced Web design features. So, open up your FrontPage Editor and get ready to create some great pages.

Text layout and formatting
Making your pages look great by effectively formatting and laying out your text.

Working with tables
Take advantage of the power of tables in your documents.

Creating lists
Using lists to create impressive, well-formatted pages.

Working with fonts
Fonts are trickier than you might expect; we'll tell you what you need to know.

Background colors and tiling
How to make your pages look really good (or bad) with background colors and tiling.

Page Design Considerations

You want your Web pages to look good don't you? You want people to visit your site and be impressed. You want them to stay awhile and read all the information you have worked so hard to prepare. You may not know it, but sometimes, even a site that looks great to you might be ugly, hard to use, or even inaccessible to a visitor. Part of this is because very few of us are trained graphic designers (my co-author Steve Banick excluded) and we have been pressed into service to create the corporate Web site. More often than not though, bad site design is due to a lack of understanding of some simple rules of page design and the mechanics of HTML.

I have no intention of boring you with all the mechanics of HTML. You probably bought FrontPage so you wouldn't have to learn it, but it would be helpful for you to at least understand the basic principles of how HTML works.

HTML is nothing but plain text. All that formatting you see on the screen when you look at an HTML page is the result of your browser software reading the HTML text and trying to make it look as close to the intended design as possible. The results will vary (sometimes dramatically) from one Web browser to another.

Look at the following three figures. They all show the same page as seen by three different Web surfers. Figure 7.1 is the screen seen by somebody surfing with the latest Netscape browser, the second is shown using an older graphical browser called Cello (see Figure 7.2), and Figure 7.3 shows a text-based browser called Lynx.

FIG. 7.1
The latest browsers will almost always display a page with all of the formatting as intended. Here is the Microsoft home page displayed in the latest Netscape browser.

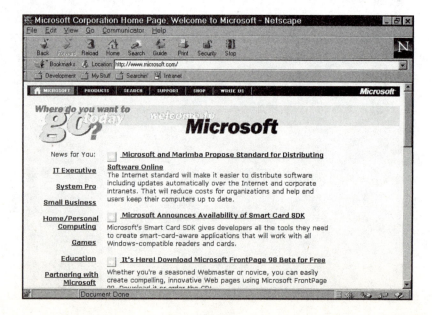

FIG. 7.2
The same page displayed in Cello, an older browser that does not support tables, background images, and a lot of other things. Yuck!

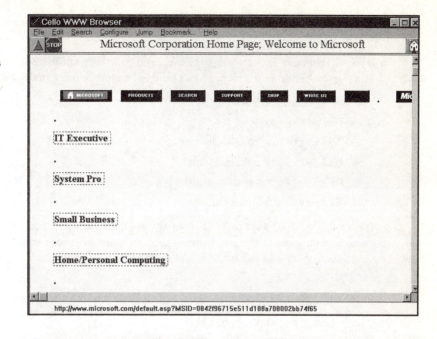

FIG. 7.3
The Microsoft home page as seen in the Lynx text browser.

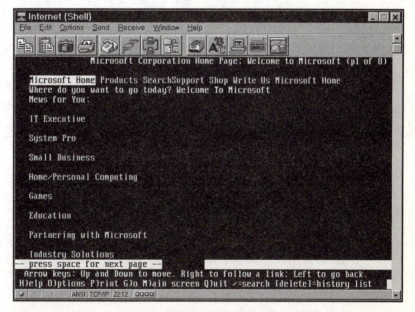

As you can see, different browsers can show pages in dramatically varying fashion. It is fairly common that Web designers build only for the latest and greatest browsers, and there are some kinds of sites where shutting out some users is just fine.

In addition to the challenges imposed by HTML, there are several other design considerations to keep in mind when working on your pages.

If you've spent any time browsing the Web, you've already encountered plenty of sites you won't revisit because the first page you went to had one or more of the following problems:

- Took too long to load
- Had no clear purpose
- Was poorly laid out or badly written
- Had obscure navigational tools
- Didn't link to other sites as it said it would
- Had no useful information

Obviously, you don't want people to have these experiences with your work. But how do you make sure they don't? The short answer is to put yourself in your visitors' shoes and think like the audience you want to have. Any author, in print, multimedia, or Web has to do this or risk failure.

Reversing our earlier list of reasons for not staying on a Web site, we get the following:

- The first page appears quickly.
- Its purpose is immediately and clearly identified.
- It's well laid out and well-written.
- Its links accurately suggest what the viewer will find if he/she uses them.
- Its links behave as advertised when the viewer does use them.
- It supplies the content the viewer expects, or a quick path to that content.

That's a page with successful hook for a Web site. Following these guidelines will go a long, long way toward making all your pages, and therefore your entire site, both pleasing and useful. In short, your key to success is a balance of presentation and content.

There's another important fact about Web authoring you need to keep in mind. With other media, the author has some control over where the audience is going to start. With a Web site, though, your readers may enter at any page, depending on what link sent them there. This means that you should design every page with the same care you lavished on your home page. And since people usually like to have a look at the home page (it helps orient them), it's a good idea to include a go-to-home-page control on all your pages. This is especially true if you have a large or complex site or one whose organization isn't obvious when a person enters it at some point other than the home page.

Web Page Layout Fundamentals

Web authoring is a young art, but already there is some agreement about its basic principles. The following guidelines deal with the fundamentals of text layout and hyperlink design.

- With a text-heavy page, use lots of whitespace.
- Avoid very long pages that require endless scrolling.

- Give your page a title that helps the user figure out where she is and what she's looking at.
- Write clearly and pay close attention to spelling and grammar. Nothing undermines a page's authority as much as confusing language and bad spelling. Even typos suggest that the author couldn't be bothered to check his work, and what does that say about the other information he's offering you?
- Keep your navigation controls uniform in appearance; for example, a go-to-home-page button should look the same everywhere on your site.

So now that we've given you a few things to keep in mind when creating your pages, let's get into the actual mechanics of doing it.

Basic Text and Page Layout

Now that we have covered some of the basic design principles for Web page creation, we will spend the rest of this chapter working with the FrontPage Editor to put them into practice. If you haven't created a Web site in FrontPage already, you should create one now or open one that you have already created.

If your Web site has no pages in it or if none of them are blank, add one by clicking the New Page button in the Explorer. Then open that page up in the FrontPage Editor by double-clicking it.

Now you are staring at a blank page. Let's fix that. Web pages, as you know, can be very elaborate. However, all you need to keep in mind now is that the bulk of every page is made up of combinations of the following three basic elements:

- Text
- Hyperlinks
- Images

There's also active content, of course, such as JavaScript, ActiveX, and so on. These aren't basic in the sense that they're required for a pleasing, functional page, so they will be dealt with in later chapters.

Adding a Title to Your Page

Even before you start adding content to your page, you should give it a meaningful title (if you want to modify the title later, you can always do so). You ought to put some thought into this because a person new to your page will usually read its title for hints about where he is and what he's looking at. The default titles usually aren't helpful. In fact, there are several reasons for taking pains with your title. First, it's what your visitor's browser will record in its Bookmark list (Netscape) or Favorites folder (Internet Explorer) if he marks the page; an informative title will jog his memory later about the nature of your site. Second, Internet search programs such as Excite read the title for indexing and retrieval purposes, and presumably, you want your site to show up in their lists.

To change the page title to a more useful one, use the following steps:

1. Choose File, Page Properties, or right-click in the workspace and choose Page Properties from the shortcut menu. The Page Properties dialog box appears (see Figure 7.4).
2. Type the new page title into the Title text box. You can use any characters you want. The title can also be any length, but remember that your visitors may be using a lower screen resolution than you are. A width of 60 characters is about the practical maximum.
3. Choose OK.

FIG. 7.4
The Page Properties dialog box lets you change the page title and other things.

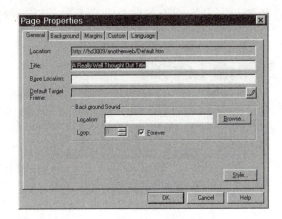

Your new page title appears in the FrontPage Editor title bar.

Remember that your home page isn't the only one in your site that needs a functional title. Every page should have such a guidepost for its viewers. A title such as "Page 31" or "Section 17" isn't much use in keeping a viewer oriented.

Remember to give every page on your site a well thought out title. Not only will this help orient your visitors, but search engines too will index your entire site, not just your home page. You wouldn't want the search engine to return "Page 15" instead of "Bob's Amazing World of Crickets."

You can use several different methods to put text onto your page. The simplest kinds of text are headings and Normal text.

Using the Format Menu to Add Headings

You use headings to mark off major divisions and subdivisions of meaning within a page. FrontPage Editor offers the six levels of headings that are standard with HTML. To place one on a page, use the following steps:

1. Type the heading text at the place you want it. Do not press Enter when you're done.
2. Choose Format, Paragraph. The Paragraph Properties dialog box appears (see Figure 7.5).

3. Select Heading 1, and then choose OK. The text changes to the largest heading style. Press the Enter key to put the insertion point on the next line.
4. To look at the other heading styles, follow steps 1 through 3, each time selecting a different heading type from the Paragraph Properties list box. Figure 7.5 shows the full range of heading styles as well as the Address and Formatted styles.

FIG. 7.5
The Format Paragraph dialog box is shown with samples of all the basic styles directly behind it.

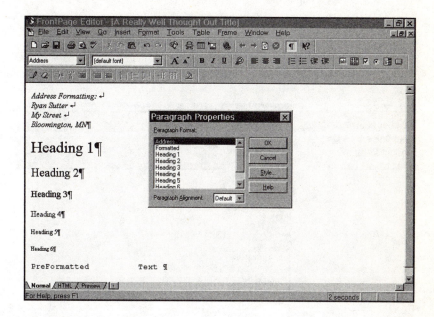

To delete a heading, use the following steps:

1. Select the heading you want to delete.
2. Press the Delete key.
3. The heading text disappears.

The line containing the insertion point will still retain the heading style. To remove this, choose Format, Paragraph. Then select Normal from the list box, and choose OK. The style of the line returns to Normal (default) style.

The heading style, unlike some of the other styles in FrontPage Editor, is not retained after you press the Enter key. When you press Enter at the end of a heading-style line, the style of the next line returns to Normal.

A faster and more convenient way to change heading levels is with the Change Style drop-down list box, which lets you choose from all the heading levels and text styles available. (If you've used styles in Microsoft Word, the technique is immediately familiar.) To see the styles, click the arrow button at the right of the Change Style drop-down list box (see Figure 7.6).

To use this method to change a paragraph style, follow these steps:

1. Select the paragraph you want to modify by placing the insertion point anywhere inside it.
2. Click the arrow button at the right of the Change Style drop-down list box. The list of styles appears.
3. Click the style you want. All the text of the paragraph takes on the new appearance.

As you've already guessed, this method works for all styles, not just for headings. In some cases, you might want to compose most of the text of your page in the Normal style (the default) and then use the Change Style drop-down list box to modify sections of it.

FIG. 7.6
The Choose Style drop down box is a handy shortcut for applying styles to your text.

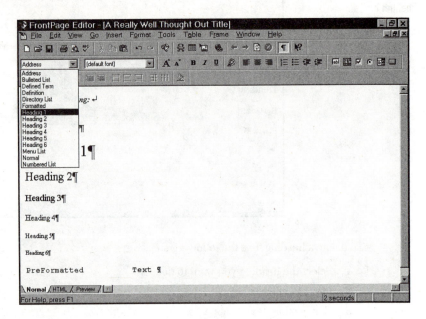

 Don't overuse the larger heading styles on a single screen. If you do, a visitor to your site may feel as if she's being shouted at. Think of headings as signaling divisions and subdivisions of content, rather than as a method of emphasis.

Adding Paragraphs of Normal Text

In FrontPage Editor, you produce most text with the Normal style. The Normal style displays in the browser in the default variable-width font at the default size. In many browsers, this is Times New Roman, but selecting Normal does not mean that Times New Roman will be the displayed font. It only tells the browser to use its default font.

Basic Text and Page Layout | 109

To write your text, use the following steps:

1. Place the cursor where you want the text to begin.
2. Select Normal from the Change Style drop-down list on the toolbar.
3. Start typing. When you reach the end of a paragraph, press Enter, as you usually do. This starts a new paragraph, still in the Normal style. Continue typing until you've said what you want to.

 There is a Paragraph button on the toolbar that will display a Paragraph symbol at the end of every paragraph. You can toggle it on and off.

You can see an example of Normal text in Figure 7.7. Both FrontPage Editor and browsers automatically insert a blank line before the start of each paragraph. You can't change this behavior, but you can use Shift+Enter to insert a line break instead of a new paragraph and avoid the whitespace. Also, in the Normal style, the first line of a paragraph can't be indented. The Tab key doesn't do anything, in this situation.

But what if you want extra whitespace between paragraphs? If you've used other Web page editors, you know that you can't put in blank lines merely by pressing the Enter key. The whitespace shows up in the editing window, but browsers ignore it.

FIG. 7.7
A paragraph formatted as normal text appears in the default variable-width font of the browser.

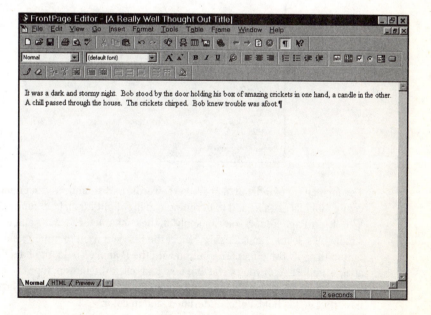

 Sometimes, you need a nonbreaking space to force two words, or a word and a number, to stay together on one line (January 17, for example). Use Shift+Spacebar to insert such a space.

Enlarging and Shrinking Normal Text

You may need to increase or decrease the size of text within a paragraph for emphasis or design purposes. You can't do this with a heading; because headings are styles, they affect all of a paragraph, not just part of it. The way around this problem is to use the Increase and Decrease Text Size buttons on the Formatting toolbar (see Figure 7.8). First, select the text whose size you want to change, and then click whichever button is appropriate. You can keep clicking till the text is close to the size you. Unfortunately, the point size of the type isn't fully adjustable, as it is in a word processor. The sizes available, in terms of points, are 8, 10, 12, 14, 18, 24, and 36.

The size of "Normal" text is 12 points by default. The seven point sizes just mentioned correspond to the seven HTML-defined type sizes.

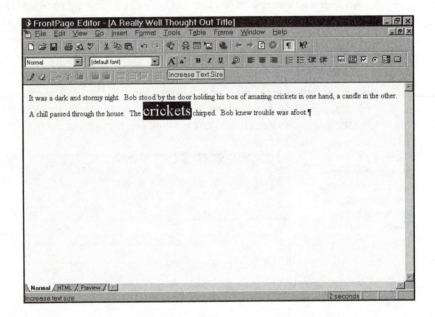

FIG. 7.8
Use the Increase and Decrease text size buttons to make your text bigger or smaller.

The formatting of individual characters, words, and sentences can enhance your page significantly. Bold face, italic, and underlining can highlight important information if not overused. With FrontPage Editor, you can apply all these character formats and change the text color simply by selecting and clicking. Select the text you want to modify; then click the appropriate button to apply the effect. The button with the B applies bold, the I applies italics, and the U applies underline. If you're starting new text, click the button, type the new text, and click the button again when you want to turn the effect off. The effects can be layered; that is, you can have text that is bold, italic, underlined, and in color.

Usage of bold, underline, and italic in page design are pretty conventional and easy to grasp. Color usage, however, is a more complex matter, and we'll consider it at length later in this chapter, in the section "Changing Backgrounds and Text Color."

If you've been experimenting with character formatting on a large section of text and have messed it up so thoroughly that you want to start over, you can easily do so. Select the offending text and choose F<u>o</u>rmat, <u>R</u>emove Formatting. Character size, font, color, and attributes (such as bold) will revert to the default normal style.

Justification

By default, all of the text you type aligns to the left side of the screen. This is fine in many instances, but you will often want to center your text or align it to the right side of the screen as shown in Figure 7.9.

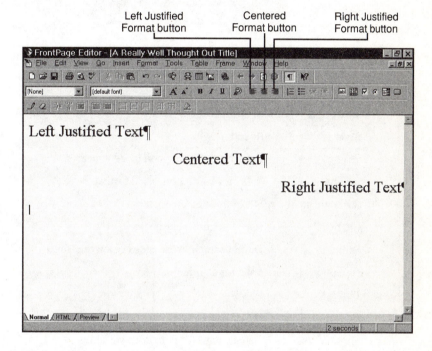

FIG. 7.9
Aligning your paragraphs to the left, center, or right is called justification.

Justification can only be applied to entire paragraphs, not individual words or sentences.

Using Logical Styles

HTML has two classes of formatting commands you can use on text: physical and logical. The distinction can initially be confusing. If a browser sees the HTML tags for italic or bold characters (physical styles), it puts italic or bold on the screen, no matter how the browser preferences are set. But if it sees the emphasis or strong HTML tags (logical styles), it checks its preference settings to see how its user wants emphasized or strong text to appear.

Choose F<u>o</u>rmat, <u>F</u>ont, and click the Sp<u>e</u>cial Styles tab to see the logical styles formatting sheet (see Figure 7.10).

FIG. 7.10
The Logical Styles tab allows you to format text according to the intent rather than the physical attributes.

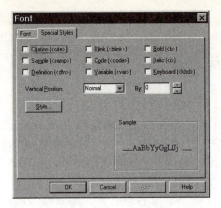

As usual, you can apply these styles by selecting text and then choosing the style you want. Table 7.1 gives you a quick rundown of the different styles.

Table 7.1	Logical Character Styles
Style	**Result**
Strong	Bold faced or other enhanced appearance
Emphasis	Italic or other emphasized format
Strike-through	Strike through characters
Citation	Italic for citing references
Sample	Output sample (resembles typewriter font)
Definition	Italic for definitions
Blink	Blinks text
Code	HTML code (resembles typewriter font)
Variable	Usually italic for defining a variable
Keyboard	Indicates user-supplied text (resembles typewriter font)

 TIP To quickly format some characters, select the text, right-click it to open the shortcut menu, and click Font Properties to make the Font dialog box appear.

Horizontal Rules

Although not technically part of basic text, horizontal rules are a standard part of HTML layout. What is a horizontal rule? It is simply a line that divides a page. Considering that HTML documents are always one big page (without page breaks), horizontal rules can help you logically separate your content.

You place a line on a page by choosing Insert, Horizontal Line. The resulting default line, which all graphics-capable browsers display, is a shadowed line that stretches the width of the browser window. Incidentally, it forces a blank line above and below it, so you can't get text to snuggle up close to it.

You can vary the line's appearance somewhat by adjusting its properties. These variations are actually Netscape extensions that FrontPage Editor supports, though not all browsers display them. To modify a line's appearance, click the line and choose Edit, Horizontal Line Properties; alternatively, right-click the line and choose Horizontal Line Properties from the shortcut menu. You can then change the line's displayed width, align it, adjust its weight by changing its height in pixels, change it to a solid, unshaded line, or give it a color.

Working with Tables

Tables are grids containing columns and rows. Each rectangle in the grid is called a cell. If you are familiar with spreadsheets, then you are familiar with tables. Tables are supported by all the major graphical browsers (Netscape 2.0 and 3.0, Internet Explorer 2.0 and 3.0, and Mosaic 2.1), so you can include them in your pages. Different browsers treat visible cell borders differently, though, so you should check to see what the borders look like in each browser before you settle on a design. Equally important, remember that many people cruise the Web at 640×480 resolution; if you create tables that take advantage of the width of a 1024×768 display, your visitors using a lower resolution may not see what you envisioned.

The cells in your table can include text, images, components, and even other tables. Invisible tables (with border width set to 0) are often used to give more precise control over page layout.

In Chapter 5, "Working with the FrontPage Editor" in the Primer section of this book, we briefly covered how to create tables and will repeat that information here before we talk about the advanced formatting you can do with your tables.

So, how do you create tables? There are two ways to do it. The first way is to select Table and then to select Insert Table. You will see the dialog box shown in Figure 7.11.

FIG. 7.11
The Insert Table dialog box allows you to easily add tables to your documents.

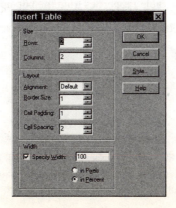

Enter the number of rows and columns you want in your table and FrontPage will create it. There are several more advanced options such as the table width, border line width, alignment, cell padding, cell spacing, and style. I entered 3 rows and 5 columns to create the table pictured in Figure 7.12.

FIG. 7.12
A table with 3 rows and 5 columns.

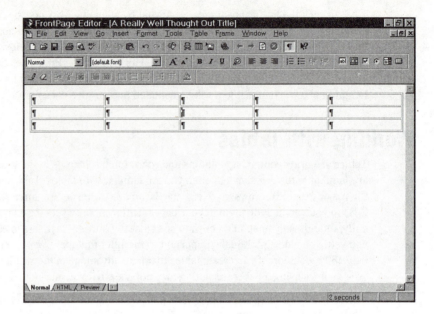

The other method of table creation is also a method of table modification. If you move the mouse cursor over the table, you will notice it change into a small pencil. This pencil indicates the Table Drawing tool. You can click and draw lines in order to split cells and rows in a "free-form" manner. When you select Table and then choose Draw Table, you can get the same tool to draw a new table at any place in your document.

Once you have created your table, you can access a large number of the tables properties by right-clicking the table and choosing Table Properties from the pop-up menu.

Let's look at Table Properties and see what kinds of formatting you can do with your tables.

Adjusting Table Properties

In Figure 7.13, you can see the Table Properties dialog box. We'll go through each item in the properties list.

First, there is the Layout group in the upper-left corner. The Alignment choice allows you to choose from a drop-down list, indicating where you want the table positioned on the page. Currently, most Web browsers only support aligning a table left or right. The Float selection allows you to choose whether you want text to flow to the right of the table, left of the table, or not at all. Border Size asks for a number, in pixels, to add a border around a table. The default border size is one.

FIG. 7.13
The Table Properties dialog box is where you can control all aspects of your table's appearance.

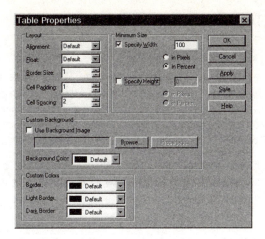

> **NOTE** A border width of zero means that no table border will appear in a Web browser; however, the FrontPage Editor displays dotted lines around cells when border size is zero to show you the layout of the table. When you use a table for laying out a page, set the border size to zero so the table is invisible.

To adjust the space around each cell in the table, use the Cell Padding field. Simply enter a number, in pixels, to set the space between the contents and inside edges of cells. You can only set the cell padding for an entire table. The default cell padding is one. In Cell Spacing, you enter a number, in pixels, to set the spacing of the cells in a table. Cell spacing determines how much space is placed between all the cells in a table. You can only set the cell spacing for an entire table. The default cell spacing is two.

Just below the layout options in the dialog box is the Custom Background group of options. You can use the options in this section to select a background image or color for the table. Check the Use Background Image box to choose a background image for a table. A table can have a different background image from the page containing it. If you want to find the background image, click Browse. If you have chosen a background image, you can edit its properties by clicking the Properties button. Finally, there is the Background Color option. Just select a color from the drop-down list to be used for the background of the table. A table can have a different background color from the page containing it. To define a custom color, select Custom from the drop-down list. You can set a background image, a background color, or both.

The Custom Colors group at the bottom of the box is for choosing colors used for the Table border. You can specify two colors for a table border to give the border a three-dimensional look. Specify one color for a solid border.

Then there is the Minimum Size group. You can set the minimum display size of the table here. If the content is larger than the minimum size, the table will usually expand to display the content, but this is where you can make sure that it is always at least the size you would like.

Check the Specify Width box to specify a minimum width for a table. If you do not specify a width, a Web browser might resize the table and change how the contents of cells fit within the cells. To fix the appearance of a table on a page, specify a table width.

You can specify the width in either pixels or percentage. Pixels will result in the same size table at any resolution, while percent will make the table a certain percentage of the overall page width. For example, if you choose 50 percent, the table will span 50 percent of a Web browser's window, regardless of how a user resizes the window. When you specify a percentage width for a table, the width of each cell in the table is the same. The default table width is 100 percent of the window.

The Specify Height choice works exactly the same as Width, only for the Height, obviously.

Click Apply to view any changes you made to a table's properties before you close this dialog box.

Cell Properties

When you right-click a cell in a table, the pop-up menu also contains a menu choice for Cell Properties. Basically, individual cells in a table can have separate formatting from the table for many, but not all, of the table attributes. Figure 7.14 shows the Cell Properties dialog box with a description of the choices.

FIG. 7.14
The Cell Properties box lets you set many of the same options you set for your table for individual cells.

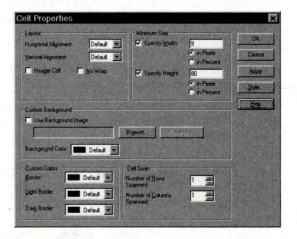

Use the Cell Properties dialog box to set and view properties of a cell. First, there is the Layout portion of the dialog box. You can use the options in this section to position the contents of a cell and create headings for a cell. Use the Horizontal Alignment drop-down list to select the horizontal alignment for the contents of a cell. Unlike the table, you also have a Vertical Alignment option for cells. Here you select the vertical alignment for the contents of a cell from the drop-down list.

If the cell is supposed to be a column header, you should click the Header Cell box, and if you want to make sure that the text in your cell does not wrap onto the next line when it is too long, click the No Wrap check box.

Cells can have their own Custom Backgrounds as well, and this works exactly the same as the Table Custom Background.

The Border options also work exactly the same as the Table Border options but apply only to the selected cell.

As with the Table Properties, you can specify a Minimum Width and Height for your cell in the Minimum Size group.

The last part of the dialog box is the Cell Span group. To understand cell spanning, take a look at Figure 7.15.

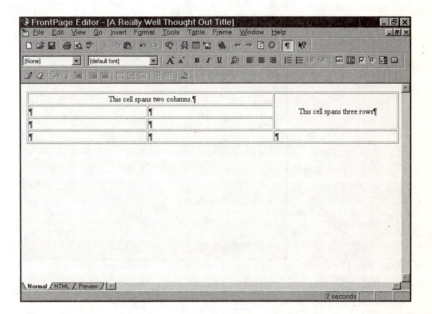

FIG. 7.15
Cells can span multiple rows or columns, as in the table shown here.

Notice how one cell is the width of two columns with no line in the middle to divide it and another cell is the height of three rows with no dividing lines. These are examples of cell spanning. You can accomplish this by either setting the Number of Rows or Number of Columns spanned values in the Cell Span group of the Cell Properties dialog box, or you can use the Eraser tool on the Table Drawing toolbar to just delete the lines you don't want.

Creating Lists

We covered the basic types of lists in Chapter 5, "Working with the FrontPage Editor," but did not cover the formatting of lists. For review, here is the procedure to add a list to your page.

To create a numbered list, you simply click the Numbered List button. It is the button with the numbers 1, 2, and 3 and three lines on it. Next to this button is another button with three small squares and three lines on it. Clicking that button creates a bulleted list.

While editing a list, FrontPage assists by providing sequentially numbered line items, bullets, and indents as applicable to the style of list being created. You can also create nested lists by inserting a list within a list, or you can insert a paragraph in a list. To end any list, press the Enter key twice or press Ctrl+Enter.

Is there anything more that can be done with lists you ask? Yes, there are quite a few List formatting options available. Figure 7.16 illustrates some of the variations available by changing the list properties.

FIG. 7.16
You can format lists in many different ways beyond the basic bulleted or numbered list.

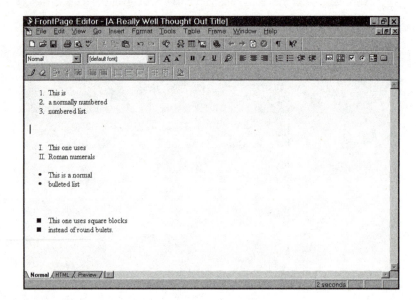

You can change the properties of how lists appear by right-clicking the list and choosing List Properties. The dialog box displayed in Figure 7.17 appears.

The first three tabs allow you to change the style of the numbers or bullets used while the fourth tab in the dialog box lets you change the type of list altogether.

There is a List Item Properties dialog box that displays only one of the tabs (depending on the type of list the item is a part of) and lets you change the style for an individual list item. It is accessible by right-clicking the list item you want to change and selecting List Item Properties.

After you have made the changes you want, click OK to apply the changes and Cancel to discard them.

FIG. 7.17
Change the bullet types, number types, and even the kind of list being displayed with the List Properties dialog box.

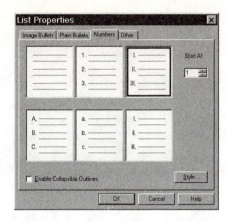

Working with Fonts

I am a font junkie. I admit it. I have 1,600+ fonts installed on my computer and don't even care that it causes Windows to take five minutes to start. So, when I found out about the HTML Font tag, I immediately started thinking of ways to use it on my site. Before you get too carried away with using fonts on your site, here are a couple of things to keep in mind.

1. Fonts with the same names will look similar from one platform to another, but not necessarily identical.
2. Fonts included on your pages are NOT transferred to the computer that is viewing the page. If the viewing computer doesn't have a font by the same name installed, your page will not display with the font you intended.
3. Many browsers do not recognize the font tag and will, therefore, not correctly display the page.

An example of the hazards of using fonts for page design is shown in Figures 7.18 and 7.19.

You can easily change your font to anything you have installed by using the font drop-down box on the toolbar. Any text you have selected will change to the new font, and anything you type now will be in the new font face. Just don't use much more than the most common fonts (Arial, Times New Roman, Courier) if you want to be sure that your pages display correctly. Anything that uses interesting font faces is better done with graphics. There is a chapter later about some new advances in page design and layout including Dynamic HTML, Style Sheets, and Portable fonts. You should take a look at that chapter before doing too much with fonts.

Another thing people attempt to do with fonts is use an International character set such as Korean or Japanese. This rarely works as intended and is not the right way to solve this particular problem. Instead, you should right-click the page and choose Page Properties. Then click the Language tab, and change the HTML encoding for the page to use the correct international character set.

FIG. 7.18
The cool Alien font makes this page look dramatic to the person who built it.

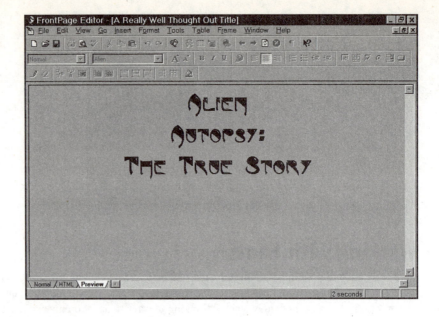

Changing Backgrounds and Text Color

Both these changes can be made at once from the same dialog box, so we'll consider them together. You will be working with the dialog box shown in Figure 7.19. To change either color, use the following steps:

1. Right-click the page and select Page Properties from the pop-up menu.
2. When the Page Properties dialog box appears, click the Background tab to bring that sheet to the front.
3. Click the button at the right of the Background drop-down list box. A drop-down list of available colors appears.
4. Click the color you want. If you now click OK, the dialog box will vanish, and your page background will immediately assume that color.
5. If you want to use a background image instead, click the Background Image check box, and enter the location of the image you want to use as a tiled background. This is similar to Windows wallpaper.

You can also use the previous procedures to change the colors of various types of hyperlinks on your page by selecting different colors for Hyperlink, Visited Hyperlink, and Active Hyperlink. If you select the Get Background and Colors From Page option, you can select another page that already has the background and colors you want to use, and those colors and background will be automatically brought into your page.

FIG. 7.19
The Background color or image, as well as the text colors, can be set from within the Page Properties dialog box.

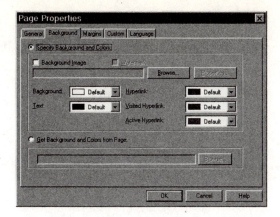

There are a couple of things to keep in mind. First, custom colors may look great on your machine but may display differently on a machine with, say, a 16-color depth. I once had a custom light blue that showed up as white on a white background on a 16-color monitor. Needless to say, that effectively made the page unusable. Another thing is that wild purple on a bright green color scheme may look great to you, but it may be totally illegible—or give other people a headache. The number one rule with background colors and images is "exercise restraint." ●

CHAPTER 8

Enhancing Pages with Graphics and Multimedia

There was an Internet before the advent of the World Wide Web. It had tons of information, searchable databases, lots of documents, and other resources. FTP was there, UseNet was there, as were other protocols such as Gopher. What was missing from the Internet? The browser. Web browsers brought two important innovations to the Internet that caused it to become the global phenomenon it is now. First, the browser provided a single interface to all of the various Internet resources. Secondly, and just as importantly, the Web browser brought graphics to the Internet. It wasn't long before it also brought animation, music, video, and games to the Internet as well. This chapter will tell you what you need to know to start spicing up your pages with graphics, audio, and video. ∎

Using images in your Web pages
Images can greatly enhance your pages; learn the rules for using them effectively.

Working with JPG, GIF and PNG image files
Different file formats are good for different things; here you'll learn about the different file formats.

Working with image maps
You can link your images to resources on the Web with Image Maps.

Adding sound to your page
Learn about the different ways you can incorporate music and speech into your pages.

Working with MIDI, RealAudio, WAV, and AU sound files
Different audio formats are good for different things—learn what to use for your needs.

Working with AVI and RealVideo files
Learn to work with the default Windows video format, as well as how to stream video with RealVideo.

Using Images on Your Web Pages

Graphics inserted into a Web page are called *in-line images*. The two most common graphic file formats for Web publications are GIF (Graphics Interchange Format), and JPEG (Joint Photographic Experts Group). All graphics-capable browsers support these two formats and display them without fuss. A new format called PNG (pronounced "ping") is starting to catch on and has several advantages over both GIF and JPG. We will discuss all of these formats in the next section of this chapter. Several other formats exist, for example TIFF, PCX, and BMP. Web browsers are capable of viewing these formats as well by launching separate programs called helper applications that can read these files. Since these files are not natively supported by any of the major Web browsers, we will not discuss them further here.

Some images, especially of icons and buttons, are available on the Internet for free use. At the end of this chapter, I have included links to several good sites on the Web where you can browse and download free graphics. However, to individualize your own Web site, you'll likely want unique graphics. Original artwork can be produced either with graphics packages, such as the Image Composer software included with FrontPage 98 (covered in Part V, "Creating and Adapting Graphics with Image Explorer), or by more traditional means such as paint or photography. Photographs and artwork must be scanned to make the required graphics files, which you can then insert into your pages.

Putting an Image onto a Page

Within each Web you create in FrontPage, there is an images folder. This is the most convenient place to keep the graphics for your Web, since FrontPage automatically displays the images folder when you choose Insert and then select Image. Of course, having all your images in one place also makes it easier to stay organized.

> **CAUTION**
>
> When you reference a graphic that is stored outside the current Web, and then save the page that displays the graphic, FrontPage Editor will ask if you want to copy that graphic to the current Web. If you say yes, the graphic ends up in the Web's root directory, not in the images folder. To copy the graphic to the images folder, you must supply the relative path name for that folder.

You can insert graphics into your pages without having copied them over into the images folder; it is just a nice thing to do. You can insert a graphic into any page by doing the following:

1. Place the cursor where you want the image to appear.
2. Choose Insert and then select Image. The Image dialog box appears as shown in Figure 8.1
3. If the image file you want is shown, select the image file by clicking its name in the list.
4. If it is not shown, you can select Clip Art to browse the Microsoft Clip Art collection shipped with FrontPage; click the Scan button to acquire the image from a scanner

(if you have one connected); enter the Internet URL of the image you want to insert; or click the button with the folder icon to browse your hard drive for the image file. These options will be covered later.

5. Choose OK. FrontPage Editor inserts the image into the page.

FIG. 8.1
The Insert Image dialog box gives you the ability to insert images from multiple sources.

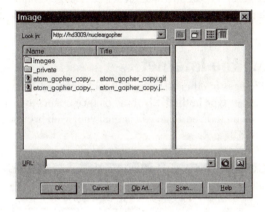

 TIP If you want to make changes to your image beyond those that you can do within the FrontPage Editor, double-click the image. This opens Image Composer or your favorite image editor.

Deleting an Image

You will occasionally want to delete an image from your page. To get rid of it, first click it to select it (you know it's selected when the sizing handles appear on its borders). Then press the Delete key. The image vanishes. Alternatively, you can right-click the image and choose Cut, which will place the image on the Windows Clipboard for insertion elsewhere on the page.

Inserting an Image from Your Hard Drive

Sometimes, the image file you want isn't in the images folder of the Web you're working on or anywhere else in the current Web. It may need to be scanned in. Sometimes, it is somewhere else on your hard drive, or maybe on the Web. FrontPage gives you a quick way to import images from somewhere else. First, let's look at how to add a file to your site from somewhere on your hard drive. Place the cursor where you want the image, and use the following steps:

1. Choose Insert, and then choose Image so that the Image dialog box appears.
2. To insert an image stored elsewhere on your system, use the Explorer button (the one with the Folder icon) to open the next dialog box, which is a standard Windows 95 file-opening dialog box.
3. Find and select the name of the image file you want, and then choose Open. All dialog boxes close, and the image appears on your page at the cursor position.
4. Choose File, Save. The Save Image to FrontPage Web dialog box appears.

5. To save the new image to the root folder of the current Web, simply choose Yes. To save it to the Web's images folder, type **images/** (with a forward slash) into the Save as URL box, right ahead of the file name, to make the proper path. If you've inserted more than one graphic and want them all saved to the Web's root folder, choose Yes to All.

If you now check Explorer's Folder View and click the images folder (or the root folder, depending on the path name you saved with), you'll see that the graphic has been added to your Web.

Getting Images from the Internet

You can also access images at other sites, both in Webs on your local host and on the World Wide Web. You can either type in the URL of the picture or surf to it. To do this, click the button with the Globe icon on it. FrontPage will launch your Web browser and it should look something like Figure 8.2.

FIG. 8.2
FrontPage lets you surf the Net for pics. As soon as you find the image you want, switch back to FrontPage and the URL will be filled into the Insert Image dialog box.

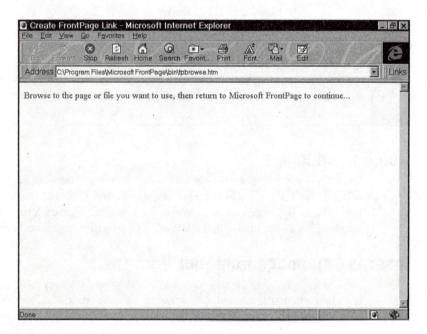

There are a few things to be aware of when using images from the Web:

- Most graphics are copyrighted and should not be used without the permission of the person who owns the image. Ask before you use anything.
- Links to graphics on the Web do not make local copies of the images, they just make links. If that image is changed, deleted, or renamed, it could break your link or change the way it appears on your page.
- By using an image from another person's server, you are putting more load on his server and he may not appreciate it.

As a general rule, using images you find on the Web is fine as long as you have permission and you make a local copy first.

Adding a Clip Art Image

FrontPage 98 gives you access to Microsoft Office clip art; if you don't have MS Office, FrontPage 98 does include six categories of clip art of its own: backgrounds, bullets, buttons, headers, lines, and miscellaneous. To use them, do the following:

1. Choose Insert, Image to open the Image dialog box. Click the Clip Art button. This launches the Microsoft Clip Art Gallery.
2. Browse the collection until you find the image you want.
3. Click the image to select it and then choose OK. The graphic is inserted into your page.

Figure 8.3 shows the Clip Art Browser, which allows you to view and select the Clip Art at your disposal.

FIG. 8.3
The Microsoft Clip Art Gallery contains a variety of image for you to use in your Web documents.

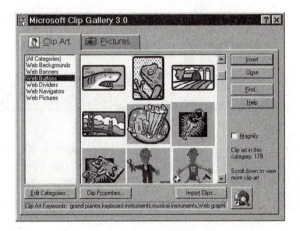

Scanning an Image

If you are one of the lucky few who have a TWAIN compliant scanner hooked up to your system, you can click the Scan button, and FrontPage will let you grab an image from the scanner.

Modifying an Image

After an image has been inserted into your page, FrontPage lets you modify it in all sorts of cool ways without even using a separate image editor. You can change the height, width, contrast, and all sorts of other things about your image right within the page by using the Image Editing toolbar. This toolbar appears on the bottom of the Editor window whenever you click an image, along with a series of little black squares that will appear along the sides and on the corners of your image.

Chapter 8 Enhancing Pages with Graphics and Multimedia

Figure 8.4 shows you what can be done by clicking the black squares and dragging them. This resizes the image.

FIG. 8.4
Images can be displayed larger or smaller than their actual size in browsers that support width and height attributes for images.

 TIP Not all browsers support changing the width and height of your images via HTML, so your pages may look funky in those browsers. To avoid this, it is a good idea to display your graphics at their actual size. Another problem with changing the width and height is that some graphics, such as animated GIFs, will usually display wrong.

The toolbar has the following buttons going from left to right:

Table 8.1 The FrontPage Editor Image Manipulation Toolbar

Button Name	Description
Select Hotspot on Image	This button helps you create imagemaps.
Draw a Rectangle Hotspot	Also imagemap-related. Creates rectangle hotspots.
Draw a Circular Hotspot	Again, used in the creation of imagemaps for circular hotspots.
Draw a Polygon Hotspot	Used to create polygon-shaped hotspots.
Highlight Hotspots	Shows hotspots instead of image.
Create a text label or hotspot	Creates a text label on your image that can be a hotspot.

Button Name	Description
Make Transparent	Select a color in the image that should be transparent
Crop	Lets you trim your image down to just the part you want to display.
Washout	Creates a washed version of the image suitable for a background that you can read text over.
Black & White	Removes the color from your image.
Restore	Returns the image to it's original saved state.
Rotate Left	Rotates the image 90 degrees to the left.
Rotate Right	Rotates the image 90 degrees to the right.
Reverse	Flips the image horizontally.
Flip	Flips the image vertically.
More Contrast	Increases the image contrast.
Less Contrast	Decreases the image contrast.
More Brightness	Adds brightness to the image.
Less Brightness	Lowers the brightness level of the image.
Bevel	Adds a bevel to the image that makes it look like a button.
Resample	Resamples the image to match its current size.

Try selecting an image and experimenting with the various effects. You can always click the Restore button to undo your changes.

Positioning Text Around an Image

If you've experimented with simple pages where you put blocks of text with an image, you'll have noticed that the text lines up with the image's bottom edge. Sometimes, this is what you want, but it's typographically limiting. You need more than that to lay out a good-looking page. What about centering images, putting them at the right margin, and getting multiple lines of text to flow down an image's side? FrontPage Editor lets you do all these things.

As we previously observed, if you add Normal text beside an image or insert an image into an existing line of Normal text, the text lines up with the image's bottom edge. If you don't want this effect, you can change it. To do so, use the following steps:

1. Select the image by clicking it.
2. Right-click the image and select Image Properties.
3. Choose the Appearance tab. In the Layout area, click the arrow button at the right of the Alignment box.

4. Select the alignment you want from the drop-down list (see Table 8.2 for an explanation of the various alignment choices).
5. Choose OK. The text moves to the appropriate position beside the image.

Table 8.2 Alignment Choices for Images

Alignment	Result
Default	Aligns the image using the default settings of the Web browser. This is the same as the baseline option.
Left	Aligns the image in the left margin and wraps the text that follows the image down the image's right side.
Right	Aligns the image in the right margin and wraps the text that precedes the image down the image's left side.
Top	Aligns the top of the image with the surrounding text.
Texttop	Aligns the top of the image with the top of the tallest text in the line.
Middle	Aligns the middle of the image with the surrounding text.
Absmiddle	Aligns the image with the middle of the current line.
Baseline	Aligns the image with the baseline of the current line.
Bottom	Aligns the bottom of the image with the surrounding text.
Absbottom	Aligns the image with the bottom of the current line.
Center	Aligns the center of the image with the surrounding text.

An example of some of the different type of alignment is shown in Figure 8.5.

Often, you'll want to wrap text around an image. To make an image float against the left or right margin so that existing or future text wraps around it, select the Left alignment or Right alignment options as shown in Figure 8.6.

Spacing Between Text and Image

You know that whitespace is an important component of any page, and you may dislike the way text gets crowded close to your images. Fortunately, you can adjust the text-to-image spacing with the Horizontal Spacing and Vertical Spacing boxes in the Appearance sheet of the Image Properties dialog box. The values you fill in here determine the spacing in pixels.

Adjusting Image Size from the Appearance Sheet

Earlier we showed you how to adjust image size by dragging the little black squares on the corners and edges of images. However, you can also adjust image size on the Appearance sheet; you can mark the Specify Size check box to set the width and height of the graphic in pixels or percent. Fiddling with this can give weird results, especially if the image is a floating image. The adjustments don't affect the size of the image file, either; you'll still need a graphics editor to do that. It's most useful for making minor adjustments to balance the relationship of image and text.

FIG. 8.5
You can align images many different ways within your pages.

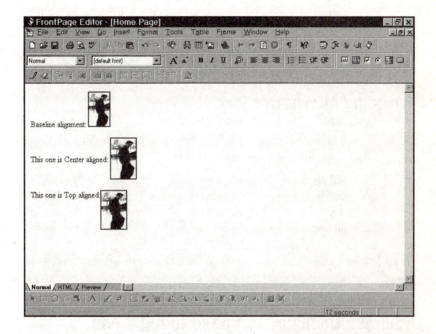

FIG. 8.6
Images can be floated to the left or right of the text on your page.

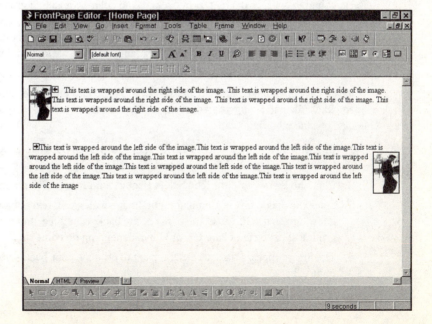

Adding Borders to an Image

You might want a visible boundary around a graphic, although such boundaries aren't used a lot. When they are, they're often understood to indicate a clickable image. If you want one, there's not much variety; you're stuck with a simple black-line rectangle. You can vary its line thickness, but that's all. To add a border, go to the Appearance sheet of the Image Properties dialog box, and type a nonzero value into the Border Thickness box.

I often use this to set the border to 0 on hyperlinked images where I do not want to show a border.

Providing Alternative Text

Remember when we showed you how different a page can look when viewed with either a text-based browser or even a graphical one with the image loading turned off? This is how you make sure that your page is still usable.

You add alternative text by using the General sheet of the Image Properties dialog box. In the Alternative Representations section, use the Text box to type the word or phrase that stands in for the graphic, and then choose OK. (Remember to test the results!) Don't, by the way, try to give an elaborate description of the picture. A few well-chosen words are plenty.

 There is an additional advantage to providing an alternate text description. When the mouse is moved over the image in most of the new Web browsers, the alternate text pops up as a ToolTip style menu.

Adding a Background Image Using a File

Background images, as distinct from background colors, are actual graphics that sit behind your text and your foreground images. You use them to add texture, color, site identification, or other visual effects to your pages. Aesthetics and legibility are important here; remember, a background is just that. If the page is not readable with the background image, your page will not be valuable to visitors.

You can place any image into your background. FrontPage Editor does this by treating the image like a tile and laying enough identical tiles to cover everything in sight. To put in an image, use the following steps:

1. Choose File and then select Page Properties to open the Page Properties dialog box. Click the Background sheet tab and mark the Background Image check box.
2. Click the Browse button. The Select Background Image dialog box appears.
3. Since the dialog box is identical to the Image dialog box (except for its title) you already know how to use it. Select the name of the background file, and return to the Background sheet by choosing OK or Open, depending on context.
4. The image appears tiled across the page to produce your background as shown in Figure 8.7.

FIG. 8.7
A speckle-textured background on the page is legible and looks sharp.

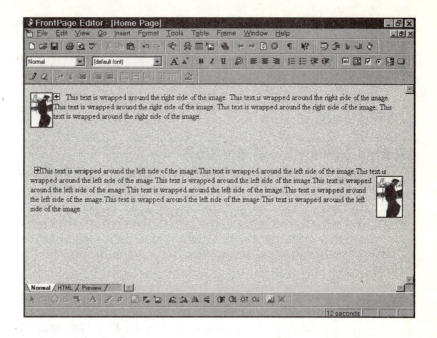

 A real time-saver is using the Get Background and Colors from Page check box in the Background sheet of the Page Properties dialog box. This copies all the color choices and the background image from another page into the current one. It's very handy for keeping your pages' appearance consistent.

Remember that using a background image from another site puts your page's appearance at someone else's mercy. If the site's URL changes or its Webmaster deletes the image file, you'll lose your background. You're better off downloading the image and storing it locally.

 When you use a background image, also set the page's background color so that it's close to the predominant hue of the image. Why? So that a browser running with images turned off (which will include background images) displays your page with something like its intended appearance.

Using Watermarked Background Images

Your background images will scroll in a browser, along with the foreground objects and text. Marking the Watermark check box on the Background sheet will keep the background image still, while the foreground material moves across it. This is not supported by all browsers but looks sharp on Netscape and Internet Explorer.

Using Images As Hyperlinks

If you know how to make a text hyperlink, you already know how to construct one from an image. Do the following:

1. Insert the image into the page, using any of the methods you learned earlier.
2. Select the image by clicking it. Then choose Edit, Hyperlink to open the Create Hyperlink dialog box.
3. Put in the URL you want to link to and click OK.

That's all there is to it! To edit the link, select the image and choose Edit; then select Hyperlink.

Making Navigational Controls

People will want to move around your site quickly and easily. They like to have a sense of where they are and how to get back to where they were. Navigational controls will go a long way toward helping your site appear professional. Buttons are the most common navigation symbols, and there are dozens of places on the Web that offer these simple images for free-use downloading. Put them into your page in an organized way, link them to their destinations, and they'll tie your site together so that it'll be a pleasure to visit.

Be consistent with button usage, though; a button that has function x on one page shouldn't have function y on another. Always provide alternative text for buttons, in case your visitor has images turned off or is using a text browser. And consider putting a visible text label with each button. It makes life easier for your visitors—and they'll like you for it.

Using Thumbnails

You may wonder how you can show all those great family photos you want to display on your site and still allow your visitors to download the page before they die of old age.

In two words: use thumbnails. Thumbnails are smaller copies of the images that download quickly and link to the original image. The FrontPage Editor lets you automatically create thumbnails of large images by doing the following:

1. Insert an image as previously described in this chapter.
2. Click the image to select it.
3. If the image is large, the Auto Thumbnail menu choice on the Tools menu will be available. Select it.
4. FrontPage will automatically resize the image.

I have created a page that uses several thumbnails in Figure 8.8.

FrontPage will automatically create a link to the original image file from the thumbnail. You don't have to do another thing except save the page. In the case of the page I created previously in Figure 8.8, the images all came from other places on my hard drive, so all of the images in the page need to be saved to the Web. The file save dialog box shown in Figure 8.9 clearly shows the original files and their thumbnail counterparts, which bear the same names with the addition of _small on the file name.

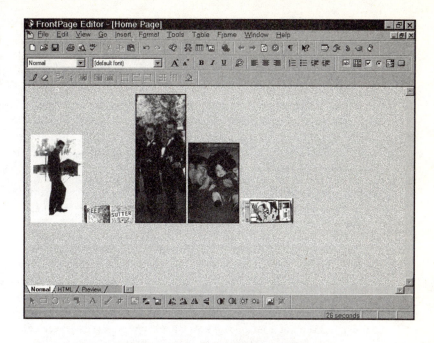

FIG. 8.8
Thumbnails allow you to create indexes of images with links to the actual larger files. These smaller images download much faster.

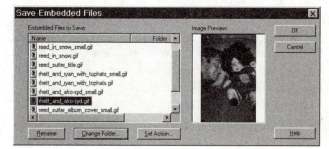

FIG. 8.9
All of the thumbnails and images from my page will be saved into my Web site.

Working with JPG, GIF, and PNG Image Files

Many people are unaware that there are literally hundreds of different image formats in existence. Until recently, there was basically a separate image file format for just about every program and operating system. CompuServe saw the need to create a platform-independent graphics format for its members a long time ago and developer Graphic Interchange Format, or GIF. JPEG was developed later by the Joint Picture Experts Group (JPEG) as a highly compressed way to store photographic images. PNG (pronounced "ping") is a fairly recent development and is not yet fully supported by most browsers. It is intended to replace GIF as a file format. Why should you select one type of image format over another? Well, they all have their strengths and weaknesses.

The biggest advantage of GIF is that it's the bread-and-butter format for the Web, at least for now. Browsers decompress it quickly, so it's reasonably brisk about showing up on your visitor's screen. It's the format of choice for line art; that is, art without continuous shading of tones (photographs, for instance). It provides up to 256 colors and can simulate more by dithering. Or you can go in the other direction, since a useful characteristic of GIFs is that you can use image editors to reduce the number of different colors in them. This reduces the file size. Then again, you can simply reduce the size of the image with a graphics editor; this is a possibility with JPEGs, too. GIFs can be "interlaced," which means that the image can be displayed as it loads as a series of lines that get filled in better with each pass. This characteristic can make the page load more quickly even if the images are not entirely present and accounted for.

There are two kinds of GIF files: GIF87 and GIF89a. Interlacing, transparency, and several other features of GIFs (including multiple image animated GIFs) are part of the GIF89a specification.

What about JPEG? GIF image files do tend to be larger than equivalent JPEG ones, so what you gain in fast GIF decompression you lose (somewhat) in having to store bigger files on your site. On the other hand, JPEG files, while they're smaller, decompress more slowly than GIF files. Their advantage over GIFs is that they support up to 16.7 million colors, so that continuous-tone images reproduce better on-screen. However, there's no point in using actual High Color or True Color images on a Web page; few people use these color depths on their systems, so the extra quality is wasted.

With JPEG images, you can also adjust the compression level (in FrontPage Editor, this is referred to as quality) to reduce the size of a graphic. If you do this, inspect the results, since the higher the compression, the more the image will be degraded. You have to find the right balance of size and quality. The compression method used by GIF is called lossless compression because the image quality is never degraded.

NOTE For best results, you should scale the compression of a JPEG graphic using a native graphics program (such as Lview or Image Composer) rather than FrontPage Editor's Quality command.

PNG files have many advantages over both GIF and JPG. First, PNG files compress smaller than GIF images without any loss of image quality (as happens with JPG). Secondly, PNG files can contain more colors than either of the other two formats. PNG files support various types of progressive display (interlacing, layering, and other options) as well as embedded descriptive information about an image file itself. These are features that neither of the other two formats can claim. Another advantage to PNG is that while GIF files can have one pixel color that displays as transparent, every pixel in a PNG file can be assigned any of 256 degrees of transparency from totally clear to opaque. All of these capabilities make PNG the image format of the future for the Web. Netscape has included PNG support via a plug-in with their Communicator 4.0 browser, and Microsoft has also included support for the format in their IE 4 browser. Therefore, if you want to do some very advanced imaging, PNG is worth looking into.

Working with JPG, GIF, and PNG Image Files   137

Making the Most of Image File Formats

Web images are almost all JPEG or GIF files, with the balance, at the moment, tending heavily toward the GIF format. You can manipulate these formats, to a limited degree, with the tools FrontPage Editor gives you (see Figure 8.10). You do this to control image quality and influence download speed.

FIG. 8.10
You can do some image conversion and alteration within FrontPage 98.

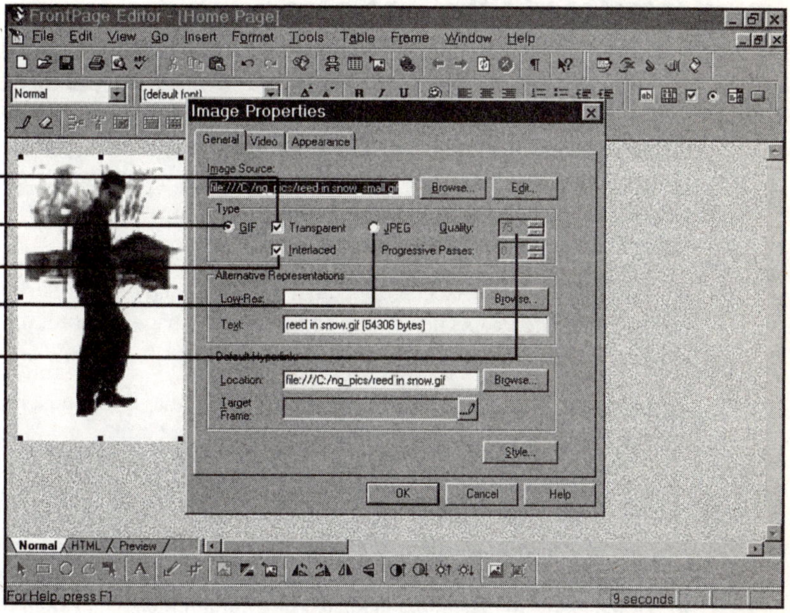

- Indicate Transparent
- Store as GIF
- Indicate Interlaced
- Store as JPEG
- Specify image quality (1-99)

TIP If you are serious about imaging, the tools within the FrontPage Editor will not be enough for you. You will want to use Image Composer or some other image editing tool to convert and modify your images.

Converting Image File Formats

When you insert an image, FrontPage Editor checks to see if it's GIF or JPEG. If it is neither GIF nor JPEG, and it is 256 colors or less, FrontPage Editor automatically converts it to GIF. If it is more than 256 colors, FrontPage Editor converts it to JPEG.

If you want to store a file in the other format, you mark the appropriate check box for GIF or JPEG. Then when you save the page, the image is converted. If you go from GIF to JPEG, you also get a chance to adjust the quality of the stored JPEG image by typing a number from 1 to 99 into the Quality box (75 is the default). With the best quality (99), you get the lowest file compression and slowest downloading; with the lowest quality (1), you get the highest file compression and the fastest downloading. There's no free lunch, is there?

> **CAUTION**
> Once you' set the Quality setting and save the image, you can't change that setting again, even if you delete the image and reinsert it from the saved page. So if you're experimenting, keep a backup.

Using Interlaced GIFs for Speed

One of the first things I learned about optimization of computer programs was that it was not as important to make a system run fast as it was to make it appear to run fast. A JPG file is almost always smaller than an equivalent GIF, but will usually not display until it finishes loading. On the other hand, an interlaced GIF builds up an image in four passes, with the picture becoming clearer with each pass. On the first pass, the text and links of the page also appear, so that the viewer can start reading (or clicking a link) without waiting for the image to be completed. Again, it's all in the interest of speed.

You can create an interlaced GIF from a noninterlaced one by marking the Interlaced check box in the Image Properties dialog box. When the page is saved, the image is stored as an interlaced GIF.

If you want to produce your own interlaced GIFs, Image Composer saves its GIF files in this format.

Using Low Res for Speed

Another tool in your speed-up kit is the Low Res (low resolution) option. To employ this, first use a graphics program to make a lower-resolution version of the original, and then save that graphic to your images folder. This version should be smaller than the original; a common trick to achieve this is to change it to black and white.

When you want to use the Low Res option, use the following steps:

1. Select the original, full-resolution image and go to the General sheet of the Image Properties dialog box.
2. In the Low-Res box in the Alternative Representations section, insert the name of the low-resolution image (the Browse button is handy here).
3. Choose OK.

Now when someone goes to the page, his browser loads the low-resolution image and the page text first; only after that does the browser go back and display the high-resolution version of the image. This speeds things up. Notice that you don't have to do any linking here, as the HTML generated by FrontPage Editor takes care of everything for you.

Making Transparent Images

Remember how I mentioned earlier that you can make a particular pixel color in a GIF image transparent? Why would you want to do that? Think about this. Every picture on the entire Web is rectangular, even pictures that appear to be round. If you see a graphic on a page that shows a sphere without any square around it, you are looking at a partially transparent image. Everything but the sphere is invisible. This is great for page design; after all, who wants to have nothing but square images? A transparent image lets the page background appear through parts of the graphic, as though the picture were painted on acetate instead of paper. Still not sure about what I am talking about? Look at Figure 8.11.

FIG. 8.11
The figure on the left has a normal, solid background while the image on the right has been made partially transparent.

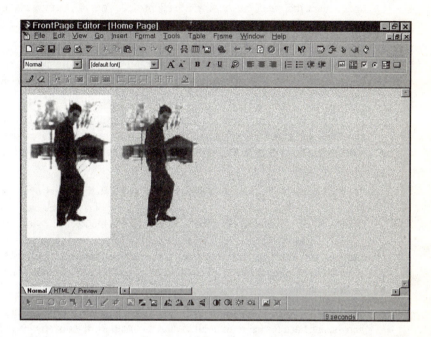

If you feel that a graphic looks better if a particular color in it is transparent, you can get this effect with the Make Transparent tool from the Image toolbar. To make a particular color invisible, use the following steps:

1. Select the graphic and click the Make Transparent button.
2. Put the cursor (it looks like the eraser end of a pencil) on the color you want to do away with, and click. All instances of that color in the graphic become transparent.

 When you first look at the image properties for some graphics, the Transparent check box is grayed out because the graphic contains no transparent colors. To establish a transparent color, use the Make Transparent tool from the Image toolbar.

Conversely, you may want to make a transparent graphic into an opaque one. To achieve this effect, select the image and then go to the General sheet of the Image Properties dialog box. Clear the Transparent check box in the Type section. Choose OK, and the graphic will be rendered opaque. You can't check the box again, though, to bring back the transparency. To do that, you have to use the Make Transparent tool, as previously described.

Setting Up Imagemaps

Imagemaps are a way to make various parts within an image link to different places on the Web. Creating an imagemap by hand-coding it in HTML can be tedious. FrontPage's capability to help you make imagemaps and link them easily is one of its most powerful features. The image maps it creates, by the way, are client-side. That is, the information about the map structure is embedded in the Web page that's downloaded to the browser client; the information does not reside on the server.

What is an *imagemap*? Functionally, it's a graphic that has hotspots in it; when a viewer clicks a hotspot, she's automatically sent to another location on the Web or in the current site. To put it another way, imagemaps are graphics with embedded hyperlinks.

Before you start working on you imagemap, think about what the graphic should look like, and especially remember that hotspots don't stand out as such in a browser window. This means you have to be careful to let people know where the hotspots are and what will happen if they're clicked.

The first thing to do, then, is to design the graphic so that it has obvious "clickable" areas. Often the best way to do this is to make those hotspot regions look like buttons. Another thing to consider is whether the destination of the link is made clear by the hotspot. If it isn't, you should consider adding text to describe what will happen if someone follows the link. Alternatively, modify the image itself to make its destination clearer. Try hard to see the imagemap as if you were coming across it for the first time, and try even harder to imagine how it can be misunderstood.

Another thing: don't jam too many hotspot links into one image. Small hotspots, a few pixels across, are hard for users to point to, and an image with a dozen clickable regions is confusing.

Finally, set up text links that duplicate the imagemap's hotspot destinations. This is for people who are running their browsers with images turned off.

> **CAUTION**
>
> If your Internet service provider (ISP) doesn't have the FrontPage server extensions installed on the server, your imagemaps probably will not work properly when you copy your Web from your PC to the server. If that happens, go to FrontPage Explorer's Web Settings dialog box in the Tools menu. The Advanced tab gives some alternate imagemap styles; try Netscape. If this also creates problems or you're concerned about browsers that don't support Netscape-like behavior, contact your ISP administrator to discuss using the CERN or NCSA styles.

Creating an Imagemap

To make an imagemap, you need an image. It can be in any file format, though you should remember that GIF or JPEG are the formats recognized by all browsers, without the need for plug-ins or helpers. Begin by inserting the image into the page, select it, and use the following steps:

1. Decide whether you want the hotspot to be a rectangle, a circle, or a polygon. From the Image toolbar, select the appropriate drawing tool.
2. Put the cursor on the image. The cursor changes to a crayon.
3. Hold down the left mouse button, drag to get the outline you want, and then release the mouse button (the black rectangles on the outline are sizing handles). The Create Link dialog box appears (see Figure 8.12).
4. Establish the link using the Open Page, New Page, Current Web, or World Wide Web tab.

N O T E If you can't see the Image toolbar, choose View, Image Toolbar to toggle it on. When it appears in the toolbar area, drag it to the place you want.

FIG. 8.12
The Create Link dialog box lets you link to another Internet resource by clicking the hotspot portion of an imagemap.

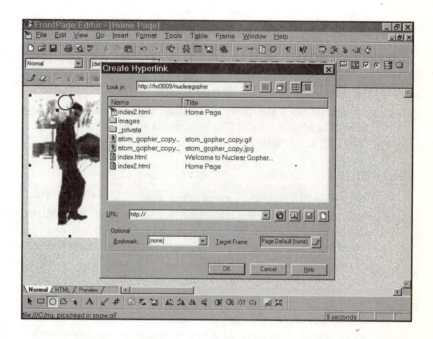

Believe it or not, that's all you need to do. If you want to edit the link, select the image, click the hotspot, and then choose Edit, Link.

 A quick way to edit an imagemap link is to right-click the hotspot and select Image Hotspot Properties from the shortcut menu.

The nature of imagemaps is to have more than one hotspot in the graphic. To get them neatly fitted, you can resize each hotspot by dragging its sizing handles, or you can move it around by putting the mouse pointer on its border and dragging it.

Deleting a Hotspot

To delete a hotspot, click the image so that the hotspot borders appear. Then click the hotspot you want to eliminate, and either press the Delete key or choose Edit, Clear.

Adding Sound to Your Page

Everything we have spoken about so far has been entirely related to visual elements on your Web site. Music actually gets little attention on most sites; this is too bad because music can greatly enhance a visitor's experience on your site. After all, imagine your favorite movie without background music or a video game without the pounding soundtrack. Okay, sound has its place but sometimes, it can be distracting, annoying, or worse. Make sure that the sound you use on your site does actually add to the enjoyment of site.

Working with MIDI, RealAudio, WAV, and AU sound Files

Just like graphics files, there are multiple ways to present sound on your Web site, and they all have their advantages and disadvantages. I am going to cover four types of audio here: MIDI, WAV, AU, and RealAudio.

MIDI Files

What are MIDI files? They are to music what HTML is to text. They are a way to store information that can be translated into music by any computer with a MIDI synthesizer. What does that mean? A MIDI file of a piano sonata would not actually be a recording of a piano sonata. Instead the MIDI file would contain the time and pitch of each note that should be played by the piano, as well as other information such as how hard the notes should be played. The MIDI synthesizer on the computer sound card uses this information to reproduce the piano sonata.

Instruments can be synthesized by a sound card in one of two ways. The first, called Frequency Modulation (FM synthesis) uses entirely computer-generated sounds that usually sound fake. The second type of synthesis is Wave synthesis, where digitized recordings of real instruments are used instead of artificially created sounds. MIDI files cannot control what type of synthesis is used; that is up to the sound card installed on each individual computer. Basically, you can have an idea about how a MIDI file will sound when played but the results will vary.

The biggest advantage to MIDI is that the files are tiny compared to other formats. A MIDI file can download very quickly, even if it is a long song, so if you want some entertaining background music, MIDI might be a good choice.

WAV Files

The default file format of waveform audio in Windows is the WAV file. Waveform audio is digitally recorded sound. All of the file types we are going to talk about now are waveform audio.

WAV files are large and take a long time to download. Even short ones of relatively poor sound quality can be so huge that your visitors will rarely listen to them. Therefore, you may want to look at an alternate format such as RealAudio if you want to present music on your site.

Here is my own experience. I run a Web site for a small record label. We wanted to present music for listening. In WAV format, we presented 30-second samples that had poor sound quality and were 600kb or more in size. This resulted in 2–4 minute download times for 30 seconds of music at 28.8 and didn't impress many people. Plus visitors could not listen to the music until the entire file had transferred. Most people didn't stick around to hear it. By going to RealAudio, we were able to have better sound quality, full-length songs, and instantaneous playback without waiting for a download. WAV is likely the format that you will use to record music on your computer, but you will want to give thought to converting it into something else before you put it on the Web.

AU Files

AU files started off as the standard audio format of the Web. Why? Because AU is the audio format of UNIX and the Internet was born on UNIX. AU files are like WAV files but the sound quality is not quite as good. The file sizes are also smaller. If you want to present your music in the lowest common denominator format of the Web, this is it.

RealAudio

RealAudio is currently the de facto standard for "streaming" audio on the Web. Streaming audio is audio that plays as it downloads instead of having to wait until the entire file is received. It is a product of Progressive Networks and is available on just about every platform including Mac, UNIX, and Windows.

RealAudio files can be streamed over the Web either with the RealAudio server from Progressive Networks or via your Web server. The former choice also gives you the ability to broadcast live events, and there are many radio stations and news sites using RealAudio to broadcast live over the Web. The latter costs you nothing and makes the sound on your site easily accessible to all visitors.

Visit Progressive Networks at **http://www.realaudio.com/.** to find out about downloading the RealPlayer and Encoder to begin creating your own RealAudio content.

Adding Background Music

Right-clicking a page, selecting Page Properties, and choosing the General Tab will display the dialog box shown in Figure 8.13. From here, you can select a WAV file, AU file, or MIDI file that will play in the background on your page. Click the Browse button to locate the file, or type in the location directly.

You can control how long the file plays by deselecting the Forever box and picking a number of times the files should loop. If you leave the Forever box checked, the file will play (you guessed it) forever. Well, at least until the user leaves the page. If you wish to remove the background sound from your page, simply delete the name of the file from the General Tab of the Page Properties dialog box where you added it in the first place.

FIG. 8.13
The General Tab of the Page Properties dialog box lets you add a looping background sound to your page.

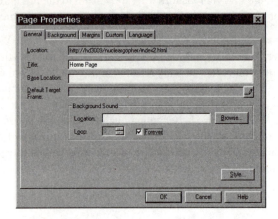

Linking to Audio Files

You can link to audio files of any type the same way you would link to an HTML document, an image file, or any other Web resource.

Adding Video to Your Site

Audio files are big and delivering them over the Web is a challenge, but one that can be handled fairly well by 28.8 modems. Video is another story altogether. Video combines images with sound and, therefore, can take a long time to download. For example, a 30-second AVI file can be 10–20 megabytes in size. I don't need to mention that most people will not download 20 megabytes to see 30 seconds of video. It takes hours.

Working with AVI and RealVideo Files

Just as WAV is the standard audio format of Windows, AVI is the standard video format of Windows. As I mentioned, AVI files are huge. You can certainly use them on the Web.

Here are some guidelines to using AVI files on the Web:

- Optimize, optimize, optimize. Anything you can do to optimize the video palette and shrink the video file will help you get more video in less space.
- Keep it short. Video files longer than a few seconds are not likely to be watched.

Several Web sites make good use of AVI files, for example, **http://espn.sportszone.com/.** where you can watch short highlights from the previous day's games.

RealVideo files are a recent development. They are basically highly compressed video files that can be streamed over the Web with varying levels of qualities. Figure 8.14 shows a page containing an embedded RealVideo file that is being streamed over the Web using a 28.8 modem.

FIG. 8.14
RealVideo files can be embedded as either a Plug-In or ActiveX control to stream video over the Web.

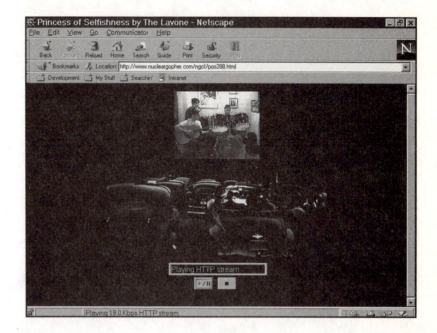

 To find out how to create RealVideo files, visit Progressive Networks at **http://www.realaudio.com**.

Other Video Formats

As you visit various sites on the Web, you will encounter other types of video: MPEG, VDOLive, QuickTime, and Xing StreamWorks among others. This chapter is not intended to teach you to create these or any other video formats but you can certainly use any of them on your Web site. This is dependent on the hardware and software you use and your particular needs. Until there is a standard video format for the Web, any one may be as good as any other. It depends on your needs. ●

CHAPTER 9

Activating Your Pages with Java, ActiveX, Scripting and More

Scripting your pages
Learn how to create interactivity on your site by using VBScript and JavaScript.

Using plug-ins and ActiveX
Embed live multimedia content into your site with ActiveX and plug-ins.

Adding Java applets
Get on the cutting edge of Web site design with Java applets that run on any computer.

Going 3-D: adding VRML worlds
Learn how to enhance your pages with virtual reality.

The World Wide Web has turned into more than just a place to publish documents. It has become a full-fledged multimedia computing system. Web pages can now include virtual worlds, embedded computer programs, and other forms of interactivity. The technologies leading this revolution are Java, ActiveX, JavaScript and VBScript. This chapter tells you what you need to know in order to use these exciting technologies with FrontPage. ■

Scripting Your Pages

Back in the early days of the Web, any and all interactivity on Web sites was accomplished by means of programs running on a Web server using complex programming languages. Nothing was ever done in the Web browser. Over time, that changed as programming languages like Java, JavaScript and VBScript have been developed.

A Little History on Scripting Languages

Netscape was the first to introduce a browser scripting language called LiveScript. After Sun Microsystems introduced Java (which is not a scripting language but does add interactivity on the client side as well), Netscape renamed LiveScript to JavaScript to increase its popularity. The renaming worked and JavaScript became popular enough that Microsoft wanted to use it in its own browser. Netscape wouldn't let them so they reverse-engineered the JavaScript language in the Netscape browser and called it JScript. At the same time they also introduced a pared-down version of their own Visual Basic language called VBScript. In case you don't see where this story is heading, there are still major issues related to using scripting on your pages. Should you code to the Netscape JavaScript standard, a version that can work with Netscape and Internet Explorer, or VBScript, which only works with Internet Explorer? It's a mess. Recently, however, JavaScript has been turned over to a standards body called the European Computer Manufacturers Association (ECMA) and rechristened ECMAScript. Standardization is therefore slowly but surely coming to page scripting. Let's hope it improves soon.

Just how exactly does scripting work? Well, HTML contains a tag called <SCRIPT>. In this tag you can specify the scripting language being used. Inside the tag you write a script, or small computer program, that the browser runs when it loads the page or in response to other actions that occur on the Web page. A very simple script might look like this:

```
<SCRIPT LANGUAGE="JavaScript">
<!-- This line opens an HTML comment
document.write("A Very Simple Script.")
<!-- This line opens and closes a comment -->
</SCRIPT>
```

The only thing this script does is write the words "A Very Simple Script" on the Web page. This isn't very useful but this script illustrates a few basic things that all scripts have in common. First, scripts are put inside a <SCRIPT> tag. Second, the scripting language is specified. Third, the script is included inside an HTML comment tag, "<!--," in order to hide the script from older browsers. This is intended to give you a basic idea of scripts' general layout and how they are put into a Web page. You get more into the actual use of a scripting language in a later section.

You might ask what is scripting good for. Well, scripts are used to present dynamic information like the time of day into your HTML pages. Scripts are also used to provide animation, change the appearance of graphics when the mouse is moved over them, scroll messages along the bottoms of pages, and a lot more. There are games written in JavaScript—even an HTML Editor. Suffice it to say that although scripts can be fairly simple, they can also be very powerful.

Using JavaScript

The JavaScript language, which was introduced by Netscape in its Netscape Navigator 2 Web browser, gives Web authors another way to add interactivity and intelligence to their pages. As mentioned earlier in this chapter, Netscape has JavaScript, Microsoft has JScript, and the standard is ECMAScript. For simplicity's sake, all here are collectively referred to as JavaScript, the popular name. You may find that your scripts need some serious tweaking to work in browsers that support JavaScript differently. This situation ought to clear up eventually (once all the major players quit arguing and agree to a standard) and allow you, the developer, to write one script that you can expect to work anywhere.

With JavaScript, code is included as part of the HTML document and requires no additional compilation or development tools other than a compatible Web browser. In this section you learn about JavaScript, get an idea of the sorts of things it can do, and learn to insert scripts into pages generated with FrontPage Editor. While FrontPage Editor on its own is an extremely capable page editor, its capabilities are enormously extended by adding scripts.

Using FrontPage Editor to Add JavaScripts to a Page   Putting a script in your page is very easy. If you don't know how to create or open a page, look to Chapter 7, "Editor Basics." Without further ado, you can insert a script as follows:

1. Choose Insert, Advanced and then select Script, or click the Insert Script button on the toolbar. The Script dialog box appears (see Figure 9.1).
2. Mark the JavaScript option button.
3. Type the code into the workspace of the dialog box and choose OK. The script is inserted into the page.

FIG. 9.1
The FrontPage Script dialog box gives you a simple way to add client-side interactivity to your pages.

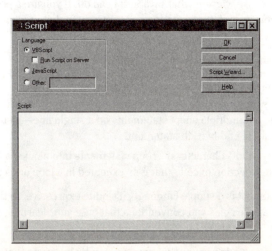

The workspace in this dialog box is just that of a text editor, and absolutely no syntax checking is done. You don't need to include the <SCRIPT> tags; they're inserted when you choose OK to close the dialog box and add the script.

Introduction to JavaScript Syntax It should be easy for people without programming experience to learn JavaScript. If you have ever programmed before, it shouldn't take long to get up to speed.

Beside some of the uses for JavaScript mentioned earlier, another important use of Web browser scripting languages comes as a result of the increased functionality being introduced for Web browsers in the form of Java applets, plug-ins, ActiveX controls, and VRML (Virtual Reality Modeling Language) objects and worlds. Each of these can be used to add extra functions and interactivity to a Web page. Scripting languages act as the glue that binds everything together. A Web page might use an HTML form to get some user input and then set a parameter for an ActiveX control based on that input. Usually this will actually be carried out by a script. You get a little into these other items later in this chapter.

JavaScript provides a fairly complete set of built-in functions and commands, allowing you to perform math calculations, manipulate strings, play sounds, open up new windows and URLs, and access and verify user input to your Web forms.

Code to perform these actions can be embedded in a page and executed when the page is loaded. You can also write functions that are triggered by events you specify. For example, you can write a JavaScript method that is called when the user clicks a form's Submit button, or one that is activated when the user clicks a hyperlink on the active page.

JavaScript can also set the attributes, or *properties*, of ActiveX controls, Java applets, and other objects present in the browser, so you can change the behavior of plug-ins or other objects without having to rewrite them. For example, your JavaScript code could automatically set the text of an ActiveX Label Control based on what time the page is viewed.

You get a very brief overview of what JavaScript can do. If you are a programmer, this will be useful to you; if you are not, it may be too brief for you. In that case you might check out Que's *Special Edition Using JavaScript*.

First, here are some basic rules for using JavaScript:

- JavaScript is case-sensitive.
- JavaScript is pretty flexible about statements. A single statement can cover multiple lines, and you can put multiple short statements on a single line—just make sure to add a semicolon at the end of each statement.
- Braces (the { and } characters) group statements into blocks; a block may be the body of a function or a section of code that gets executed in a loop or as part of a conditional test.

Even though JavaScript is a simple language, it's quite expressive. In this section, you learn a small number of simple rules and conventions that ease your learning process and speed your use of JavaScript.

You'll probably be designing pages that may be seen by browsers that don't support JavaScript. To keep those browsers from interpreting your JavaScript commands as HTML and displaying them, wrap your scripts as follows:

```
<SCRIPT LANGUAGE="JavaScript">
<!-- This line opens an HTML comment
document.write("You can see this script's output, but not its source.")
<!-- This line opens and closes a comment -->
</SCRIPT>
```

The opening `<!--` comment causes non-JavaScript supporting Web browsers to disregard all text they encounter until they find a matching `-->`; in that case nonsupporting browsers don't display your script. You do have to be careful with the `<SCRIPT>` tag, though; if you put your `<SCRIPT>` and `</SCRIPT>` block inside the comments, the Web browser also ignores them.

Including comments in your programs to explain what they do is good practice. JavaScript is no exception. The JavaScript interpreter ignores any text marked as comment, so don't be shy about including them. You can use two types of comments: single-line and multiple-line.

Single-line comments start with two slashes (`//`), and they're limited to one line. Multiple-line comments must start with `/*` on the first line and end with `*/` on the last line. Here are a few examples:

```
// this is a legal comment
/ illegal -- comments start with two slashes
/* Multiple-line comments can
   be spread across more than one line, as long as they end. */
/* illegal -- this comment doesn't have an end!
/// this comment's OK, because extra slashes are ignored //
```

You can improve the compatibility of your JavaScript Web pages through the use of the `<NOSCRIPT>` and `</NOSCRIPT>` HTML tags. Any HTML code that is placed between these container tags does not appear on a JavaScript-compatible Web browser but is displayed on one that is not able to understand JavaScript. This allows you to include alternative content for users who are using Web browsers that don't understand JavaScript. At the very least, you can let them know that they are missing something, as in this example:

```
<NOSCRIPT>
<HR>If you are seeing this text, then your Web browser
  doesn't speak JavaScript!<HR>
</NOSCRIPT>
```

N O T E JavaScript was developed by the Netscape Corporation, which maintains a great set of examples and documentation for it. Its JavaScript Authoring Guide is available online at **http://home.netscape.com/eng/mozilla/3.0/handbook/javascript/index.html**.

The most important thing you do with your JavaScripts is interacting with the content and information on your Web pages, and through it, with your user. JavaScript interacts with your Web browser through the browser's object model. Different aspects of the Web browser exist as different objects, with properties and methods that can be accessed by JavaScript. For instance, `document.write()` uses the `write` method of the `document` object. Understanding this Web browser object model is crucial to using JavaScript effectively. Understanding how the Web browser processes and executes your scripts is also necessary.

When Scripts Execute When you put JavaScript code in a page, the Web browser evaluates the code as soon as it's encountered. Functions, however, don't get executed when they're evaluated; they just get stored for later use. You still have to call functions explicitly to make them work. Some functions are attached to objects, like buttons or text fields on forms, and they are called when some event happens on the button or field. You might also have functions that you want to execute during page evaluation. You can do so by putting a call to the function at the appropriate place in the page.

Learning More About JavaScript

A few the basic things in JavaScript—expressions, operators and control structures—have been discussed. There is more to cover, including the browser and document object models, how to interact with embedded objects, and more. These things are beyond the scope of this book. If you want to know more about all of this, there are some good tutorials on the Web, as well as books available on the subject, including *Special Edition Using JavaScript* from Que. Netscape also provides a significant amount of reference material at **http://home.netscape.com/eng/mozilla/3.0/handbook/javascript/index.html**.

Using VBScript

Visual Basic and Visual Basic for Applications have been major tools for Windows development for years. They are extensions of the earlier BASIC programming language and as such are simple for beginners to use. Microsoft has taken this language and modified it for the Web and called it VBScript. VBScript was designed as a language for easily adding interactivity and dynamic content to Web pages. Just like JavaScript, VBScript gives Web authors the ability to use Internet Explorer and other compatible Web browsers and applications to execute scripts that perform a wide variety of functions. These functions include verifying and acting on user input, customizing Java applets, interacting with and customizing ActiveX controls and other OLE-compatible applications, and many other things.

> **NOTE** Although JavaScript was recently turned over to a standards body and renamed ECMAScript, thereby turning it into a true open standard, VBScript is still a proprietary Microsoft technology. Current trends are in favor of JavaScript becoming the Web's predominant scripting language, but VBScript is still one to watch. ■

Inserting a VBScript in your page is exactly the same as inserting a JavaScript. It is possible with VBScript, however, to write scripts that run on the Server by clicking the Run on Server check box on the Script dialog box. This book does not get into server-side scripting.

> **NOTE** You'll know there's a script in your page when a small script icon (J for JavaScript; movie clapboard for VBScript) appears in the FrontPage Editor workspace. If you do not see the icon, you need to choose View, Format Marks. ■

The Script Wizard, discussed later in this chapter and available through this dialog box, makes it unnecessary (much of the time) for you to type code in by hand.

Like JavaScript, VBScript allows you to embed commands into an HTML document. When a user of a compatible Web browser (currently only Internet Explorer, or Netscape Navigator with the ScriptActive Plug-in from Ncompass Labs) downloads your page, your VBScript commands are loaded by the Web browser along with the rest of the document, and are run in response to any of a series of events. Again, like JavaScript, VBScript is an *interpreted* language; Internet Explorer interprets the VBScript commands when they are loaded and run. They do not first need to be *compiled* into executable form by the Web author who uses them.

The language elements of VBScript are mainly those that will be familiar to anyone who has programmed in just about any language, such as `If...Then...Else` blocks, `Do`, `While`, `For...Next` loops, and a typical assortment of operators and built-in functions.

VBScript provides a fairly complete set of built-in functions and commands, allowing you to perform math calculations, manipulate strings, play sounds, open new windows and new URLs, and access and verify user input to your Web forms.

Code to perform these actions can be embedded in a page and executed when the page is loaded. You can also write functions that contain code that's triggered by events you specify. For example, you can write a VBScript method that is called when the user clicks the Submit button of a form, or one that is activated when the user clicks a hyperlink on the active page.

VBScript can also set the attributes, or *properties*, of ActiveX controls, Java applets, and other objects present in the browser. This way, you can change the behavior of plug-ins or other objects without having to rewrite them. For example, your VBScript code could automatically set the text of an ActiveX Label Control based on what time the page is viewed.

VBScript commands are embedded in your HTML documents, just as with JavaScript and other scripting languages. Embedded VB scripts are enclosed in the HTML container tag `<SCRIPT>...</SCRIPT>`. The `LANGUAGE` attribute of the `<SCRIPT>` tag specifies the scripting language to use when evaluating the script. For VBScript, the scripting language is defined as `LANGUAGE="VBS"`.

VBScript resembles JavaScript and many other computer languages you may be familiar with. It bears the closest resemblance, as you might imagine, to Visual Basic and Visual Basic for Applications because it is a subset of these two languages.

When you put VBScript code in a page, the Web browser evaluates the code as soon as it's encountered. Functions, however, don't get executed when they're evaluated; they just get stored for later use. You still have to call functions explicitly to make them work. Some functions are attached to objects, such as buttons or text fields on forms, and they are called when some event happens on the button or field. You might also have functions that you want to execute during page evaluation. You can do so by putting a call to the function at the appropriate place in the page. This is exactly as JavaScript works.

You can put scripts anywhere within your HTML page, as long as they're surrounded with the `<SCRIPT>...</SCRIPT>` tags. You do not have to concern yourself about that particular detail, as FrontPage 98 handles it for you.

Getting Further Into VBScript Okay, you haven't really covered enough VBScript to begin writing your own scripts yet; this book has only covered the nuts and bolts of what it can do and basically how it works. If you find yourself totally interested in learning to program VBScript better, visit the Microsoft VBScript Web site at **http://www.microsoft.com/vbscript/**.

What Scripting Language Should You Use?

As mentioned previously, JavaScript has developed into a standard called ECMAScript. Microsoft has already pledged to implement this new standard, as have Netscape and other vendors. This may make the choice of scripting language a little easier, but your choice will depend on what you need it for and your comfort level with each.

Using FrontPage Editor's Script Wizard

Now that you've explored JavaScript and VBScript as you might write it into the Script dialog box, you should investigate an easier way to do scripting. This is where the Script Wizard comes in. You still have to know your way around VBScript or JavaScript, but the wizard can save you some coding time. The Script Wizard is shown in Figure 9.2.

FIG. 9.2
The Script Wizard in FrontPage helps take some of the gruntwork out of writing scripts.

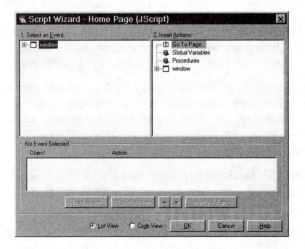

The Scripting Wizard is accessed by selecting Insert, Advanced, and selecting Script to bring up the scripting dialog box. To start the wizard, simply click the Script Wizard button.

The Script Wizard consists of three panes. Beginning in the upper left and going clockwise, they are:

- **Select an Event**—Choose the object event to which your script should respond.
- **Insert Actions**—Select the action to be triggered on that event.
- **Action List**—A list of the actions associated with the selected event.

You create scripts visually by clicking objects in your document, choosing actions that can occur to those objects, and building them all into a script. You can then view the script by clicking Code View or continue seeing it as a series of actions in the List View. Figure 9.3 shows a script in code view.

FIG. 9.3
The Script Wizard allows you to preview the code it is generating.

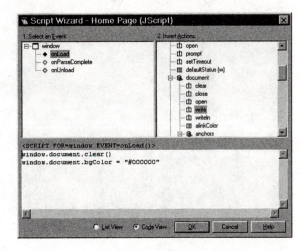

The example shown in Figure 9.3 creates a very simple JavaScript that clears the document and changes the background color to light blue. Even though you will likely need to tweak the code later, using the Scripting Wizard can save you a lot of work.

Using Plug-Ins and ActiveX

If you have ever visited a Web page that had content embedded in it, be it movies, music, or animations, you have likely dealt with either a plug-in or an ActiveX control. What are these technologies and why might you use them?

Plug-ins are a Netscape innovation that extended the even earlier concept of helper applications. A plug-in is simply a helper application that runs embedded into the Web page, inline, just like the rest of the graphics and text. Take a look at Figure 9.4, where a Web page with the RealVideo Plug-in embedded into it has been loaded up.

ActiveX controls can be used to create similar effects. In fact, the RealVideo player embedded as a plug-in on the page shown in Figure 9.4 is also available as an ActiveX control. Plug-ins and ActiveX controls are not limited to the browser, either. They can do anything that any other program can do; however, their powers come from the fact that they both have standardized ways of communicating with the browser and other applications, scripts, and Java applets. Why use them at all? Using a plug-in or ActiveX control gives you the ability to show people content that their Web browser does not understand. In essence, you extend the browser's capabilities.

FIG. 9.4
The RealVideo Plug-in allows you to create a virtual drive-in theater complete with play and stop buttons, as well as a status display panel.

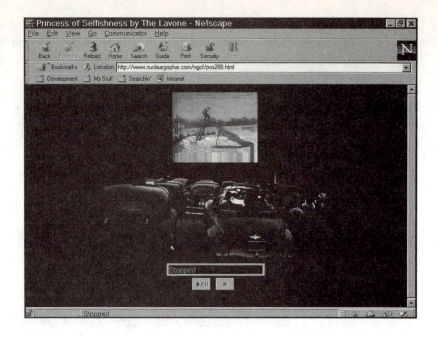

Inserting a Plug-In

You now know basically what a plug-in is. Here is how you place one in your Web page: Select Insert, Advanced, and Plug-In. Notice FrontPage inserts a picture of a giant plug into your Web page as well as opening the Plug-In Properties dialog box as shown in Figure 9.5.

FIG. 9.5
The Plug-in Properties dialog box hides the intricacies of embedding plug-ins into your pages.

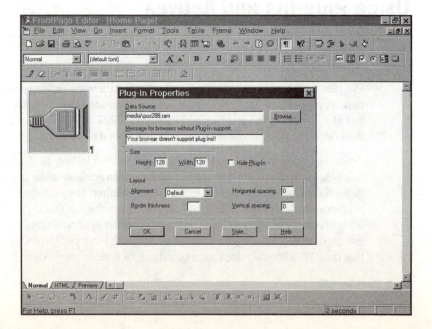

First, you need to select the data source. Just select the file you want to display with the plug-in and set some of the other options. These include:

- **Message For Browsers Without Plug-In Support**—Use this field to type HTML to display in place of the plug-in. Web browsers that do not support plug-ins display this HTML message.
- **Height**—Type the height of the plug-in, in pixels.
- **Width**—Type the width of the plug-in, in pixels.
- **Hide Plug-In**—Select the Hide Plug-In check box if you do not want a visual representation of the plug-in to appear on the page. For example, if the plug-in creates a sound, you may want it to be invisible on the page.
- **Alignment**—Sets the type of alignment between the plug-in and the text. The alignment options are the same as for images.
- **Border Thickness**—Sets a black border of the specified thickness around the plug-in, in pixels.
- **Horizontal Spacing**—Sets the horizontal spacing between the plug-in and the nearest text or other object on the current line, in pixels.
- **Vertical Spacing**—Sets the vertical spacing between the plug-in and the nearest text or other object on the line above or below the current line, in pixels.

Click OK once you have customized how you would like to see your control presented. Just in case you are wondering what surfers do if they don't have plug-in installed, don't worry—Netscape already thought of that. If the person visiting the page doesn't have the correct plug-in installed, Netscape asks them if they would like to get it and directs them to a Web page where they can automatically download the plug-in they need.

Inserting ActiveX Controls

You may have heard ActiveX mentioned in the same breath with Java. The truth is that they have little or nothing in common. ActiveX has much more in common with Netscape plug-ins. How so?

Well, like plug-ins, ActiveX controls are actually programs that you need to download and install on your machine. They are normal programs with full access to your system. They can read your files, look at your network, anything any other program on your computer can do. This is unlike Java, which has a carefully controlled security system (often called the "sandbox") to control the code being executed.

> **N O T E** Despite the similarity in the names, Java and JavaScript are not related to one another.
> Java is a programming language from Sun Microsystems that produces compiled computer programs that can run independently of a Web browser on almost any kind of computer. JavaScript is a programming language from Netscape that is interpreted and which only runs in JavaScript Web browsers. ■

Another difference between ActiveX and Java is the fact that ActiveX controls are platform dependent. An ActiveX control written for Windows will not work on a Macintosh or vice-versa. Java applets run on any platform, including those you possibly have never even heard of. It is these two major differences that make ActiveX controls analogous to plug-ins, not Java applets. If you were confused by this before, don't feel bad. The press has done a very poor job of presenting what ActiveX really does and is.

> **CAUTION**
> It should be noted that plug-ins (and Java applets) work with both Netscape and Internet Explorer 3.0 or newer, whereas ActiveX controls do not natively work with any browser other than Internet Explorer. Considering that ActiveX controls are therefore inaccessible to 70 percent of the people currently surfing the Web, it is important to have an alternative way to use the site.

So how would you go about embedding an ActiveX control in your Web page? Simply select Insert, Advanced, ActiveX. You will see the ActiveX Control Properties dialog box shown in Figure 9.6.

FIG. 9.6
You may be unaware of the number of ActiveX controls already installed on your computer.

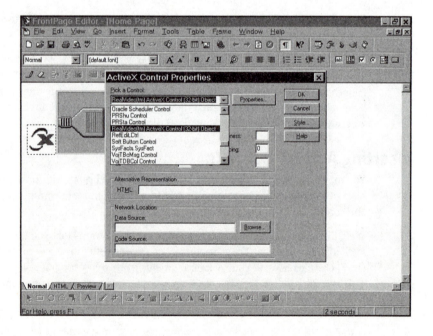

When you select the drop-down box labeled Pick a Control, you may be surprised to see a long list of available ActiveX controls. Don't be. A lot of the programs you have installed on your computer have installed ActiveX controls for their own usage. Any file with an OCX extension on your computer could technically be an ActiveX control. You cannot use most of them, however, because there are minor differences between the older-style OCX files and the current

ActiveX controls. The only way to know if you can use the control is to try. In this case, you are shown how to insert the RealAudio Control that that was shown in the previous plug-in example.

First, select the control to be inserted from the drop-down list. Then, to customize the control, click the Properties button. The screen now looks like Figure 9.7.

FIG. 9.7
The ActiveX control editor lets you set your ActiveX control's properties.

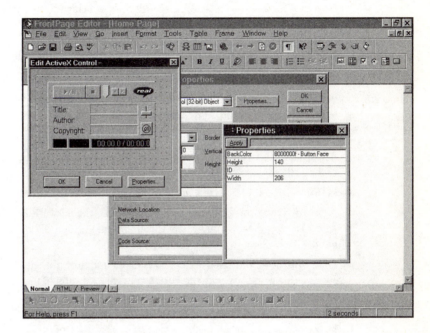

There are two boxes, one labeled Edit ActiveX Control and the other labeled Properties. The properties shown in the Properties box differ depending on the ActiveX control being edited. All of the properties shown represent various things that you can change to customize the control. The Edit box lets you modify the on-screen appearance of the control. Once you have customized the control to your liking, click OK to return to the original Insert box.

Here is an item-by-item rundown of what the various fields in the Insert dialog are for:

- **Pick a Control**—This field displays a list of the ActiveX controls installed on your computer. To insert a control, select it from this list. Some controls displayed in this list may be OCX controls that have not been fully upgraded to ActiveX protocols.

- **Properties**—Click Properties to specify parameters for the ActiveX control, if necessary. If the ActiveX control is installed on your computer and supports local editing of properties, clicking Properties opens a properties editor that you use to configure the ActiveX control. If the ActiveX control is not loaded on your computer, or if the control does not support local editing of properties, clicking Properties opens the Object Parameters dialog box. This dialog box is a simpler name/value editor. To use the Object Parameters dialog box, you must know the names of each of the control's properties, along with valid data values for each property.

- **Name**—If you want to use a custom or "friendly" name to refer to the ActiveX control within scripts on the active page, type that name here.
- **Layout**—Use the fields in this section to specify the ActiveX control's appearance and placement on the page.
- **Alignment**—Align the control. This works the same as with images.
- **Border Thickness**—Sets a black border of a specified thickness around the ActiveX control, in pixels.
- **Horizontal spacing**—Sets the horizontal spacing between the ActiveX control and the nearest text or other object on the current line, in pixels.
- **Vertical spacing**—Sets the vertical spacing between the ActiveX control and the nearest text or other object on the line above or below the current line, in pixels.
- **Width**—Type the width of the ActiveX control, in pixels.
- **Height**—Type the height of the ActiveX control, in pixels.
- **Alternative Representation**—Use this section to specify the alternative representations of the ActiveX control when viewed in a Web browser that does not support ActiveX.
- **HTML**—Type HTML to display in place of the ActiveX control.
- **Network Location**—Use this section to specify the network location of the ActiveX control and its data. If you specify this information, some Web browsers automatically get the ActiveX control when the page is loaded.
- **Data Source**—Some ActiveX controls take runtime parameters. For these controls, you can use this field to specify the URL or network location of the file containing the runtime parameters. Click Browse to browse the current FrontPage Web, the World Wide Web, or your local network or file system for the file.
- **Code Source**—You can use this field to specify the URL or network location that Web browsers should use to download the ActiveX control when the page is loaded, if the control is not on the user's computer.
- **Style**—Click this button to edit the cascading style sheet properties for the ActiveX control. Style-sheet formatting allows for precise control over spacing, alignment, fonts, and colors that is not possible with basic HTML attributes. Typically, cascading style-sheet formatting overrides attributes in HTML tags; however, the formatting displayed in a Web browser depends on the Web browser used to display the page.

Once you have edited all the values, click OK and your ActiveX control will be inserted into the page. That's all there is to it.

There is a possibility that even a visitor with ActiveX enabled on their system will not be able to use your control. This is because of security. As you may have noticed, ActiveX controls can be automatically installed and run on a user's machine without any installation programs or forethought. They can just install themselves. This could be bad if the control was, for instance, written to reformat your hard drive. Thus, Microsoft has put a code signing system in place called Authenticode. This allows a user to at least verify the origin of the code, although it still does not guarantee that the code will not misbehave once downloaded. By default, unsigned controls will not be downloaded by Internet Explorer. Therefore, if your control is not signed, many visitors may be left in the dark. For information on Authenticode, visit the Microsoft ActiveX Web site at **http://www.microsoft.com/activex/**.

Adding Java Applets

Earlier in this chapter JavaScript and VBScript—and some information on how to code them—were discussed. It's recommended that if you are interested in writing your own Java applets that you purchase Que's *Special Edition Using Java*. If you simply want to use Java applets on your site, this section should answer your questions.

Why Use Java?

You have already seen several options for adding interactivity to your Web pages—scripts, plug-ins, and ActiveX controls. Why, then, would you use Java? Well, all of those other technologies may have their place, but they also have major limitations. For example:

- Scripting languages are very limited in their capabilities and are therefore only fit for fairly simple interactions.
- Plug-ins require users to download and install software, which has to be available for their particular platform, before they can visit your site. Unless your site is something really cool, many will not bother with it.
- ActiveX controls are not supported by 70 percent of the browsers in use on any platform, and really only currently exist on Windows. Mac and UNIX ActiveX initiatives have been proposed but to date there are very few ActiveX controls on non-Windows computers. Therefore, you can be shutting out the majority of visitors to your site.

How does Java differ? Briefly, Java is a powerful programming language similar to C++ that was developed by Sun Microsystems. It can do substantially more than a lightweight scripting language like JavaScript or VBScript. In addition, Java applets automatically run in Java-enabled Web browsers without any software being installed. They are generally very small and load fairly quickly. The majority of browsers in use, from 70–85 percent, currently support Java. Java support is available not only for Windows 95, but also for Windows 3.1, Macintosh, all the UNIX flavors, Amiga, IBM mainframes, and lots of other computers you may have never even heard of. You won't be shutting all those people out with a Java applet.

Finally, Java applets run in a controlled environment on the computer. They are therefore subject to security restrictions, which limit their functionality some but also limit the threat they pose to Web surfers. Java applets are not allowed to read or write to your hard drive or network, access other programs in the memory of your computer, connect to computers other than the one they were loaded from among, other things. This makes it hard for people to write really mean Java applets.

Chapter 9 Activating Your Pages with Java, ActiveX, Scripting and More

> **NOTE** With the latest release of Java, Sun has introduced a new security model that allows Java applets to be digitally signed in much the same way ActiveX controls can be signed. This allows the user to grant rights to a particular Java applet to do things like write to the hard drive. The big difference between the new Java model and ActiveX is that the Java applets can be granted very specific permissions. For instance, you can allow the applet to write to one directory but not to view your network.

Enough about what Java applets are—how do you use them? Java applets are files with the extension of CLASS. When you have the CLASS file of the applet you want to use, assuming you also know the parameters the applet needs, you are ready insert the applet into your web page. Select Insert, Advanced, Java Applet. You see the Java Applet Properties dialog box shown in Figure 9.8.

FIG. 9.8
The Insert Java Applet dialog box lets you set parameters for your Java applets.

Here is a summary of the items in the Insert Java Applet dialog box:

- **Applet Source**—Type the name of the Java applet source file. This would be the CLASS file mentioned earlier.
- **Applet Base URL**—Type the URL of the folder containing the Java applet source file.
- **Message for Browsers Without Java Support**—Use this field to type HTML to display in place of the Java applet. Web browsers that do not support Java applets display this HTML message.
- **Applet Parameters**—Use this section to add parameter names and values for the Java applet. Because Java does not provide a mechanism for displaying what the parameters

and values are for a given control, consult the documentation that comes with the Java applet to learn the correct parameter names and the legal values for each parameter.

- **Name**—Lists the names of the parameters you have added.
- **Value**—Lists the value of each parameter.
- **Add**—Click Add to add a parameter name/value pair.
- **Modify**—Click Modify to edit the currently selected parameter name/value pair.
- **Remove**—Click Remove to delete the currently selected parameter name/value pair.
- **Size**—Use the fields in this section to control the size of the Java applet on the page.
- **Width**—Type the width of the Java applet, in pixels.
- **Height**—Type the height of the Java applet, in pixels.
- **Horizontal Spacing**—Sets the horizontal spacing between the Java applet and the nearest text or other object on the current line, in pixels.
- **Vertical Spacing**—Sets the vertical spacing between the Java applet and the nearest text or other object on the line above or below the current line, in pixels.
- **Alignment**—Just like with images, choose how the applet will be aligned on the page.
- **Style**—Click this button to edit the cascading style-sheet properties for the Java applet.

ON THE WEB

http://www.gamelan.com   Probably the best place to find Java applets for use on your site. There are hundreds of applets there for your use.

ON THE WEB

http://www.javasoft.com   Another good place to look for information on Java is the JavaSoft Web site; it's the official home of Java.

Going 3-D: Adding VRML Worlds

VRML (pronounced "vermal") is the standard file format for creating 3-D graphics on the World Wide Web. Just as HTML is used for text, JPEG and GIF are used for images, WAV is for sounds, and MPEG is used for moving pictures, VRML is used to store information about 3-D scenes. VRML files are stored on ordinary Web servers and are transferred using HTTP.

VRML files are just ordinary text files that have an extension of WRL. A Web server that serves up VRML files needs to be configured to use the MIME type of x-world/x-vrml or the newer model/vrml. If the Web server is not set up correctly to serve VRML files, the end user only sees a text file containing a bunch of scene coordinates.

When a user retrieves a VRML file (by clicking a link in an HTML document, for example), the file is transferred onto the user's machine and a VRML browser is invoked.

Figure 9.9 illustrates a VRML world found at one of the better VRML sites on the Web, **http://www.vruniverse.com**. As you can see, VRML can produce some pretty amazing results.

FIG. 9.9
Wow—it's virtual schnitzel! Who could have guessed this would be the future of Virtual Reality?

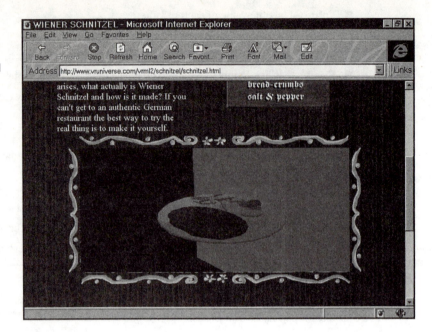

Here are a few good resources for creating your own 3-D world:

- **http://vrml.sgi.com/** Silicon Graphics has a great VRML site including links to tutorials, resources and lots of cool VRML worlds.
- **http://www.sdsc.edu/vrml/** The VRML Repository; one of the first really good VRML Web sites to show up back when VRML was just getting started. It still has lots of great links to great resources.
- **http://www.meshmart.org/vrmlup.htm** The Meshmart VRML Page; A good place to keep up to date on VRML happenings, they publish the VRML Update newsletter on this site.

Once you have found a VRML world you want to use, simply download the VRML file with the WRL extension, save it in your site and create a link to it. ●

CHAPTER 10

Using Templates, FrontPage Components, and Wizards to Build Your Web Pages

- **Using the FrontPage Templates**

  FrontPage Templates are a handy way to get a head start on both Webs and pages. Learn how templates work, how to make your own, and what the various templates do for you.

- **Using the FrontPage Wizards**

  The Wizards make complex tasks simpler. Learn about the various Wizards available in FrontPage and how you can use them.

- **Working with FrontPage Components**

  FrontPage Components are a great way to add interactivity and impressive features to your pages without programming. FrontPage Components are very powerful features.

Previous chapters have discussed creating Web pages from a template or a Wizard. The basics of using FrontPage Components have also been discussed, but this chapter gives you a guide to each of the templates and Wizards FrontPage provides. It also reviews the various FrontPage Components provided by FrontPage and shows how to include them in your Web pages. ■

Using the FrontPage Templates

Templates are Web pages that have already been started for you. They can contain formatting, layouts, and more. FrontPage includes 25 page templates and 10 frame templates. These are accessed by selecting File, New from within FrontPage Editor. You will see the New dialog box shown in Figure 10.1.

FIG. 10.1
There are 25 page templates and 10 frame templates included with FrontPage 98, giving you a lot of options for creating great pages.

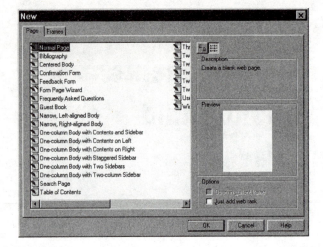

When you click the name of any of the templates, a preview of that template is shown in the small Preview box on the left. Table 10.1 shows a brief description of what each of the page templates do:

Table 10.1 The FrontPage Page Templates

Name	Description
Normal Page	Creates a basic blank page.
Bibliography	Creates a bibliography page with references to written or electronic works. Fills in a couple of fake entries to help you with correct formatting.
Centered Body	Creates a page where all the text is centered on the page.
Confirmation Form	Creates a page that thanks a user for something or confirms that an action is completed, such as a form having been successfully sent.
Feedback Form	Creates a page where users can comment on your site or organization and submit those comments to you.

Name	Description
Frequently Asked Questions	Creates a page for building a list of answers to frequently asked questions about your site, service, or company.
Guest Book	Creates a page where visitors can leave their own remarks about their visit for the world to see.
Narrow, Left-Aligned Body	Creates a page with a narrow, left-aligned body.
Narrow, Right-Aligned Body	Creates a page with a narrow, right-aligned body.
One-Column Body with Contents and Sidebar	Produces a columnar layout with text in the middle, a table of contents on the left, and a sidebar on the right.
One-Column Body with Contents on Left	Produces a columnar layout with text in the middle, a table of contents on the left.
One-Column Body with Contents on Right	Produces a columnar layout with text in the middle, a table of contents on the right.
One-Column Body with Staggered Sidebar	On the right of this layout is a column of text, and to the left is a two-column staggered sidebar.
One-Column Body with Two Sidebars	Creates a page with a column in the middle, a normal sidebar to the right, and a two-column staggered sidebar to the left.
One-Column Body with Two-Column Sidebar	Creates a page with a single column body of text and a two-column side bar to the right.
Search Page	Creates a page where users can search for keywords in all the documents in the Web.
Table of Contents	Creates a page with a list of every page in your Web site.
Three-Column Body	Creates a newspaper-style three-column body layout with a header across the top.
Two-Column Body	Creates a newspaper-style, two-column body layout with a header across the top.
Two-Column Body with Contents on Left	Creates a newspaper-style, two-column body layout with a header across the top and a table of contents to the left.
Two-Column Body with Two Sidebars	Creates a newspaper-style, two-column body layout with a header across the top, a table of contents to the left, and a sidebar to the right.
Two-Column Staggered Body	Creates a page with a body containing two staggered columns.

continues

Table 10.1 Continued

Name	Description
Two-Column Staggered Body with Contents and Sidebar	Creates a page with a body containing two staggered columns, a table of contents on the left, and a sidebar on the right.
User Registration	Creates a page where a user can self-register in a protected Web.
Wide Body with Headings	Creates a wide-bodied page with a subheadings.

After choosing any of these templates and clicking OK, FrontPage simply creates a new page with the chosen layout and fake text for replacement with your own words. Page-layout possibilities become quite interesting when you choose a frames template.

Frames Templates

There hasn't been a lot of discussion about creating frames pages in this book. There is good reason, as this is a shorter book, intended to get into FrontPage basics and designing good Web pages. Still, frames can be a valuable addition to your Web site. They can help with navigation and can allow visitors to view content from other sites while staying at your own.

What are frames, exactly? Look at Figure 10.2 to get an idea. Here is a basic frames page with two panels—a navigation panel on the left and a target panel on the right. In this case, links that are clicked in the panel on the left load in the panel on the right. Frames, then, are a way to divide the page into sections that each contain separate HTML documents. You can split a page in as many ways as you like and every part of the page can load a different page. This does get a bit confusing at times, because even in the simple example shown in Figure 10.2 there are actually three separate HTML files being shown. One defines the frame, another the navigation document, and a third the target document.

FrontPage helps you get a jump on creating frames documents by means of the ten frames templates included with FrontPage. Here is a brief description of each:

- **Banner and Contents**—This is a common Web layout. It creates a banner frame at the top to display a logo or advertising and splits the bottom portion of the screen into a contents frame on the left and a main frame on the right.
- **Contents**—This is the example shown in Figure 10.2. The left side of the screen is for a table of contents that loads pages in the right side.
- **Footer**—Splits the screen near the bottom to create a footer. Hyperlinks in the footer load in the main screen.
- **Footnotes**—This is split just like the Footer template, only the footnote space is larger and the hyperlinks in the main frame change the footer, instead of the other way around.
- **Header**—Creates a navigation header and a main frame under it.

- **Header, Footer, and Contents**—Creates a page with a header at the top, a footer at the bottom, a contents frame on the left, and a main frame on the right. The header and footer links change the contents frame which in turn changes the main frame. Complicated, huh?
- **Horizontal Split**—Creates independent top and bottom frames.
- **Nested Hierarchy**—A panel on the left changes more specific items on the top and to the right.
- **Top-Down Hierarchy**—Creates a frame on the top to contain general information that changes the main frame below.
- **Vertical Split**—Creates independent right and left frames.

FIG. 10.2
A frame splits the screen into separate, independent panes.

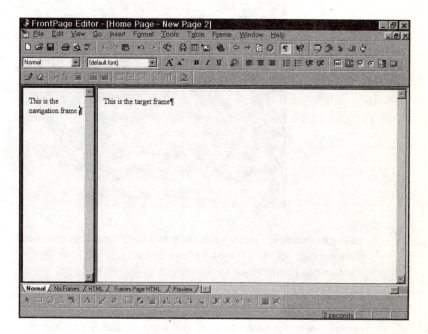

As you can see, there are quite a few frames templates from which to choose. These templates are listed on the Frames tab of the New File dialog box. To start a new document using one of them, click the template and click OK. You see something similar to Figure 10.3.

Each frame contains three buttons: Set Initial Page, New Page, and Help. What each button does is fairly straightforward. Clicking the Set Initial Page button lets you browse your site or the Internet to find the page you would like to show in this frame. The New Page button creates a new, empty page in the frame so you can start editing the page just like any other in your site. The Help button brings up help on creating frames documents.

Working with frames documents is the same as working with regular documents with a few exceptions. The first (and probably most important) is the concepts of *targets* and *names*. You are probably used to creating hyperlinks that link to other pages on the Web but have never before had to think about where those pages would load. Now you do. When a link is clicked, should the new page load in the current frame or in some other frame? This is where targets and names come in. Every pane in your frames document has a name and every link can have a target frame.

FIG. 10.3
Once the frames document is there, it is up to you to put other documents in each frame.

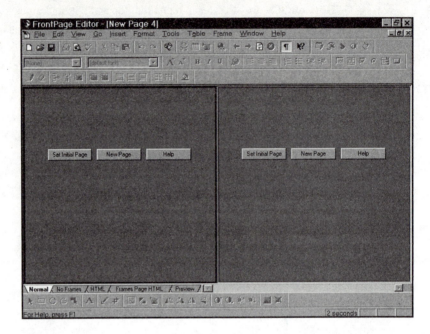

To see the name of a given frame, bring up the Frame Properties dialog box by right-clicking the frame and selecting it from the pop-up menu. You see the Frame Properties dialog box as it's shown in Figure 10.4.

The name of the frame is shown in the Name text box. Later, when you are editing the document displayed in the frame and you create a link, you need to tell FrontPage which frame should display the contents of the link when clicked. To do that, create a hyperlink as usual by selecting Insert, Hyperlink. Enter the URL of the page you want to link to and click the button with the three dots and the pencil next to Target Frame. This brings up the Target Frame dialog box shown in Figure 10.5.

On the left you see a diagram of the current page. Clicking the target frame desired in the picture changes the target. The current target is always highlighted. To the right of that you see some common targets. The first is Page Default. This loads the link into whatever target is set as default.

 TIP You can set the default target for the current frame at any time by bringing up the target box and checking the Make Default for Hyperlinks on the Page check box.

Using the FrontPage Templates 171

FIG. 10.4
The Frame Properties dialog box allows you to the change the file loaded in the frame, change the width and margins, and determine if scroll bars should be shown.

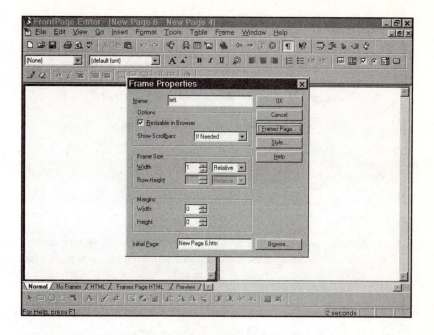

FIG. 10.5
All the frames in your page are shown, as are special targets like Whole Page, New Window, and Parent Frame.

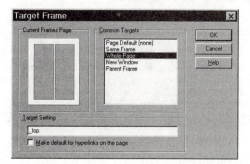

The next one is Same Frame. This loads the page into the frame where the link was clicked. Next is Whole Page. This loads the page in the current browser window full screen without frames. It effectively removes the frame environment unless the linked document provides its own frames. New Window actually opens the page in a whole new browser window independent of the current window. Finally, the Parent Frame choice specifies to display the page that is the hyperlink target in the frame that contains the current frameset tag. This is an advanced feature.

Once you can name frames and target your links, you are on your way into the wonderful world of frames.

Creating Your Own Page Templates

This is so easy you practically already know how to do it. If you have created a page that uses frames and wish to save it as a template for future Web pages, Select File, Save As (instead of Save). Then, when you get the Save As dialog box click As Template. You are prompted with the Save As Template dialog box shown in Figure 10.6.

FIG. 10.6
Creating new templates is easy. Give it a name and a description and FrontPage does the rest.

Give the template a title by which it will be displayed when you choose to create a new file. Next, fill in the actual name you would like used for the template file on the disk. Finally, provide a description of your template to be displayed when browsing the available templates. Click OK and your file is saved as a template.

Using the FrontPage Wizards

Wizards are automated assistants that break complex tasks down into a series of simple steps and walk you through those steps one at a time. You may already be familiar with the concept of Wizards, as they are found in Microsoft Office and many other major software packages as well. FrontPage 98 includes three Wizards. The Corporate Presence Wizard was discussed in Chapter 4, "Creating Your First Web Site." That leaves two FrontPage Wizards for discussion, the Discussion Web Wizard and the Form Page Wizard. There are two types of FrontPage Wizards, those that are launched from the Explorer and those that are launched from within the Editor.

The Discussion Web Wizard

The Discussion Web Wizard is launched from within the Explorer. This Wizard takes you step by step through the process of creating a threaded discussion group Web site, a table of contents, and full-text searching. In order to create a Web site with this Wizard, follow these steps:

1. From within the Explorer, select File, then choose New and finally select FrontPage Web...
2. In the New FrontPage Web dialog box, select From Wizard or Template:
3. Choose Discussion Web Wizard from the list box.
4. Enter a title for your new FrontPage Web and in the Title text box .
5. Click OK to start creation of the Web and launch the Wizard.
6. The first screen of the Wizard doesn't ask you for any information, it just tells you what it is going to do. Click Next to continue.

7. The second screen of the Wizard allows you to choose which Discussion Web features you would like to implement. It is shown in Figure 10.7.

FIG. 10.7
The second step in the Discussion Web Wizard allows you to select which Discussion Web features you would like to use. Click Next.

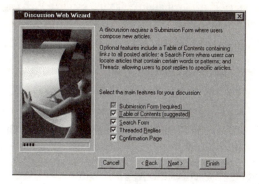

8. Follow each successive step in the Wizard. Depending on which options you checked in the second step, you will be asked different questions. If at any time you change your mind on a step, click Back.

9. Once you have gone through all of the screens, click Finish. The Discussion Web Wizard will generate your discussion Web site, exactly as you have asked it to. You can then proceed to modify the site.

Figure 10.8 shows a completed discussion Web site created using the Discussion Web Wizard with all of it's default settings.

FIG. 10.8
The Discussion Web Wizard chooses a default look and default labels for parts of your site.

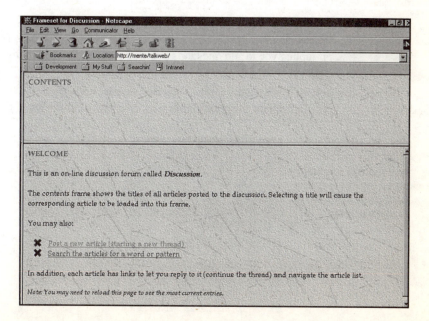

The Form Page Wizard

The Form Page Wizard is not for the creation of entire sites, rather it is for the creation of a data-gathering forms page. The information collected can to a Web page or to a text file on the Web server to be used as a database.

To use the Form Page Wizard follow these steps:

1. From within the Editor, select File and then choose New...
2. From the Page tab of the New dialog box, select Form Page Wizard.
3. The Wizard will start with a screen explaining its purpose. To continue click Next.
4. The second pane, shown in Figure 10.9, prompts you for the Title and URL of the page. Enter the information you want use and click Next.

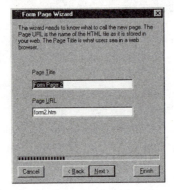

FIG. 10.9
You can either enter a descriptive title and a different file name or keep the Wizard defaults.

5. When you arrive at the third screen, there is an empty list box. There is also text prompting you to add questions to the page. Click the Add button to add at least one question to the list.
6. You will then see the screen shown in Figure 10.10. There are several types of input to choose from for the question shown in the list box at the top of the screen. Choose one.

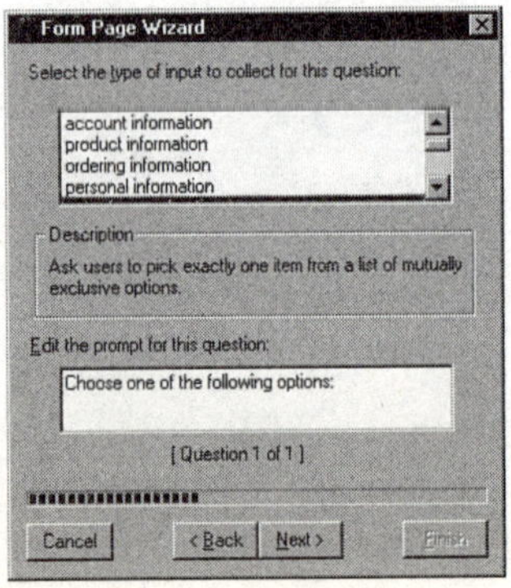

FIG. 10.10
You can use the Form Page Wizard to create all of the common types of questions and answers for your Web based forms.

7. After choosing a type of input from the top list, the bottom text box will change to reflect the text of the question. Change it to be whatever you want. When you have selected an answer type and set the question text, click Next.

8. Depending on which input type you choose, you will come to another screen that lets you further customize how you would like that information to be gathered. After filling out that screen, click Next.

9. You will be returned to what was before an empty question list but now contains the question you just added. Add, edit and remove questions until you are happy with the question list. Then click Next.

10. You will then be prompted for presentation options for displaying your questions on the form. You can choose to display them as paragraphs or as various type of lists. You can also decide whether or not you want a table of contents and whether you would like the page laid out using tables. Click Next after you choose these options.

11. Finally, you will be prompted for the manner in which you would like to save the results of this form. You can choose to save it to a Web page, a plain text file or a custom CGI script. Most often you will want to do one of the first two, as the third choice requires programming. Choose a storage method and click Next.

12. Last but not least, click Finish to have the Wizard generate your page.

Upon completion of the Wizard, you can customize the resulting form to contain different descriptive text or other paragraphs of information. A very simple form created with the Form Page Wizard is shown in Figure 10.11.

FIG. 10.11
The Fruit Feedback Page is a basic, one question form created with the Form Page Wizard and customized after creation.

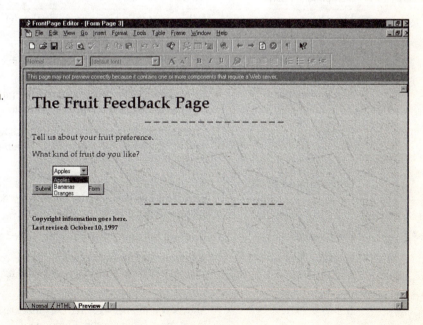

Working with FrontPage Components

FrontPage Components are a key part of FrontPage because they automate certain procedures that other Web authoring tools require you to hand-code in HTML or in a scripting language such as PERL. FrontPage puts several different kinds of components at your disposal.

But what's a component? Well, simply put, it represents a chunk of programming that gets embedded into the HTML code of a page when you insert the component. Depending on the component type, the program it represents executes when one of the following happens:

- The author saves the page.
- A visitor to the site accesses the page.
- The visitor clicks an interactive portion of the page, such as the Submit button, for a form.

You use some FrontPage Components only with forms; others are what you might call "utility" components because they carry out useful, routine tasks that streamline page and site creation. A few are almost invisible; they execute automatically when you tell FrontPage Editor to do something, and they show up neither in FrontPage Editor nor in a browser.

The available FrontPage Components, and their functions, are shown in Table 10.2.

Table 10.2 The FrontPage Components and their Functions

Component Name	Function
Timestamp	A Component that is replaced by the date and time a page was last edited or updated.
Table of Contents	This Component inserts an automatically updated Table of Contents for your site.
Navigation Bar	A Component that creates a navigation bar on your Web page that has links to other pages in your site.
Comment	This Component inserts a Comment that you can read as you develop the page, but that will be invisible to people browsing the page.
Confirmation Field	A FrontPage Component that displays the contents of a form field. This can be useful for confirming data entered by a user such as their name.
Hit Counter	Displays the number of times the page has been accessed.
Include Page	A Component that is replaced with the contents of another page in the Web. This lets you update parts of many pages in one step.
Insert HTML	Allows you to insert HTML tags that are not recognized by FrontPage. By using this Component, FrontPage will not attempt to verify the accuracy of the tags.

Working with FrontPage Components

Component Name	Function
Scheduled Image	A Component that is replaced on the page by an image for a specified time period. This is useful for displaying graphical information that has a limited lifetime, like a limited time offer banner advertisement.
Scheduled Include Page	A Component that is replaced by another page in the Web for a specified time period.
Substitution	A Component that is replaced by the value of a selected page or Web variable.

Most of the FrontPage Components are found in the Insert FrontPage Component dialog box, shown in Figure 10.12.

FIG. 10.12
Eight of the eleven available FrontPage Components are available from within the Insert FrontPage Component dialog box.

Microsoft has chosen to move three of the most commonly used Components into the main Insert menu. Those three Components are the Timestamp, Table of Contents, and Navigation Bar Components. We will know look at how to use each of these Components.

The Timestamp Component

The Timestamp Component will insert either the time the document was last changed or the time the document was last automatically updated. To use the Timestamp Component, do the following:

1. From within the FrontPage Editor, select Insert.
2. Select Timestamp. The Timestamp Properties dialog box (shown in Figure 10.13) will be displayed.

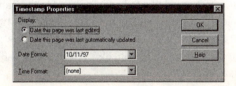

FIG. 10.13
The Timestamp Properties dialog box allows you to create two different type of timestamps on your pages.

3. Select the type of Timestamp you would like to create and the format you would like to have the information displayed in.
4. Click OK.

At this point, you will see today's date and time inserted into your page. when you move your mouse cursor over the date and time, it will turn into a small robot icon, indicating that this isn't just a date you typed, but rather a Timestamp component.

> **N O T E** The reason for the robot icon in FrontPage 98 is because in FrontPage 97 Components were referred to as Web Bots, or Bots for short. The robot icon is one of the holdovers from FrontPage 97.

If you should decide that you would like to change the way the Timestamp is displayed simply double-click it to bring up the Timestamp Properties dialog box again and change the options. To remove it, highlight it and hit the Delete key as you would any other piece of text on your page.

The Table of Contents Component

The Table of Contents Component creates a table of contents page in your site that is automatically updated whenever you edit pages on your site. Like the Timestamp Component, it is located on the Insert menu. Adding a Table of Contents Component to your page is accomplished by doing the following:

1. From within the FrontPage Editor, select Insert.
2. Choose Table of Contents. The Table of Contents Properties dialog box, shown in Figure 10.14, will be displayed.

FIG. 10.14
The Table of Contents Properties dialog box controls all of the display characteristics for the Table of Contents Component.

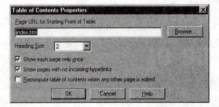

3. In the Page URL for the Starting Point of the Table: text box, fill in the filename of the first page in your site you would like to have displayed in the Table of Contents. For a table of contents that encompasses the entire FrontPage Web, type or browse to the URL of the FrontPage Web's home page.
4. Check the boxes of the options you would like to use for the Table of Contents Component. When complete, click OK.

That is all there is to it. The Table of Contents on the page will automatically be kept up to date as you modify your site.

The Navigation Bar Component

Use the Navigation Bar command to insert a page element that contains hyperlinks to other pages in the FrontPage Web's structure. To navigate the structure of a FrontPage Web, users follow hyperlinks from one page to another. FrontPage manages these hyperlinks with navigation bars.

To change the hyperlinks or button labels on a navigation bar, use the Navigation View in the FrontPage Explorer and rename the page title you want to change. To insert the Navigation Bar Component follow these steps:

1. From within the FrontPage Editor, select Insert.
2. Select Navigation Bar from the Insert menu. This is bring up the Navigation Bar Properties dialog box shown in Figure 10.15.

FIG. 10.15
In the Navigation Bar Properties dialog box, you can customize the behavior of the Navigation Bar Component.

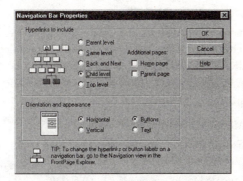

3. The first group of options is Hyperlinks to Include. Selecting various choices in this group will change the level of pages in the Web that will be displayed as links in the Navigation Bar. Select the group you would like to use.
4. The second group of options is Orientation and Appearance. You can change the appearance of the Navigation Bar by changing it from Horizontal to Vertical, or by alternating between displaying buttons and text.
5. Once you have set the properties for your Navigation Bar, click OK.

You can change the Navigation Bar properties at any time by double clicking on the Navigation Bar Component in the FrontPage Editor. This will bring the Navigation Bar Properties dialog box up again.

The Comment Component

The Comment Component is inserted into a page differently than the previous three components. It is a Component for your use as a developer, not for the display of information to a person visiting your site. The Comment Component displays a comment in your page that is invisible to people visiting the page over the Internet. It can be useful for making notes to yourself regarding changes that you have made to a page. Insert the Comment Component as follows:

> **NOTE** Despite the fact that comments are not displayed by a Web browser people can still view your source code (and therefore any comments within) while online or save the page to their hard drive and open it up in a text editor. This is actually a good way to "deconstruct" a Web page that does something you find interesting.

1. From within the FrontPage Editor, select Insert.
2. Choose FrontPage Component.
3. From the Insert FrontPage Component dialog box, select Comment. Click OK.
4. In the Comment dialog box, type the text of your comment and click OK.

The resulting text will be purple and prefaced by the word Comment:. When you look at your page in Preview the Comment will not be visible.

The Confirmation Field Component

This is a special component, in that it cannot be used on just any page. It is only for use on form confirmation pages. After creating a form page, you can select a confirmation form that displayed the contents of the form fields back to the user so that they can verify that the information on the form are correct. Insert a confirmation field component as follows:

1. From within the FrontPage Editor, select Insert.
2. From the Insert Menu, select FrontPage Component.
3. From the Insert FrontPage Component dialog box, select Confirmation Field.
4. The Confirmation Field Properties box will be displayed. Enter the name of the field whose values you would like to see displayed. Click OK.

The Hit Counter Component

The Hit Counter Component inserts a graphical display of the number of times your page has been loaded. Each time the page is loaded by somebody visiting the page, the counter is incremented by one. Inserting a Hit Counter Component is done as follows:

1. From within the FrontPage Editor, select Insert.
2. From the Insert Menu, choose FrontPage Component.
3. From the Insert FrontPage Component dialog box, select Hit Counter. Click OK. You will see the Hit Counter Properties dialog box shown in Figure 10.16.
4. Select the style of hit counter you would like to have on the page. You can also reset the counter to 0 from here or limit the number of displayed digits by clicking the checkboxes next to those two options. After you have chosen how you would like to display the counter, click OK.

Every time your page is accessed, the hit counter will now automatically be incremented.

FIG. 10.16
FrontPage offers a variety of graphical styles for the display of a hit counter on your page.

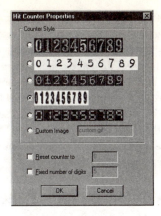

The Include Page Component

The Include Page Component includes the contents of another page from your Web into the current page. It can be useful for updating your site in multiple places at one time. To use the Include Page Component, follow these steps.

  1. Open the Insert FrontPage Component dialog box and select Include Page. Click OK.
  2. Enter the URL of the page you would like to include into the text box in the Include Page Component Properties dialog box. Click OK.

The contents of the other page will now be included into the current page at the location of the Include Page component.

The Insert HTML Component

The Insert HTML component is useful if you know HTML and would like to use a tag not supported by FrontPage. Inserting this Component is done as follows:

  1. Open the Insert FrontPage Component dialog box, select Insert HTML. Click OK.
  2. Enter the HTML markup you would like to insert and click OK.

FrontPage will not check the accuracy of the HTML entered in this Component. This can be useful for including tags that FrontPage might remove thinking that they are errors.

The Page Banner Component

The Page Banner Component inserts a banner with the page title as either text or an image. To insert this Component, follow these steps:

  1. Open up the Insert FrontPage Component dialog box.
  2. Select Page Banner. Click OK.
  3. From the Page Banner Properties dialog box, select Image or Text. Click OK.

The banner created will depend on whether or not the page uses themes or shared borders. If the page does not use a theme or shared borders, the page banner inserts only the page title as large, bolded text. Choosing Image has no effect. However, if the page uses a theme but does not use shared borders, choose Image to insert the page banner using the font and banner image from that theme; choose Text to insert only the page title as large, bolded text using the theme font, but without a banner image. If the page uses a top shared border, a page banner is automatically created in the top shared border; you do not need to insert it. If the page does not use a theme, the page banner displays the page title in the top shared border as large, bolded text without a banner image. If the page uses a theme, the page banner displays in the top shared border using the font and banner image from that theme.

The Scheduled Image and Scheduled Include Page Components

Both the Scheduled Image and Scheduled Include Components insert information in your page that is only supposed to be displayed for a limited time. That information can be either an image or the contents of another page in the Web. To insert either one, follow these steps:

1. Open the Insert FrontPage Component dialog box. Select Scheduled Image or Scheduled Include Page. Click OK.

2. Both of these components display almost the exact same dialog box. The Scheduled Image Properties dialog box is shown in Figure 10.17.

FIG. 10.17
The Scheduled Image dialog box allows you to select an image that will only be displayed for a limited time.

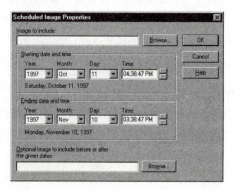

3. Enter the URL of either the page or the image you would like to display.
4. Select a start time and end time for display of the information.
5. Optionally, enter a URL of a page or image you would like to display instead before and after the display time.
6. Click OK.

Once inserted into your page, either of these components will display the information only during the times you specified.

The Substitution Component

The last FrontPage Component that will be covered in this chapter is the Substitution Component. The function of the Substitution Component is to insert the contents of a page variable, such as the author name, who last modified the page, the description of the page or URL of the page. It is inserted as follows:

1. Open the Insert FrontPage Component dialog box. Select Substitution. Click OK.
2. From the drop-down list in the Substitution Component Properties dialog box, select the item you would like to have inserted. Click OK.

The contents of the variable you selected will now be inserted into your page whenever the page is loaded and automatically changed when those pieces of information change. ●

PART IV

Managing Your Web with the FrontPage Explorer

11 Basic Operations of FrontPage Explorer   187

12 Managing Your Web Site   205

13 Advanced Web Site Creation   223

CHAPTER 11

Basic Operations of FrontPage Explorer

Website infrastructure

Learn how to manipulate FrontPage Webs within the Explorer. With the added control, you'll be cursing the old days of Telnet and FTP.

Using views

FrontPage 98 has several different view options, which can aid in organizing your Web.

Configuring FrontPage Explorer

Learn to configure FrontPage Explorer to grant the functionality you desire.

The FrontPage Explorer is a powerful piece of software in its own right, and is easily the centerpiece of the FrontPage 98 suite. In order to use the Explorer properly, you need to know the basics of its operation. These basics can include many things, from traditional file manipulation to publishing an entire Web site. Regardless of the actual operation however, is the underlying philosophy behind its implementation. You need to know how to do things in FrontPage Explorer, and why you'd do them. ■

Loading a Web Site

By default, the first thing you see when running the FrontPage 98 Explorer is the Open FrontPage Web window (shown in Figure 11.1), which lets you select which Web you want to work on. The first thing you should know is that Webs aren't loaded from your hard drive as a normal application file is. Instead, they're obtained from a remote server, which must support the FrontPage Server extensions.

FIG. 11.1
From the Open FrontPage Web window you can connect to an existing Web, or create an entirely new one.

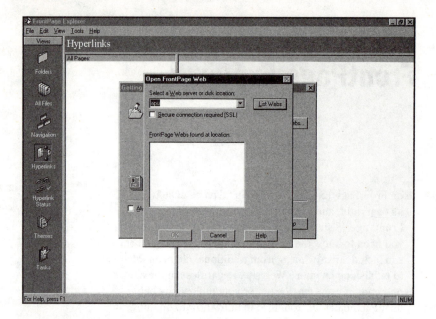

It's important to understand this remote access, because the FrontPage Explorer handles files in a fashion that traditional products do not. The most important aspect to remember is speed; no matter how fast your computer, you can only retrieve information at the speed of your connection. Assuming you're working remotely, when you load an existing Web, it may take some time for the FrontPage Explorer to obtain it and store it locally on your hard drive. The Explorer doesn't download the entire site, but rather the header and navigation information that allows FrontPage Explorer to show you how a site is structured. The more complex a site, the more time it will generally take for its organizational information to be obtained from the server.

> **NOTE** FrontPage 98 organizes its projects by Webs. You can have several sites within a Web, and can in fact have Webs within Webs. Try to think of it as a meta-folder for Web sites, but not as a Web site itself. A FrontPage Web is a specific series of files stored or created within FrontPage 98 that represents collectively a Web site or series of Web sites.

The default Web in the Open FrontPage Web window is always whatever Web you've worked on last. If you haven't worked on a Web yet, the default is your own machine's local server, assuming you have one running. There's no such thing as "offline" mode in FrontPage 98. If you don't have a connection to the Internet at large, then you have to work from your own machine. This isn't a problem, as many people use FrontPage as a local development tool, but in order to use it as such you *must* have a local Web server installed. Otherwise, you have to rely on a remote server, which usually requires a good connection.

If you want to always bypass the Open FrontPage Web window by always working on the previous Web, click the Always Open Last Web check box. This circumvents the window and allows you to dive right into working on your previous project, which can be handy for large Webs.

In order to connect to an unlisted Web, you must:

1. From the File menu, select the Open FrontPage Web ... option.
2. In the resulting dialog (Getting Started), click the More Webs ... button.
3. In the Select a Web Server or disk location: entry field, type the name or IP of the server your new Webs are located on. When done, click the List Webs button to bring up a list of the Webs on that server.
4. Select the Web you want to work with and press OK.

You can access the Open FrontPage Web command at any time from the File menu, which lets you load a Web the same as outlined previously. However, the Open command only works on Webs that you or someone else has created within FrontPage already. If you have a Web site or series of Web sites that already exist, you need to import them into FrontPage. In order to import files, you must:

1. Navigate your way to where you want the files to be imported. Your "virtual" location within the All Files, Folders, Navigation, or Hyperlinks view is where the files will be imported.
2. From the File menu, select Import.
3. Add files to your list of import items using the Add File, Add Folder, or From Web buttons (as shown in Figure 11.2), depending on how you want to add the file and where it is.
4. After you've completed your list, click OK to bring the files into your FrontPage Web (this may take a little while).

 You can also import files and folders to a Web through drag-and-drop. With a Web open in FrontPage Explorer, simply drag files or folders from Windows Explorer into either pane of the Explorer window and drop them. FrontPage immediately uploads the file to the Web server, even if the server is on a remote machine. Once the files are in place, you can provide links to them or manipulate them as you manipulate other files in your Webs.

FIG. 11.2
The Import window lets you bring any existing Web site you may already have into the FrontPage organizational fold.

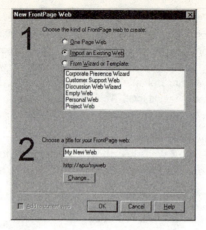

 If the site you want to import is already on the remote server, it can save you a bit of waiting. When you import the Web, the files are already present, and therefore FrontPage doesn't have to upload them. However, every file you work on within the Editor will have to be downloaded to your local machine, anyway. If you are going to import a site entirely and do little work on it, it might be smarter to have the files already on the server (if you can achieve local access). If you're importing files and then totally revamping them, you might as well add the Web in the traditional sense, because the amount of traffic will be roughly the same.

If you import files created in Microsoft Office, FrontPage Explorer creates icons for these files that reflect the program of origin. When you double-click these files instead of loading FrontPage Editor or Image Composer, the two standard editing programs, the file loads into the appropriate Office application instead. Keep one important thing in mind; unless your visitors are using Microsoft Internet Explorer 3.0 or Netscape Navigator (with the appropriate Office viewers plugged in) as their browser, they won't be able to view these Office documents. For this reason, importing Office files directly is best reserved for private intranets, in which the choice of browser can be guaranteed.

FrontPage also provides an Import Web Wizard, which is available only if no Web is currently loaded into FrontPage Explorer. In such a case, selecting File/Import reveals the Import Web Wizard series of dialog boxes, in which you can select individual files or entire folders for import. The wizard can also be selected from the Getting Started with Microsoft FrontPage dialog box that appears on start-up. The wizard allows you to import an existing site and make it your "root" Web, instead of having to create a Web and then importing your files.

Publishing a Web Site

One aspect of FrontPage 98 that makes it so useful are the streamlined publishing options. In the old days you had to access your remote server via a messy FTP account to manipulate and upload files. Now, FrontPage handles all the file activity for you in an interface that is familiar and easy to use. Most importantly, all of this is unified into one interface instead of a separate FTP or Telnet program. In order to publish your Web onto a server, you must:

1. From the File menu, select Publish FrontPage Web.
2. In the resulting Publish FrontPage Web dialog box, enter the name or IP of the destination server and click OK.
3. You should then have to enter the administrator password for the server. After verifying the password, FrontPage copies over the entire content of the Web to the remote server.

Once you've specified a server, the next time you go to publish, FrontPage assumes you'll want to publish to that server. You can get around by clicking on the More Webs button, just as you would when trying to load a new Web at start-up.

In addition, if you are copying the root Web from your current server, you can tell Explorer to copy the child Webs to the destination as well. The root Web is created automatically by Explorer on your server, and the child Webs are all other Webs you create on that server. By copying the root Web and the child Webs, you are, in effect, copying all Webs from your current server.

> **NOTE** Transferring an entire Web is an extremely bandwidth-intensive procedure. Don't expect it to take place immediately, and try to ensure that you have a speedy connection to the server. Depending on how much content you have to send, the entire process may take several minutes over a traditional modem connection.

Using the View Panel

What makes FrontPage 98 so powerful is the fact that it grants an intuitive interface to managing your Web files. It does this by filtering the raw file structure information into several different organizational structures, or *views*. You can control which view you are using by either clicking the appropriate icon in the Views pane or selecting a view in the View menu. Each view is a special interpretation of the data sent to FrontPage from the server. For example, the Hyperlinks view displays an assortment of information about which file leads to which, but very little about actual file locations and sizes. Each view lets you control FrontPage in a new and different way, and each has its own specific use.

The first view is the Folder view, which shows your Web in a Windows Explorer fashion. Folder view exists for Webmasters who want to see the Web as a series of individual files in various folders. Essentially, it lets you view an entire Web as you would by exploring it under Windows 95. This is a useful feature since the remote server might not even be a Windows 95 machine.

 The term "*folder*" is instantly recognizable to Windows 95 and Macintosh users. If you're more familiar with UNIX, MS-DOS, or Windows 3.x, think of folders as "*directories*" instead. Also, in the Contents frame of Folder view, "Name" really means "file name."

You can access the Folder view either by clicking the Folder View icon on FrontPage Explorer's toolbar, or by selecting Folder View from FrontPage Explorer's View menu.

As shown in Figure 11.3, Folder view offers two separate panes: All Folders and Contents. The latter is referred to here as *"Folder Contents"* to make its function more apparent. Essentially, the All Folders pane shows the folders for that Web, which were the folders FrontPage created when it built the Web you're working with. The Folder Contents page shows the files and subfolders within the folder selected in the All Folders pane.

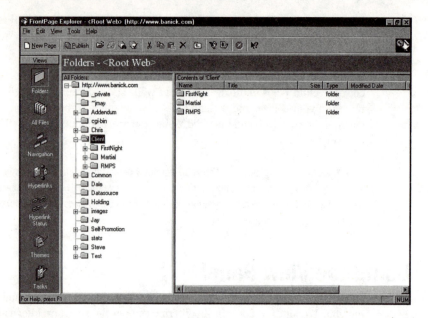

FIG. 11.3
The Folders view is very useful for file-related functions applied to your Web, such as delete or rename.

In other words, Folder view is very much like the Windows Explorer file viewer found in Windows 95 and Windows NT 4.0. The only difference between the two views is that Windows Explorer shows all hidden directories, while FrontPage Explorer shows only the _private hidden directory. In order to see hidden folders in the Folder view, you must:

1. Select the Web Setting option from the Tools menu.
2. Click the Advanced tab.
3. Click the Show documents in hidden directories checkbox on.
4. Click the Apply button and then click Yes to refresh the server connection.
5. Click OK to exit.

The third potential view is the Navigation view, a useful new feature exclusive to FrontPage 98. Essentially, the Navigation view is a hybrid mixture of the Hyperlinks view and the Folders view, with added functionality. Traditionally, the Hyperlinks view has been a display-only view; you could look at the various relationships between files, but couldn't touch them. The Navigation view lets you organize and adjust your site's structure to your heart's content. An example of the Navigation view is shown in Figure 11.4.

N O T E The Navigation view changes apply *only* to documents that use the FrontPage Editor to define their navigational elements. You can use the Navigation view to plan and forecast the structure of your site, but unless you are using the FrontPage Editor Insert option to place your navigational elements, no code will be changed in your page.

FIG. 11.4
Navigation view is a new feature that allows you to manipulate a Web's structure in almost any way, including printing it.

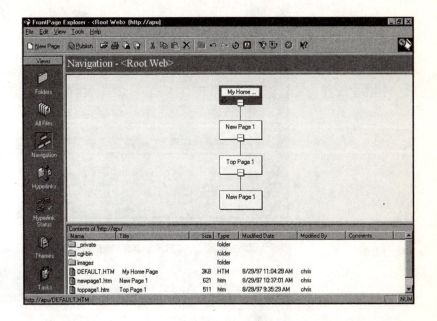

The two main sections of Navigation view are the Navigation pane and the Folder pane. The Navigation pane has all the graphic interface bells and whistles; you can shape, create, and modify from here. If you right-click within the Navigation pane (but not on a file), you can do any of the following:

- **Size to Fit**—This adjusts the scale of the Navigation pane. Especially large or complex structures might not fit properly unless you size to fit.

- **Rotate**—Changes the orientation of the structure from vertical to horizontal, or vice-versa.

- **Expand All**—Expands any compressed items (for example, those with a "+" sign on them).

- **New Top Page**—Creates a new page with no links to any of the existing files.

- **Apply Changes**—Applies changes made to the hierarchy to your final product. Remember, changes aren't implemented until applied. This won't appear unless there are actual changes to be applied.

- **Web Settings**—Lets you change the various Web-specific options within FrontPage.

The ability to manually orient and place pages is a powerful one, as it lets you plan sites in a very intuitive fashion. Instead of the old fashioned pen and paper approach, you can scheme and plan using the Navigation pane, as evidenced in Figures 11.5 and 11.6.

FIG. 11.5
When using the Navigation view you can easily turn this...

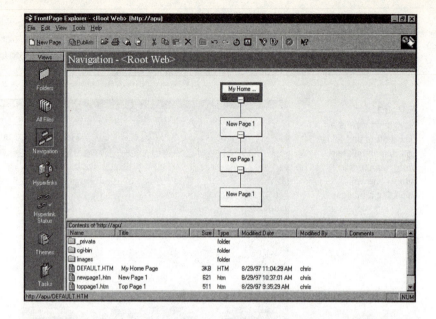

FIG. 11.6
...into this.

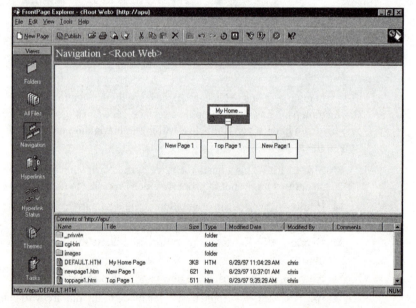

> **NOTE** The Up One Level command is the only way to navigate *back* a layer while inside the Navigation view. Highlighting and clicking files in the Navigation pane simply brings up the editor associated with them.

Making changes to your Web's structure in the Navigation view is both easy and somewhat fun. All you need to do is drag things around. Experiment with it for a while to determine the quirks that determine what file goes where. There are two things to keep in mind when working with the Navigation view. The first is that the "top" page can never be moved below its current level without disassociating it from its existing structure. To move the top page around you need to first remove it from your existing hierarchy. You can do this by dragging "out" any of the pages that depend from it. Otherwise, the top page won't budge regardless of how much you try to drag it. The second thing to remember is that a page's eventual position can vary greatly depending on where you drag it. Watch the preview lines that appear when you're dragging a page; they'll denote the page's eventual position. Take note of the fact that you can embed pages in any visible layer, regardless of original position, as long as you're not dragging the top page. Embedded structures also retain their shapes when dragged into other layers.

You can also add files to a navigation scheme by dragging them in from the Folders pane found beneath the Navigation pane.

If you want to print out the organizational schema of your Web, all you have to do is select the Navigation view and choose File, Print Navigation View. From there you print just as you normally would.

The fourth Explorer view is the Hyperlinks view. It has two parts: All Hyperlinks on the left, and hyperlinks for the currently selected page on the right. The latter view will be known here as the *Individual Hyperlinks* pane. Hyperlink view's purpose is to provide both an outline-like perspective and a visual-style perspective of your Web site.

Hyperlink view is accessible through Explorer's View/Hyperlink View command, and also by clicking the Hyperlink view icon in Explorer's toolbar.

Figure 11.7 shows the All Hyperlinks pane expanded by sliding the vertical separator fully to the right edge of the screen. This figure demonstrates how All Hyperlinks functions: It's very similar to the outline feature of word processors or personal information managers, showing the various headings and subheadings distinguished from one another by indentation. In this figure, some of the visible headings are fully expanded, as indicated by the minus signs (-) beside the main topic headings. By contrast, other topic headings remain unexpanded (closed), as indicated by the plus signs (+) beside them.

Actually, the division is not topic and subtopic. Instead, the All Hyperlinks pane shows links among pages. Main links lead to sublinks, sublinks to further sublinks, and so forth.

Note that as Figure 11.7 also shows, as you move the pointer up and down the All Hyperlinks view, the topic you're currently pointing at is highlighted to show where you are in the view. This helps you orient your way through the hierarchy of topics.

The fifth Explorer view option is the Hyperlink Status view. This is an invaluable maintenance tool for determining whether all your links are accurate, and whether they lead an operating server. Essentially the Hyperlink Status view displays all your potential links within your pages. From there it goes on to show whether they are "broken" links by displaying their status in the Status column. There are three possible states: Broken, OK, and Unknown. A Broken link is exactly that; it leads nowhere and should be fixed before end users see the page. An OK link works fine. An Unknown link can be either, but you won't know until you check it. Links are Unknown when the link's address is pointing somewhere outside your local server. In order to determine the true state of an Unknown link, you must verify it. The Hyperlink Status view, along with some link states, is shown in Figure 11.8.

FIG. 11.7
The All Hyperlinks pane is essentially an analog to the All Files view discussed previously.

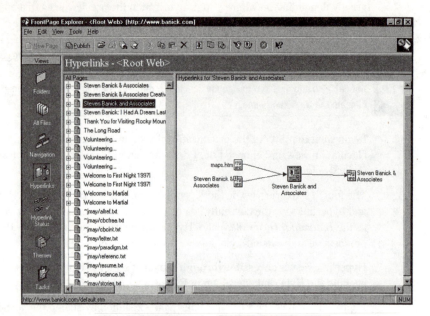

There are two main ways to influence the Hyperlink Status view. The first is to right click on a file within the pane, the second is the right click somewhere within the pane not on a file. The options available by right clicking on a file are:

- **Verify**—Verifies an Unknown link by sending out a quick request to determine if that link is "up." Only available when the link is Unknown.
- **Edit Hyperlink**—Lets you edit the actual hyperlink within the file without having to open the FrontPage Editor. You can also "globally" fix that hyperlink in case of large-scale changes. In this case, "globally" means within the confines of that particular Web.
- **Edit Page**—Edits the page within the FrontPage Editor.
- **Add Task**—Adds this file to the Tasks list.

The power of the Edit Hyperlink command is obvious. It lets you change the reference to the file within any other file in which the reference might occur. Many editors offer a global search-and-replace function, but because FrontPage keeps track of your hyperlinks anyway, there are no wasted resources searching out every "`<A HREF=...>`." Not only that, you can browse to the file's new location, or even decide to edit the page yourself. All of these options are shown in Figure 11.9, which details the Edit Hyperlink window.

FIG. 11.8
The Hyperlink view can help you quickly diagnose what is normally a very time-consuming problem.

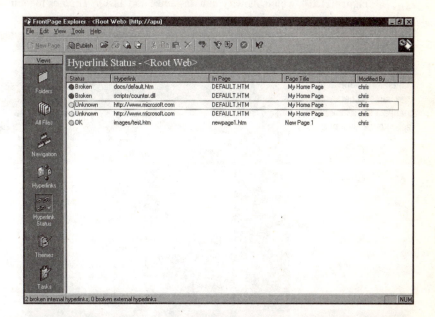

FIG. 11.9
By editing hyperlinks directly you can save yourself an incredible amount of time and resources.

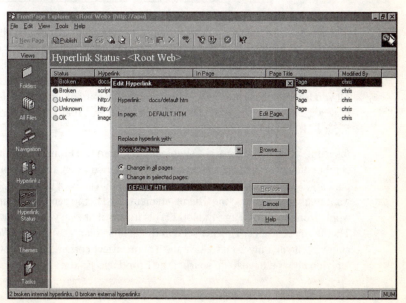

The next two Explorer views aren't the same as the previous five in the sense that they help you organize data from the Web server. Instead, they play a supplementary role in the larger sense, by helping you work better. The sixth view option is the Themes view (as shown in Figure 11.10), which allows you to organize and assign Themes to your work.

FIG. 11.10
Themes can help you create a basic Web site in literally no time at all. They can also help you change a site's look and feel with the click of a button.

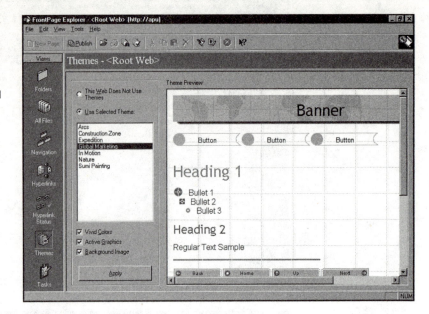

A *Theme* is essentially a predetermined layout template that can be applied to several pages after they've been written. If you don't want to bother designing your own page from scratch, you can just create "vanilla" pages and apply a theme to them. The Theme fills in most of the graphical elements of the page, such as background, button graphics, headers, and font types. All you have to do is supply the basic underlying content, and the Theme is laid over. To illustrate what sort of changes can be wrought between a themed and non-themed page, look at Figure 11.11 and Figure 11.12.

Inserting Theme elements is a simple matter from the FrontPage Editor, and usually involves a combination of simple insert commands supplemented by the judicious use of FrontPage Components. The radical changes Themes implement can be a bad thing, though, especially if you want to undo or remove the Theme elements. A Theme can only be applied to a Web as a whole from the FrontPage Explorer. This means that every file within that Web will reflect the Theme's appearance. This is useful in that it lets you mass-produce Web pages, but it can be annoying if you only want to have the Theme affect certain files. If you want to apply a Theme individually, you have to do so from the FrontPage Editor.

Using the View Pane

FIG. 11.11
Without a Theme the general page looks pretty boring.

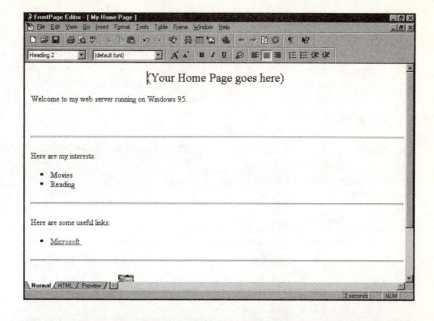

FIG. 11.12
However, once you add a Theme, it adds a bit of sparkle.

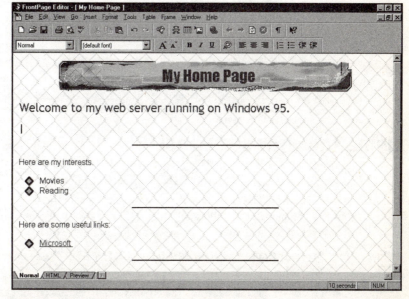

> **CAUTION**
> While Themes are a powerful addition to any designer's toolbox, it is possible for them to be overused. Keep in mind that every user of FrontPage 98 will have the potential to use the same themes you do. To prevent uniformity you should try to be creative in how you apply certain theme elements, and which ones you decide to use in the first place.

Chapter 11 Basic Operations of FrontPage Explorer

The last Explorer view option doesn't effect how your finished pages look at all, except for refining the process you use to create them. The seventh view is the Tasks list, which is essentially a shared "To Do" list that can be viewed and modified by multiple authors. The power of the Tasks list is obvious; it lets you assign and complete tasks dynamically. You may be editing one series of files at the same time someone else is working on another part of the site. You can communicate and keep track of who's done what by assiduously updating the Tasks list, as shown in Figure 11.13.

FIG. 11.13
The Tasks list can make a multi-user communications nightmare into a pleasant chore.

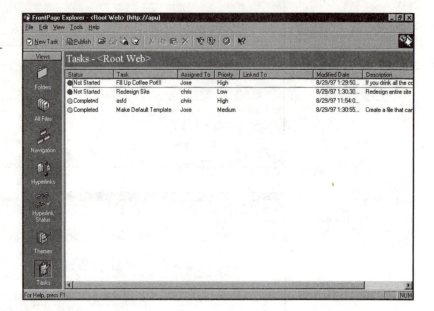

Using the Browser Panel

Once you reach a file you want to work with, in any Explorer view, you can work with it by clicking it. At this point, you have several choices. Double-clicking opens that page in its associated editor, where you can edit and save it directly back to the Web (even if you're editing it on a remote computer). Depending on which view and pane you're working in, right-clicking the icon reveals a pop-up menu with some of the following five options:

- **Move to Center**—Centers the Individual Hyperlinks pane on that page's icon (Hyperlink view only).
- **Open**—Loads the page into the editor you have specified for that file.
- **Open With**—Loads the page into an editor you select from the resulting Open With dialog box.

- **Cut**—Removes the page or folder from the display and places it in the Clipboard, making it available for pasting elsewhere. Simultaneously erases links to other pages and restores them when you paste. Use Cut to move files or folders.
- **Delete**—Permanently erases the file from the Web and simultaneously erases links to other pages.
- **Copy**—Copies the page or folder to the Clipboard and makes it available for pasting to other locations.
- **Rename**—Lets you change the file's or folder's name and simultaneously changes names in links to that item.
- **Properties**—Opens the Properties dialog box.
- **Add Task**—Lets you add this file or folder to the Tasks list.

Beyond that, any work you do on individual pages occurs through FrontPage Editor, not the Explorer. The point of the Explorer is to let you see your Web and keep track of it, not to alter or edit individual pages.

Reconfiguring Explorer

It's important to be able to work effectively within a program, regardless of its original settings. For this reason, the FrontPage Explorer comes with an array of configuration options to make your use of the program that much easier. There are two primary methods of configuring the Explorer. The first simply requires you to select Tools, Options. The second modifies the Explorer by use of the FrontPage Standard Developer's Kit.

However, the amount of change you can bring to the FrontPage Explorer by changing the Options is still considerable. The general options are shown in Figure 11.14.

FIG. 11.14
The general options tab lets you configure the more basic behaviors of the FrontPage Explorer. Take note of the ability to disable the "Getting Started" dialog that appears at every start up.

The general options are explained in the following list:

- **Show Getting Started Dialog**—Toggles whether you're presented with the Getting Started window that forces you to load or create a Web as soon as you start the FrontPage Explorer.
- **Show Toolbar**—Switches upper toolbar on and off.
- **Show Status Bar** Switches lower status bar on and off.
- **Warn When Included Components Are Out of Date**—Displays a warning when you attempt to use a component that is no longer current.
- **Warn When Text Index Is Out of Date**—Displays a warning when you attempt to use a file that is no longer current.
- **Warn Before Permanently Applying Themes**—Displays a warning that tells you applying a Theme is an irreversible process that may permanently change your page's formatting information.

The second tab to be found on the Options dialog box is the Proxies tab. From here you can control how FrontPage interacts with your proxy server, if there is one. You can also set addresses that are to be processed without the proxy server's intervention. The third and final tab is the Configure Editors, as shown in Figure 11.15.

FIG. 11.15
You can link any program you like to FrontPage's "Open" command using the Configure Editors tab.

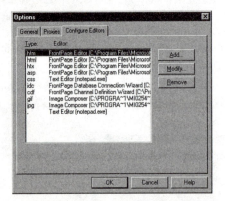

By configuring the editors you want to use within FrontPage you gain a lot of flexibility over what kind of work you do within it. If you have your own third-party editor you can include it and use it interchangeably within the Explorer. The process itself is easy to undertake, as all you have to do is fill out the dialog box pictured in Figure 11.16:

1. Select the Options item from the Tools

The first field, File Type, should be filled by the extension of the file you want to edit with that program. Remember not to include the period. The second field, Editor Name, is the shorthand label you use for that particular editor. The last field is the most important; Command contains the actual command line expression that you need to use to execute the editor. FrontPage takes care of inserting the file information. All you need to do is browse to the executable's location and link to it.

FIG. 11.16
Adding a new Editor type within the FrontPage Explorer.

CHAPTER 12

Managing Your Web Site

With your Web site created and attracting the attention of millions on the Web, you are usually faced with the daunting task of managing your site. Managing a successful site usually entails ongoing maintenance (changing content, fixing mistakes) as well as ensuring the integrity of the site itself. Microsoft FrontPage 98 makes that management a considerably easier job than it used to be, thanks in part to the carefully planned out FrontPage Explorer component. It is safe to assume that 90 percent of your Web site management will have you using the FrontPage Explorer. In the previous chapters, you have learned how to use the FrontPage Explorer for your site creation. This chapter introduces you to FrontPage Explorer's site management features so that you can use this tool to its maximum potential. ■

Making a list

Web site management can be chaotic and hectic. To help alleviate some of the difficulty, FrontPage Explorer gives you a well thought out "To Do" list that can be used to track your tasks.

Checking hyperlinks

Are your visitors tired of the infamous "Error 404, Not Found"? Maintaining the integrity of a large Web site is a headache few want, but the job has gotten easier with FrontPage Explorer's hyperlink validation service. Dead links no more!

Managing structure

When you are looking to reorganize or manage your Web site's structure, FrontPage 98's new Navigation view can make your life easier. This drag and drop method for planning and management will surely make city planners envious.

Stamping a shared identity

Consistency is one of the hallmarks of a good Web site. Creating a constant look for your Web site is easy with a shared set of borders that appears on each page. Create it once and FrontPage handles the rest.

Using Tasks

Users of computers are familiar with scraps of paper strewn about with handwritten notes. Perhaps you have a spiral bound notebook at your side, or you rely on Post-It notes lining your desk. Regardless of what you use, everyone needs a means of tracking what they have to do. Integrated into FrontPage 98 is an effective means of tracking your tasks with a "To Do" list called the Tasks view. Unlike your handwritten notes, the FrontPage Explorer's Task view is capable of automatically creating and monitoring certain tasks (let's see your spiral bound notebook do that!). The Tasks view in FrontPage 98 has improved its usability over previous versions and is ideal for tracking what you have to do, and in what priority. Figure 12.1 illustrates the Tasks view at work, with a list of prioritized jobs complete with a description and an assigned person for the job.

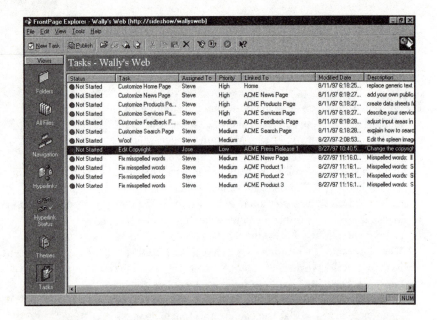

FIG. 12.1
Tasks view lists each job that needs completing, along with a status, priority, and a description. You can assign tasks to specific authors for your Web site.

Each FrontPage Web (your Web site) can have its own Tasks list to help you keep track of individual goals and objectives. When a task has been completed, you can mark it completed, archive it, or delete if from the list. Some of the FrontPage Explorer wizards and FrontPage Editor commands add and link tasks automatically, letting you concentrate on what has to be done. Tasks view displays each task in a number with a number of columns. These columns give you details on each task. The columns used are:

- **Status**—The first column is Status. Using this column you can quickly scan for tasks that are incomplete, complete, or under way.
- **Task**—The task's title is listed under the Task column. This is typically a brief description of the task for quick identification purposes, such as "Customize Search Page."

- **Assigned To**—When you are working with multiple authors for a site, it is convenient to be able to delegate certain tasks to particular authors. Using the Assigned To column, you can list who is responsible for a particular task.
- **Priority**—There is no doubt that some jobs are more important than others. When you are faced with a task that has a greater importance, assigning priorities becomes crucial. The Priority column lists the tasks priority, be it High, Medium, or Low.
- **Linked To**—When a task is created automatically by a FrontPage wizard or command, the task is typically tied to a particular page in your Web site. If your task is directly linked to a page, this column lists the page by its title.
- **Modified Date**—The date of the last modification is always listed under the Modified Date column. You can use this column to determine when a task was created or last worked on.
- **Description**—Typically a task name like "Customize TOC Page" wouldn't ring too many bells. To make sure that understanding of your task is clear, you can edit a more comprehensive description of the task under the Description column. As a task is completed or being worked on, the description can be changed to reflect its current objectives or related notes.

To use FrontPage Tasks, you must first switch to Tasks view. To switch to Tasks view, click the Tasks button in the Views panel, or choose View, Tasks. The main window display changes to reflect your choice.

Some of your actions in the FrontPage Editor and FrontPage wizards automatically add or modify tasks to your list without any intervention. However, when you have a new job that doesn't involve a wizard, you'll likely want to add a task to the Tasks list on your own. If you think of the Tasks list as your own digital notebook, you can use it to keep track of almost anything pertaining to work on your Web site. Examples of how you can use the Tasks list include:

- *Creation of new pages for your site.* Too often the mess of pages you are responsible for grows enough that you lose track of your objectives. By keeping track of each page you need to add to your site, and what exactly each page will include, you can make sure you stay on track.
- *Updates for existing pages and content.* Keeping your Web site fresh is crucial to keeping visitors. If you post reminders to keep content up-to-date and with what changes have to be made, you are less likely to forget. You can also use the FrontPage Tasks list to keep track of what updates you have already done.
- *Future goals and plans for your site.* Ideas flash in a lightning strike. Don't forget them. Instead, make note of them in the Tasks list. You can use tasks to map out future plans and new ideas so that you won't forget them at a later time. As your ideas are refined, use tasks to keep notes.
- *Implementation schedules.* Not every aspect of your Web site can be completed overnight. It is important to keep a schedule for your Web site, marking dates for completion of

certain sections and material. Use the Tasks list as your own personal scheduler, detailing when a project or task is supposed to be started and completed. Then go back and use it as a means of tracking your progress and your timeline.

- *Debugging and testing information.* Whenever you or your authors encounter problems or issues with your Web site, make note of it in the Tasks list. The tasks you create can then be modified to become goals for completion to make sure that all problems are corrected.

What you put into the Tasks view is only limited to how much you want to use this tool. If you are looking for a means of tracking all of your responsibilities without incurring a bigger paper trail, the Tasks view is likely a good choice—especially when you're working with multiple authors. Adding a new item to the Tasks list is a simple effort, as demonstrated in the following steps in the FrontPage Explorer:

1. Switch to Tasks view by clicking the Tasks button in the Views panel, or choose View, Tasks.
2. Click the New Task button, or right-click in the Tasks view and choose New Task from the pop-up menu. This opens the New Task dialog box, as shown in Figure 12.2.

FIG. 12.2
The New Task dialog box is very straightforward and lets you assign a task to a particular author, assign a priority for the task, and enter a comprehensive description.

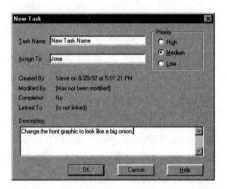

3. Enter a descriptive name for your new task in the Task Name text box. For example, if you were creating a task for changes to your site's table of contents a task name could be "*Customize TOC.*"
4. By default, the Assign To text box has the current author's name (presumably you). If you want to assign this task to a different author, enter the author's name in the text box. Make sure you enter the author's proper user name.
5. The Priority radio button group lets you assign an importance to the new task. You can choose High, Medium, and Low.

 Use task priorities to keep track of the importance of your jobs. Obviously, some things are more pressing than others, so make sure that you are working on the most crucial tasks first. You can use priorities to encourage and guide other authors to working on the most appropriate and applicable area first.

6. With your task name being so succinct, you may want to provide a more detailed description in the Descriptio<u>n</u> box. You may want to enter an itemized list detailing the task, or perhaps a description of the changes that should be made.

7. Click OK to close the dialog box and add your new task to the list.

Tasks with detailed descriptions are the most useful. When you fail to detail the task, other authors may not understand your objectives. In fact, this may happen to you after a late night Web development session.

NOTE You can go back and modify your task at any time by either double-clicking it in the Tasks list, or by right-clicking the task and choosing <u>E</u>dit Task. This opens the Task Details dialog box where you can edit the description, priority, assignment, and name. ■

You can also add a task in the FrontPage Explorer that is directly related to a page in your Web site. This is called "*linking*" your page to a task. By linking a page to a task, you can automatically jump to the linked page from the task itself. To create a task with a linked page from within the FrontPage Editor, choose <u>E</u>dit, A<u>d</u>d Task. The task you create using the standard New Task dialog box is linked to your Web page. You can go back and look at your newly added task at any time in the FrontPage Explorer.

With your page linked to a task, any time you select it from the list you can choose to <u>D</u>o Task (by either right-clicking it or double-clicking it to open the Task Details dialog box). By doing so, the linked page is automatically opened in the FrontPage Editor, ready for your changes.

Upon completion of a task, mark your job as complete. To do so, right-click your task in the Tasks list and choose <u>M</u>ark as Complete. Your task is then removed from the tasks list and frees you to do other work. At any point in time you can look back at previous tasks by choosing <u>V</u>iew, Task Histor<u>y</u>, or by right-clicking in the Tasks list and choosing Task Histor<u>y</u>. You can remove completed tasks from the Task History by also right-clicking on the task and choosing <u>M</u>ark as Complete.

You can use the Task history to track your progress and accomplishments. You can also use it to monitor the work history of other authors. Use the Tasks history to create productivity reports so that you can be more accurate in your predictions for the next project.

Spell Checking

Few things can be more embarrassing in a Web site than spelling mistakes. Whether it was a quick and simple typo or a complex confusion of words, spelling mistakes scream "unprofessional!" and can ultimately affect your image. FrontPage includes a useful spell checker that can be used from both the FrontPage Editor and the FrontPage Explorer. The power of the spelling checker's integration with the Front Page Explorer is its ability to check selected documents or your complete Web site. Additionally, the spelling checker can optionally create a task in the Tasks list for any pages containing mistakes. The FrontPage spelling checker (shown in Figure 12.3) is very similar to the spelling checker found in Microsoft Office, mostly because it shares the same functionality. Use of the spelling checker will ultimately improve your site (and credibility) without causing a bunch of extra work on your part.

FIG. 12.3
The FrontPage spelling checker can help you catch those embarrassing mistakes that often slip by, especially in late night editing sessions. The spelling checker even knows not to check your Web page's HTML code.

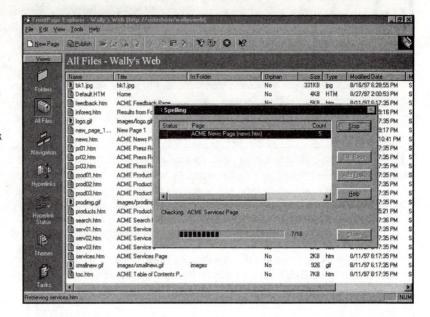

Using the FrontPage spelling checker is a simple chore. If you are currently editing a document in the FrontPage Editor, the spelling checker is accessible from the Tools, Spelling Checker menu (or by pressing F7). The spelling checker scans your current document. If it discovers any errors, the Spelling dialog box appears (shown in Figure 12.4) and lists suggestions based on your mistake. You have the option to Ignore the mistake, correct the mistake by selecting a suggested word and hitting the Change button, or adding the misspelled word to the dictionary by clicking the Add button.

To check your spelling from the FrontPage Explorer, follow these steps:

1. In any view that lists your Web site contents (that is, all views except Themes, Tasks, and Hyperlink Status) select the document(s) to be spell checked.
2. Either click the Cross File Spelling button in the toolbar or choose Tools, Spelling. This opens the Spelling options dialog box, as shown in Figure 12.5.
3. If you want to check the spelling of all pages in your Web site, choose the All Pages radio button. If you would rather check selected pages' spelling, choose the Selected Pages radio button.
4. If you want FrontPage to automatically add a task to the Tasks list for each page with a spelling mistake, select the Add a Task for Each Page with Misspellings check box.

Spell Checking 211

FIG. 12.4
The Spelling dialog box provides you with a list of suggestions based on your mistake.

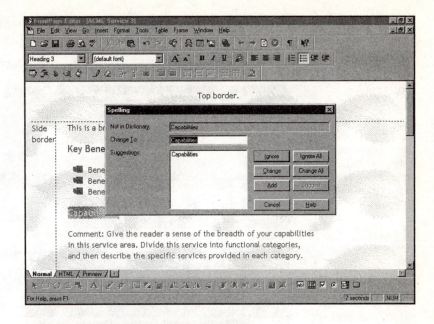

FIG. 12.5
This Spelling dialog box lets you choose to spell check all pages of your Web site or only the selected pages (if any). Optionally, you can have a new task added for each page with spelling mistakes.

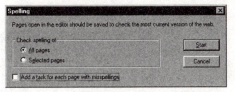

5. Click the Start button to begin the spell checking.
6. After scanning your pages, FrontPage reports its results. If you choose not to have a task added for each page, you are given a Spelling dialog box like the one shown in Figure 12.6. This dialog box lists each page with mistakes and gives you the option to Edit Page or Add Task. If you choose to have a task created for each page with misspellings, you are given a result of how many tasks were added. Click the Close button when you are done.

 TIP When you add a task for misspellings, FrontPage is kind enough to give you the misspelled word(s) in the task description. Use this to spot your mistakes at a glance when completing a task.

To check your spelling inside the FrontPage Editor, follow these uncomplicated steps:

1. Open the page that you want to spell check with the FrontPage Editor. Make sure that you are in Normal view.

2. Choose Tools, Spelling to begin the spelling check. The spell checker scans your entire document and prompts you with any spelling mistakes with the dialog box shown in Figure 12.7.

FIG. 12.6
FrontPage reports the number of misspellings found in your pages. You have the option of editing each page, adding a task for each page, or dismissing the dialog box.

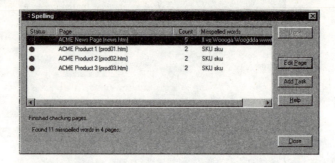

FIG. 12.7
The Spelling dialog box lists suggestions based on your mistake. As no dictionary will ever be fully accurate, be sure to add commonly used new words to your personal dictionary. Notice how the misspelled word is selected in the Editor.

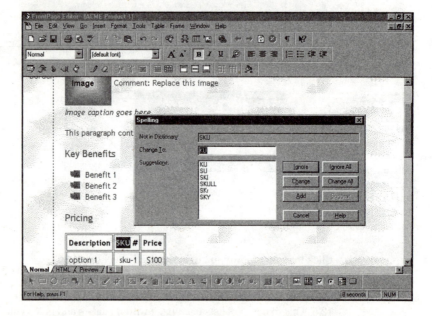

3. Either enter the correct spelling in the Change To box or select a word from the Suggestions list and click the Change button. Keep in mind that if the dictionary does not contain any suggestions, none appear in the list.
4. If you are sure you've spelled the word correctly and it doesn't appear in the dictionary, click the Add button to add the word to the dictionary. Any future spelling checks recognize the word as correct.

TIP The FrontPage Editor gives you another tool: a thesaurus. You can use this tool to avoid repetitious wording in your content. To use it, make sure you are in Normal view and select a word in your text and choose Tools, Thesaurus from the menu bar in the FrontPage Editor, or press Shift+F7. Synonyms for your selected word are provided so that you can make changes for the better.

Checking Hyperlinks

Without a doubt, the biggest headache in maintaining a Web site is ensuring the integrity of the site's hyperlinks. Hyperlinks are the heart of every Web site, linking pages and content files together. If you rename a file or a resource becomes unavailable, your site's integrity is compromised and visitors are greeted with the not-so-friendly "Error 404, Not Found" message. In the past, validating your Web site's links involved tedious manual checking and correction for each page. To make your job easier, Microsoft has included powerful hyperlink checking and indexing in FrontPage 98.

NOTE Hyperlinks don't just include links from one Web page to the next, they also include links to your Web site's graphics, multimedia files, and any external files that are referenced within. Hyperlinks can point to a resource within your own Web site, or a resource in a different Web site altogether. Remember, it's from hyperlinks that the World Wide Web gets its name—all the links crossing one another like a great spider web.

All pages in your Web site are automatically indexed by FrontPage to create a global index of hyperlinks. FrontPage uses this index to check the validity of your hyperlinks. Indexing of your pages is an automatic process and carried out each time you open your Web site and add a new page. You may optionally rebuild the index yourself in the FrontPage Explorer by choosing Tools, Recalculate Hyperlinks. The process of re-indexing your hyperlinks and text can take a few minutes, depending on the size of your Web site and content. By recalculating your index, you are always making sure that FrontPage is using the most recent information when checking hyperlinks.

When you recalculate your site's hyperlinks, FrontPage does more than create an index. In fact, it can repair internal hyperlinks that point to the wrong resource. Pages that use the `Include Page` component or text indices from a search form can be updated, as can any pages that point to a resource that has been moved, renamed, or deleted. This command does not check the status of any external hyperlinks—links outside your own Web site. FrontPage gives you another command to do so—the Verify Hyperlinks command.

Checking Internal Hyperlinks with Hyperlink View

Before you begin checking your hyperlinks, you should familiarize yourself with two important FrontPage Explorer views—Hyperlinks and Hyperlink Status. These two views were specifically designed to monitor and manage your site's hyperlinks. In addition to these two views,

FrontPage 98's new Navigation view can also prove useful. To begin, switch to Hyperlinks view by clicking the Hyperlinks button in the Views panel (or optionally choose View, Hyperlinks). The view changes to the Hyperlinks display, as shown in Figure 12.8. Hyperlinks view is used to check the hyperlinks within your own Web site.

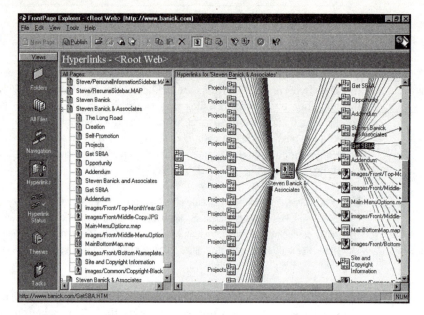

FIG. 12.8
Hyperlinks view gives you a firsthand look at your Web site's internal hyperlinks. You can use this view to check exactly what page is going where in a global view.

Hyperlink view is very straightforward. The view window is split into two regions. The left is a list of all of the pages and resources that comprise your Web site, sorted by title. The right is a graphic representation of the hyperlinks for the selected page or resource. When you select a page or resource from the list, the display updates to reflect how the selected resource is linked within your Web site. You can use the mouse to drag the display around the screen. You can also click any page with a plus sign (+) in the top-left corner to expand the view for hyperlinks related to it. From the hyperlink display, you can double-click any resource to open it, or right-click it to choose different options, such as the resource Properties.

The hyperlink display can be controlled from the View menu. There are three options for the hyperlink display:

- **Hyperlinks to Images**—With this option selected, the hyperlink display shows all the hyperlinks to images in your Web site. Additionally, it displays the images in the resource list. Without this image selected only Web pages are displayed.

- **Repeated Hyperlinks**—By default, if a page has multiple hyperlinks to another page, FrontPage only shows you one hyperlink. If you choose to display repeated hyperlinks, you see all the hyperlinks to another resource.

- **Hyperlinks Inside Page**—When you create a page that has hyperlinks pointing to itself (for hyperlinked topics, for example), FrontPage by default does not display it in the

Hyperlink view. With this option selected, the Hyperlink view shows hyperlinks that the page has to itself.

 TIP You can also control the Hyperlink view options by right-clicking in the Hyperlink view area and choosing the options from the pop-up menu.

Checking External Hyperlinks with Hyperlink Status View

As useful as Hyperlinks view is for visualizing your site's intricate interrelationships, it cannot help you verify hyperlinks to outside resources. Using the Hyperlink Status view, FrontPage 98 can check each outside link in your Web site to make sure it is active and available. Hyperlink Status view, shown in Figure 12.9, lists each external hyperlink in your Web site, broken up by a few columns.

FIG. 12.9
Hyperlink Status view lists each external hyperlink and broken internal link in your Web site and its status. You can choose to have it display all hyperlinks in your Web site.

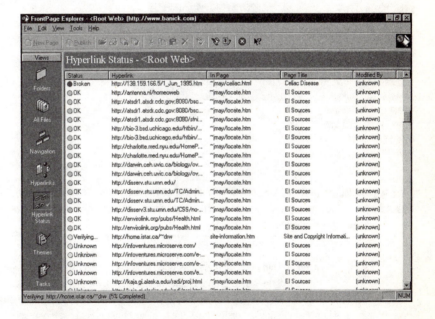

The columns Hyperlink Status view uses are:

- **Status**—The status of an external hyperlink can be either Broken (the link doesn't exist), OK (the link exists and is available), or Unknown (the link has not been checked).
- **Hyperlink**—The hyperlink's actual URL is listed in the Hyperlink column. You can use this information to verify the links on your own with a Web browser.

- **In Page**—To help you identify what page may have a troublesome hyperlink, FrontPage lists the actual page name in the In Page column. This is the actual file name of the Web page in your site.
- **Page Title**—The Web page title for the page containing the hyperlink is listed in the Page Title column.
- **Modified By**—In multi-author environments, the name of the author who last modified the Web page is listed in the Modified By column.

To verify your site's hyperlinks, choose Tools, Verify Hyperlinks. You are prompted with a Verify Hyperlinks dialog box (shown in Figure 12.10) where you can choose to verify all hyperlinks, resume a verification that has already begun, or verify selected hyperlinks (if any). Clicking the Start button begins the verification process. During the verification process, your Web server tries to contact each link and substantiate its existence. Valid hyperlinks are marked OK, while unavailable hyperlinks are marked as Broken. If a site is unavailable, you are prompted to confirm to continue.

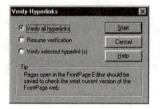

FIG. 12.10
The Verify Hyperlinks dialog box lets you verify either all external hyperlinks in your site or selected links. To verify only selected links, select them from the hyperlink list and then choose to verify hyperlinks.

 By default, Hyperlink Status view only displays the external hyperlinks for your Web site as well as broken internal links. If you want to list all hyperlinks, including links within your own Web site, choose View, Show All Hyperlinks.

N O T E Keep in mind that FrontPage has to be able to connect to the external Web server to verify the link. If the server is unavailable for any reason, the link will not be verified and instead will be identified as Broken. You may want to try verifying the link at a later time to ensure that the link is indeed broken and not just unavailable due to a server or network related problem. ■

If you encounter a broken link, you can correct it from within the FrontPage Explorer without even opening the page. To correct a link, follow these simple steps:

1. Select the link from the Hyperlink Status list and right-click it. Choose Edit Hyperlink from the pop-up menu.
2. The Edit Hyperlink dialog box (shown in Figure 12.11) appears. Enter your new hyperlink in the Replace Hyperlink With text box. You may optionally choose to Browse to a particular page instead.

Checking External Hyperlinks with Hyperlink Status View

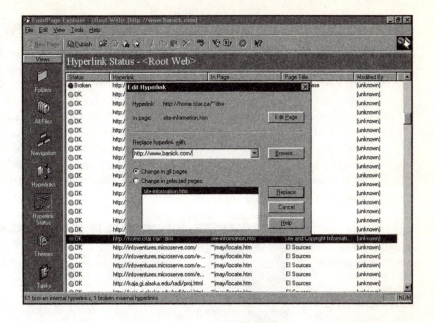

FIG. 12.11
The Edit Hyperlink dialog box lets you change your hyperlink without opening the page in the FrontPage Editor. You can also change all occurrences of the URL in your Web site.

3. If you want to make this change in all pages that use the original hyperlink, select the Change in <u>A</u>ll Pages radio button. If you would rather make the change only in selected pages, choose the Change in <u>S</u>elected Pages radio button and select the pages from the list.

4. If you want to edit the Web page in the FrontPage Editor, click the Edit <u>P</u>age button. Otherwise, click the <u>R</u>eplace button to make the change to the selected page(s).

 You can edit the Web page that contains a hyperlink by right-clicking the link and choosing Edit <u>P</u>age from the pop-up menu. You can also add a new task to the Tasks list by right-clicking the hyperlink and choosing <u>A</u>dd Task from the pop-up menu.

 Considering how often sites are changed and updated on the World Wide Web, you should verify your external hyperlinks often. Visitors, especially neophytes, are typically frustrated or put off by broken links. If a link becomes temporarily unavailable, make sure to temporarily point it to another resource. You may want to create a default "Resource Unavailable" page for your Web site that you can link to in such cases. When the resource becomes available again at the same address (or a new one), you can change the hyperlink to point to the right address. This way your visitors never encounter an error page.

N O T E Hyperlink Status and the verification of outside hyperlinks requires that your Web server have the FrontPage Server Extensions installed and operational. Although you can check the links within your own Web site (Hyperlink view) without the extensions, external links require server participation for link verification. ■

Managing Structure with Navigation View

Navigation view, new to FrontPage 98, lets you create, display, and change the navigation structure of your Web site. Using a folder-like view, you can drag and drop pages into your site structure. You can use this view to effectively manage your site and manipulate your internal links. Although not strictly a tool for link management, it is a powerful and useful new way to control your site's structure. The Navigation view, shown in Figure 12.12, is broken into two distinct areas. The top area is the actual Navigation view, displaying each page in your site as a box in a flow chart-like tree. Each page can be expanded or minimized by clicking it. When you expand a page, any links to subsequent pages are shown below it. The bottom part of the view is the resource list for your Web site. You can use this list to drag and drop resources into your Web site structure.

FIG. 12.12
Navigation View makes it easy to reorganize your site's navigational structure. Each page automatically has its hyperlinks updated to reflect the changes.

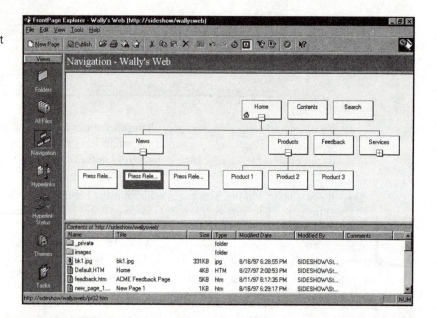

To link move an existing page's link in your navigational structure, select it in the Navigation view and drag it to its new position. When you drag it close to another page, a line appears to represent a hyperlink. You can move the page freely until the line rests where you want it. If you want to have a page that is not hyperlinked to any other page, drag it far enough away from every other page until the line disappears.

 Think of Navigation view as a magnetic board. Each page in your site is a magnet that you can slide freely to a different position. The actual order of the pages is irrelevant, all that matters is to where the line links the page.

If you create a page that is not linked to any other page, visitors must enter that page's exact URL to view it. This may be necessary for some sites, but typically is not advisable. You usually want visitors to be able to link to any page and get to another from there.

When you need to add a new page to your Web site, you can click the New Page button in the tool bar. This creates a new page in your Navigation view that floats independent of all other pages until you link it. Finally, you can also drag a resource from the resource list at the bottom of the window and link it to any existing page, just as if it were already there. This resource can be a page, a graphic, or any other resource file.

 You can use a few tricks to help you in Navigation view. From the View menu, you can choose to Rotate the navigation view. This changes the orientation from vertical to horizontal, which is very useful for large sites. You can choose Rotate again to return the orientation to vertical. If the Navigation view is too large to fit in your window, you can choose View, Size to Fit to shrink the display to fit in your current window space. Finally, if you want to quickly expand all levels of your navigation tree at once, choose View, Expand All.

N O T E Navigation view requires that your Web server have the FrontPage Server Extensions installed and operational. ▪

Creating Shared Borders

Many Web sites share a common navigational scheme in all pages. In fact, successful sites always maintain a consistent interface. FrontPage 98 lets you create a shared set of borders for either your entire Web site or selected pages. Your borders may be a header or footer, or even the left or right sides. For example, if you wanted to have a site copyright message and disclaimer appear on each page, as well as your company's name and address, you could enable a shared border for your entire Web site. Then, in the FrontPage Editor, you would customize your border to contain the information and save it once. The change would appear automatically on all pages in your Web site that use the shared border. The changes that you make to the shared borders apply to all pages in your Web site that use the shared borders. An example of shared borders is shown in Figure 12.13.

Shared borders are used if:

- Your Web site was created using one of the FrontPage templates or wizards. Shared borders are automatically created and enabled for you.
- You created your Web site page-by-page in the Navigation view. In doing so, FrontPage automatically creates navigation bars and shared borders for your site. The shared borders are also automatically enabled.
- You activated shared borders. If you did not use any wizards or templates to create your site, you can enable shared borders using the Shared Borders option in the Tools menu.

N O T E Shared borders are *not* frames. You can use frames and shared borders, but be aware of potential problems of duplicated interface elements or confusion in the layout. Shared borders are an elegant solution that are supported in every tables-capable Web browser, whereas frames are only available to newer browsers. ▪

FIG. 12.13
Both of these Web pages use shared borders. You only need to make changes to the border once, then it automatically permeates into every page that uses the borders.

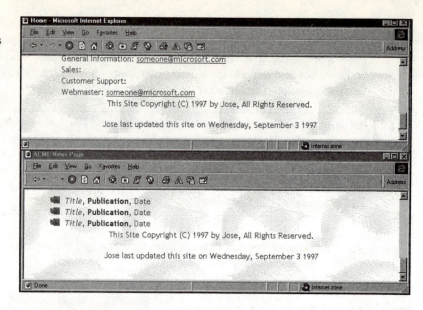

To begin using the shared borders, activate them by choosing the Shared Borders option from the Tools menu. If you choose this option from the FrontPage Explorer you are controlling the borders for your entire Web site. If you choose this option from the FrontPage Editor you are controlling the borders for the page you are editing. Regardless, when you choose this option the Shared Borders dialog box appears, as shown in Figure 12.14 (from the Explorer) and Figure 12.15 (from the Editor).

FIG. 12.14
The Shared Borders dialog box lets you choose what borders are used. You can choose to use a header or footer, right or left, or any combination thereof.

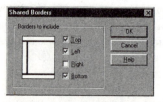

FIG. 12.15
When you open the Page Borders dialog box from the FrontPage Editor you may choose to apply the changes to the current page or to the entire Web site.

Using the check boxes in the dialog box, you can select what borders you want to use. The diagram updates itself to reflect your selections. Keep in mind that if you are using this dialog box from within the FrontPage Explorer you are controlling the borders for your entire Web site. If you want to control the borders for particular pages, choose this option from the FrontPage Editor while editing the page.

Once you have established what borders you want to use, you have to create the contents of the border(s) itself. To do so you need to open one of your Web pages using the FrontPage Editor and follow these steps:

1. The borders for your Web page are represented by dotted lines along the edges of your page. Click just outside the dotted line to select a border to edit. Remember that if you want to edit a border that doesn't exist, open the Shared Borders dialog box from the Tools, Shared Borders menu.

2. When you select the border, it changes to a box representing your editing area (as shown in Figure 12.16). Edit the border's contents to your satisfaction using FrontPage Editor's features.

FIG. 12.16
When a border is selected it becomes a solid-lined box. This represents your editing area for the border. Notice that unselected borders are marked with a dotted line bordering the page.

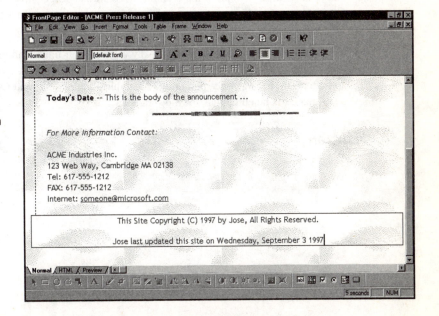

3. Repeat Step 2 for each border that you want to have shared in your site.

4. When you are done editing your borders, save your page by choosing File, Save. Close the FrontPage Editor. You may be prompted to save the individual borders. As you save the borders, FrontPage updates each page that uses the shared borders to reflect your changes.

Once you have created and saved your shared borders, they appear on every page that uses the shared borders feature. Whenever you change the border in one Web page, it is automatically copied to every other page using the borders. Shared borders is an effective feature that lets you control your site's appearance and interface more precisely without relying on a lot of hand work. Some uses for FrontPage shared borders include:

- **Navigation bars**—Shared borders are ideal when you want to create a common navigational bar for your Web site. You only need to modify the shared border once and then have it duplicated to each page in your site.
- **Disclaimers**—Legal disclaimers and notices are increasingly common on the Web. You can insert a legal disclaimer once in a shared border without having to copy it manually to each page.
- **Copyright messages**—Theft of content on the Internet is a common problem. If you use shared borders to mark a copyright message on your site, you are clearly telling visitors who owns the content.
- **Modification dates**—Many Web sites have a "last updated on" tag on their Web pages so visitors know when new material has been added. You can use shared borders to create a note on all of your pages informing visitors when you last carried out updates to the site.

Because shared borders are applied universally without your intervention, you only have to create an effective interface or appearance once to have it mimicked throughout your site. The care and attention that was once demanded for duplicating similar material in a Web site can now be reduced to one edit and a few mouse clicks.

> **CAUTION**
> Remember that any change you make to a shared border replicates itself to all other pages using the borders. You shouldn't make any page-specific borders.

CHAPTER 13

Advanced Web Site Creation

Once you have created your Web site, you may want to investigate ways to enhance your site. Your Web site can become a richer experience for your visitors if you consider some of the more advanced features of FrontPage 98 and Web site creation. Specifically this chapter focuses on new Web technologies, such as Cascading Style Sheets, Dynamic HTML, and CDF. The material in this chapter assumes that you have an existing site and are looking to enhance it. The functions in this chapter are entirely optional and are not required for a successful Web site. Read this chapter at your leisure and consider the impact that it could have on your Web site. ■

Applying formatting with stylesheets

Stepping closer to print typography, the advent of Cascading Style Sheets lets you incorporate more complex control over your site's text and appearance.

Using Dynamic HTML

Web pages don't need to be static any more. Your pages can adjust and respond to user input without complex programming, all thanks to FrontPage 98's support of Dynamic HTML.

Push publishing with CDF

Broadcast your Web site with Microsoft's CDF Push standard. Now your visitors can subscribe to your site and receive updates automatically, without needing to go to the site first.

Using Cascading Style Sheets

A new addition to the Web standards, Cascading Style Sheets (or CSS) gives you precise control over the text formatting in your Web site. Traditionally HTML does not give you a lot of control over your Web site's text; with CSS you can control not only fonts in precise faces and sizes, but also positions and margins. CSS acts as an extension to HTML, allowing for graceful degradation. Visitors that do not have a browser that is capable of viewing CSS see normal HTML text without formatting. Visitors with a CSS-capable browser, will see the formatted text, margins, and borders. Features and benefits of CSS include:

- **Alignment control**—Cascading Style Sheets let you define full margins for text (left and right, top and bottom), as well as padding for the alignment and floating text.
- **Borders**—Regions of CSS text can have borders defined for the left/right and top/bottom. These borders can be any of a variety of line styles and colors.
- **Font control**—Unlike HTML, with CSS you can precisely control your text's fonts. You can define primary and secondary fonts (that is, if the primary font is not available to a visitor, it will try to use the secondary) and precise point sizes instead of relative sizes.
- **Attachments**—Just as you can define background and attributes for a Web page, you can define colors and images for a region of CSS text. You can choose a foreground/background color and background image. You can also control how the image is tiled and positioned.
- **Text control**—Aside from font control, CSS also gives you control over the text weight and style, decorations (such as underlines, small caps, alignment, and indentation).

Cascading Style Sheets have the advantage of portability. Style Sheets can be used in three different ways:

- **External**—where the style sheet information is stored in an external file (somewhere on the Web) that is referenced in the Web page. These styles can then be applied to particular pages or your entire Web site for a uniform appearance. External styles can be applied to any element in any Web page by linking to the external style sheet and referring to a style by name.
- **Embedded**—refers to style information stored within the Web page itself, and not in an external document. Embedded styles are only accessible within the Web page, and not from other documents. Embedded styles can be applied to any element in the Web page by referring to its style name.
- **Inline**—is used to apply styles to individual elements on a Web page. The style is not stored in an external file or embedded in the page, instead it is applied directly to a page's element. Inline styles can not be applied to more than one element without duplicating the entire inline style information.

> **WARNING**
> If a page is linked to an external style sheet, the embedded or inline styles that you create for that page will either extend or override properties specified in the external style sheet.

Style Sheets can be used to apply formatting to existing HTML formatting commands, such as headlines (H1, H2, and so on). When used to do so, CSS-capable browsers see the formatting tag with the enhanced style properties. Browsers not supporting the CSS attributes downgrade to displaying the standard formatting attributed to the tag. Style sheets define the styles that can be applied to your Web pages. Each style is a rule or definition that consists of a *selector,* or identifier, that is used as the name for the style, followed by the properties of the style itself. Styles themselves can be broken up into subclasses, each inheriting the attributes of the parent. If you were to look at a style sheet file in a text editor, you would see something similar to this:

```
[ic: psc]
H1 { font-size: x-large; color: green }
H2 { font-size: 32pt; color: blue }
.note { font-size: small }
```

Creating Styles

Each style begins with a selector, followed by the properties enclosed in curly braces. When more than one attribute is being applied to the style they are separated by semicolons. To begin using style sheets in your Web site you need to begin by creating some styles to use. You can then use these styles by embedding them in your page(s), or storing them in an external .CSS file. To start with, you will define your own styles to embed in a Web page.

To begin, follow these steps in the FrontPage Editor:

1. Choose F̲ormat, S̲tylesheet from the menu bar to open the Format Stylesheet dialog box, shown in Figure 13.1.

FIG. 13.1
The Format Stylesheet dialog box lets you directly enter style sheet information. To begin creating style sheets, click the S̲tyle button to use a dialog box to define your styles.

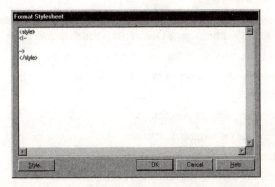

2. This dialog box lets you immediately enter your new styles, between the <!— and —!> tags. Begin with typing a name (selector) for your new style. For example, if you wanted to create a new style named "lead", you would enter this as the selector.

 TIP If you want to override a different style or an HTML tag's formatting, enter its name as the selector. For example, to override the default formatting for the <H1> tag, enter H1 as the selector.

TIP If you are creating a subclass of an existing style, precede the selector with a period (".").

3. If you know the style rule information already, enter it after the selector. Otherwise click the Style button to open the Style dialog box, shown in Figure 13.2.

FIG. 13.2
The Style dialog box gives you five tabs for controlling the properties of your new style. Each tab represents a different aspect of the style definition.

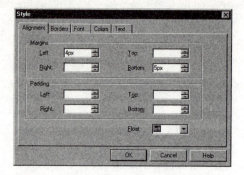

With the Style dialog box open, you can now begin to define your style's Alignment.

1. Starting out with the Alignment tab, you can begin defining your style. The Margins box lets you define the margins for all text using this style. Use the spin wheels beside each margin text box (Left, Right, Top, Bottom) to enter a margin value, or directly enter it into the respective text box(es). Margins can have negative values.

   NOTE Values for style sheets can be specified in either relative or absolute length units. Valid relative length units are:
   - **em** specifies the height in ems. An em is the height of the elementary font. This term should be familiar to anyone experienced in traditional print layout.
   - **ex** specifies the x-height. The x-height is the height of the letter "x."
   - **px** specifies pixels, relative to the screen resolution.

   Valid absolute length units are:
   - **in** specifies the height in inches.
   - **cm** specifies the height in centimeters.
   - **mm** specifies the height in millimeters.
   - **pt** specifies the height in points (traditional font points).
   - **pc** specifies the height in picas.

   You can also specify a percentage by typing the value followed by the percentage symbol, such as 50%. ■

2. To specify the distance between the borders of your style's element and the element's content, you can control the padding by a relative or absolute length, or as a percentage

of the element's width (just like margins). Padding cannot be specified with a negative value. You can set the padding for the L<u>e</u>ft, <u>R</u>ight, T<u>o</u>p, and Botto<u>m</u>.

3. Use the <u>F</u>loat drop box to choose how surrounding text wraps around the element. You can choose to have wrapping set to None, Left, or Right.

The next step in defining your style is to control the borders and fonts.

1. Click the Borders tab to display the next page, as shown in Figure 13.3.

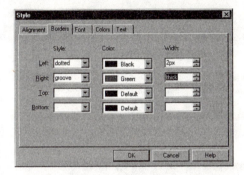

FIG. 13.3
The Borders tab lets you specify the borders for an element using this style. You can control the border for the top, bottom, left, and right.

2. Use the drop boxes to select the border(s) for your style. You can choose from a variety of styles, colors, and widths. You may apply a line style to any edge of a border (Left, Right, Top, Bottom).

3. Click the Font tab to switch to the next page, shown in Figure 13.4.

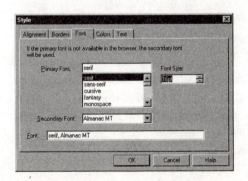

FIG. 13.4
You can set both the primary and secondary style font in the Font tab. The secondary font is only used if the visitor does not have the primary font.

4. From the <u>P</u>rimary Font list box, select the font for your style. You may choose a particular face, or a style of font (such as Serif, Sans-Serif, or Cursive). Select the secondary font from the <u>S</u>econdary Font drop box. This updates the <u>F</u>ont text box with the order of your fonts. You may edit this text box to add additional fonts to use in this style, separated by a comma.

> **WARNING**
>
> When you choose a particular font face, always consider if your visitors are likely to have it. If visitors do not have a font face, they will not see the page as you intended. Instead of specifying a particular face, consider specifying a font style or family, such as Serif (fonts resembling Times New Roman), Sans-Serif (Arial or Helvetica), or Cursive (Zapf Chancery). The visitors computer will then try to match an appropriate font to the style. When you use this method, you are always sure that a visitor will see your page as it was intended.

5. Specify the size of the font, in points, in the Font Size text box. You can also use the spin wheel beside the text box to enter a value.

Now that you have your style's alignment, borders, and font settings defined, you can set up the style backgrounds and colors.

1. To specify background and foreground colors for your style, as well as background image properties, click the Colors tab. This page is shown in Figure 13.5.

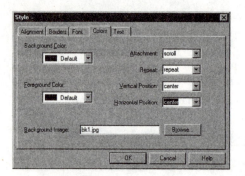

FIG. 13.5
The Colors tab is a blanket page for deciding on the properties of your style's background and foreground. You can specify a color or an image for a background and control its behavior.

2. If you want the colors for your style to differ from the page defaults, choose a color from the Background Color and Foreground Color drop boxes. If you would rather have the background of your style contain an image, choose the image in the Background Image text box by clicking the Browse button.

3. To add the background image (if any) to the page background, choose Fixed from the Attachment drop box. If you would rather the background scroll with the text in the browser, choose Scroll from the same drop box.

4. If you want the background image to repeat behind the text, choose Repeat from the Repeat drop box. You may choose to tile the background image horizontally only by choosing Repeat-X, or vertically by choosing Repeat-Y. If you don't want the image to repeat at all, choose No Repeat.

5. Using the Vertical Position and Horizontal Position drop boxes, choose how the background image will be positioned behind the text. You may choose to have it positioned vertically by the Top, Center, or Bottom. Horizontally you may choose to have it positioned by the Left, Center, or Right.

The final stage of creating your style involves your text settings and adding it to the Style dialog box list.

1. Click the Text tab to switch to the final page, shown in Figure 13.6.

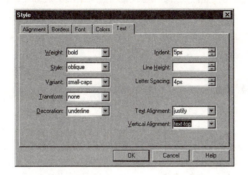

FIG. 13.6
The Text tab lets you fine tune your text presentation in the style. You can choose the font weight, style, spacing, and even alignment.

2. Use the Text page to control how your text appears in this style. You can control the Weight of the font (the thickness of the lines), the Style (Normal, Italic, Oblique), the Variant (Normal or Small Caps), the capitalization (from the Transform drop box), the Decoration (underline, overline, and so on), as well as the Indent, Line Height, and Letter Spacing. Each option can be specified using the appropriate drop box.

3. Define the style's horizontal alignment by choosing from the Text Alignment drop box and the vertical alignment by choosing from the Vertical drop box.

4. Click the OK button to add your style information to the Style dialog box. The style information is appended to the line containing your style name.

5. Edit the style to your satisfaction. When you are done, click the OK button to close the dialog box.

 Once you have created your embedded styles, it's easy to move them to an external style sheet. To save your style into an external CSS file, first cut or copy the individual styles from the Style dialog box and paste them into a blank text document using Notepad. Keep in mind that you only need to copy the style information, and not the preceding or trailing <STYLE></STYLE> or the <!-- and --> tags. Save the CSS file and import it into your Web site using the FrontPage Explorer.

Linking to an External Style Sheet

Once you have created your external style sheet file, you still have to point your Web pages to it before you can use its styles. Linking to an external stylesheet is a very simple process, but it does require you to switch from the What-You-See-Is-What-You-Get editing mode to the HTML editing mode. To link an external CSS file to your Web pages, follow these steps:

1. Open the Web page in the FrontPage Editor and switch to HTML view, as shown in Figure 13.7.

FIG. 13.7
HTML view is necessary for linking to an external style sheet. Note that the link to the style sheet appears in the beginning of the page, between the <HEAD></HEAD> tags.

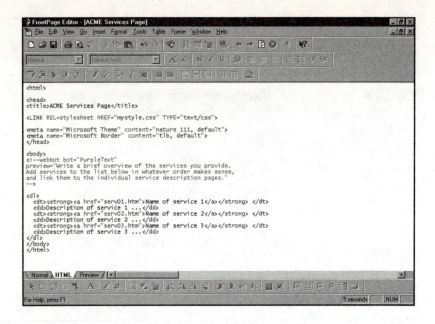

2. If your page does not contain an embedded style sheet, insert a reference to the external style sheet between the beginning and the ending of the <HEAD></HEAD> tags. Your reference should look something like this:

   ```
   <LINK REL=stylesheet HREF="mystyles.css" TYPE="text/css">
   ```

   Be sure to replace mystyles.css with the proper filename and path to your external stylesheet.

3. If your page does contain an embedded style sheet, choose Format, Stylesheet to open the Format Stylesheet dialog box, shown in Figure 13.8. At the beginning of the style definitions insert an import tag as follows:

   ```
   @import URL(/mystyles.css) ;
   ```

   Where /mystyles.css is replaced with the proper filename and path to your external style sheet.

FIG. 13.8
To link your page to an external style sheet when you already have embedded styles, you must use an SGML (Standardized General Markup Language) directive in your <STYLE> tag.

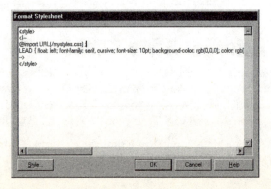

4. Freely use the external style sheet's styles in your page. Repeat the process for each page in your site where you want to use this external style sheet.

 External style sheets let you update your styles for the entire site in one place. You can apply universal changes to your Web site by using external style sheets, as opposed to embedded or inline styles.

Using your Defined Styles

When you are ready, you can now begin to use your new styles in your Web page(s). Because the style information is either stored in the page (embedded) or in a linked file (external), the styles themselves become available to you in the FrontPage Editor. If you have used the FrontPage Editor, you are likely familiar with the Change Style drop box in the Formatting toolbar. Traditionally this drop box lists the default HTML styles, such as Headings (<HR1>, <HR2>, and so on). When you define a style by either embedding it in the page or by linking to an external CSS file, this drop box updates with your new styles. To use these styles, follow these two simple steps:

1. Select the text in your page to which you want to apply your CSS style.
2. From the Change Style drop box choose your style. Styles are listed alphabetically, including the standard HTML styles.

Using Inline Styles

If you want to quickly apply a "one-off" style to a selection of text, you could use inline style definitions. These styles only apply to the selected text and are not available to the rest of your Web page(s). To use an inline style, follow these instructions:

1. In the FrontPage Editor, select a paragraph of text to which you want to apply a style.
2. Right-click the selected text and choose Paragraph Properties… from the pop-up menu. This opens the Paragraph Properties dialog box, as shown in Figure 13.9.
3. Click the Style button to open the Style dialog box (discussed earlier in Creating Styles). Use this dialog box to create your style and click OK.
4. Click OK to close the Paragraph Properties dialog box and apply your style.

 You can also apply an inline style to a selection of text when it is not a paragraph. To do so, select the text and right-click to choose Font Properties… from the pop-up menu. You can also hit ALT+ENTER with the text selected.

Beyond HTML: Dynamic HTML

With the advent of Microsoft Internet Explorer 4.0, Web pages have taken a great leap forward in functionality and interactivity. In the past, all forms of interactivity in the browser relied on complex coding and objects (such as Java applets or ActiveX components). Internet Explorer 4.0 introduced Microsoft's own extension to HTML (proposed as a standard) called *Dynamic HTML*. Simply put, dynamic HTML lets you create a page that responds and alters itself based on user interaction. Dynamic HTML (or DHTML) was created to extend the Web's functionality to make it comparable to a custom programming environment. With DHTML, anything that was possible before in a specialized client/server program (done in C++ or Visual Basic, for example) is possible within a Web browser.

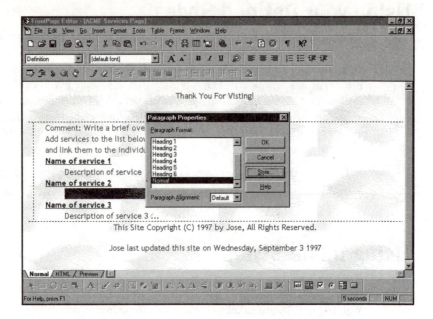

FIG. 13.9
The Paragraph Properties dialog box lets you define a format for your paragraph, an alignment, and a style to attach to it.

To take true advantage of DHTML, you must be able to program in Visual Basic Script. VBScript is used to control events and objects within your Web page. For those of us who aren't programmers, thankfully FrontPage 98 introduces some elements of DHTML without needing to enter a single line of code. FrontPage 98 supports the following Dynamic HTML features:

- **Collapsible Outlines**—With DHTML, your lists don't need to be long, dry piles of data. Using collapsible outlines, you can create lists that require user interaction to expand different trees of data.

- **Form Field Extensions**—If you've been looking to make your Web site's forms a little easier to use, the Form Field Extensions will make you happy. Using these extensions, you can now control the tab order of form fields (that is, what order the cursor will move to fields when pressing the TAB key) as well as create keyboard shortcuts for fields.

- **Page Transitions**—Users of Microsoft PowerPoint will be familiar with this feature. Now you can liven up your Web pages with cinematic transitions, such as fades and wipes.

■ **Text Animations**—For those times that you want your text to stand out, DHTML introduces animated text without relying on a Java applet or ActiveX control. Also a carryover from PowerPoint, you can now define how text will appear in your Web site through animation.

> **WARNING**
> These Dynamic HTML features require a Dynamic HTML capable browser, such as Microsoft Internet Explorer 4.0 (or higher). Unfortunately, Netscape's own dynamic HTHML (dHTML) with a lower case 'd' is not the same standard, and is not supported in IE, and DHTML is not supported in Netscape Communicator/Navigator.

DHTML: Creating a Collapsible Outline

Creating a collapsible outline is a simple process in FrontPage 98. Collapsible outlines are in fact only an extension to a standard list that you create in the FrontPage Editor. Why would you want a collapsible outline? Typically to save space and make your page more readable. Visitors can expand the "trees" of your list as they need, without causing a large list to dominate your page. To create a collapsible outline, follow these steps in the FrontPage Editor:

1. Create a list using the instructions provided in Chapter 5, "Working with the FrontPage Editor" on page 67.
2. Now, under each item in your first list, create a new "sub-list". This creates the separate trees for your outline. You can demote sub-lists further down in the tree by selecting them and clicking the Increase Indent button in the Formatting toolbar.
3. Repeat Step 2 for each branch in your outline tree.
4. Select the entire list (including the parent list) and right-click to choose List Properties from the pop-up menu. This opens the List Properties dialog box, shown in Figure 13.10.

FIG. 13.10
The List Properties dialog box lets you choose how your list will appear. You can choose image bullets, numbers, or standard HTML formatting.

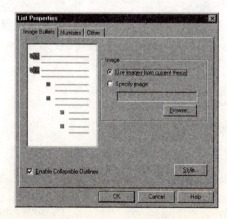

5. Select the Enable Collapsible Outlines checkbox.
  6. Click OK to confirm and close the dialog box.
  7. If you want the sub-lists to be collapsible also, repeat Steps 4-6 for each sub-list, instead selecting the child list.

DHTML: Using Form Field Extensions

Forms can be confusing for visitors. Navigation through the fields can be complicated and frustrating. Dynamic HTML introduces new form field extensions that make forms navigation easier with a little work on your part. With form field extensions you can change the tab order of the fields, assign keyboard shortcuts for particular fields, and also create clickable labels. All of these features combined let you create a form that is easy and pleasant for visitors to use. To use form field extensions you must already have a form created (refer to the FrontPage 98 on-line help).

To modify the tab order of your form fields, follow these steps:

  1. Select one of your form fields and right-click to select Field Properties from the pop-up menu. You may also press ALT+ENTER. This opens the form Properties dialog box for your particular field type. An example of the Text Box Properties dialog box is shown in Figure 13.11.

FIG. 13.11
Each form field type has a slightly different Properties dialog box. This dialog box is for the Text Box field type. Each dialog has the Tab order text box for you to define the tab order.

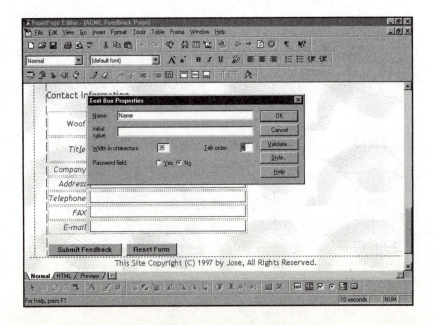

  2. Enter the tab order value in the Tab order text box. The lower the number, the sooner that the TAB key takes the visitor to that field.
  3. Click OK to close the dialog box and apply your changes.

To create a clickable label for users to access a form field, follow these instructions:

1. Click the insert cursor just before your form field and type the label for your field. For example, you could type "E-mail" for a field that you want visitors to enter their electronic mail address into.
2. Select both your newly entered label text and the form field, then choose Insert, Form Field, Label from the menu bar. This creates the label for your field, as represented by a dotted box around the label text.

If you want to assign a keyboard shortcut (such as ALT+<KEY>) to your newly created label, follow these steps:

1. Select the letter of your text label to which you want to assign a keyboard shortcut. This is the key that will be used in combination with the ALT key to select this field.

> **CAUTION**
>
> Be careful not to choose a keyboard shortcut that is already in use by the browser or another form field. If you choose conflicting shortcuts, your form field shortcut will not work.

2. Underline the character by clicking the Underline button in the Formatting toolbar. Your keyboard shortcut then appears underlined on the screen to indicate its hotkey.

DHTML: Using Page Transitions and Text Animations

Users of presentation software, like Microsoft PowerPoint, have been using animated page transitions and text for several years. These effects can contribute to your Web page's appeal without relying on a Java applet or ActiveX component. Use of these features is very simple, but be sure to select your effect carefully so you don't clutter your page's presentation. Page transition effects can be set to be used at certain events:

- **Page Enter**—when the visitor first sees your page
- **Page Exit**—when the visitor exits the active page or follows a hyperlink to another
- **Site Enter**—when the visitor initially enters your Web site by visiting the active page
- **Site Exit**—when the visitor exits your Web site from the active page

To apply a page transition to your Web page, follow these instructions:

1. In the FrontPage Editor, choose Format, Page Transition from the menu bar. This opens the Page Transition dialog box, shown in Figure 13.12.
2. From the Event drop box, choose when you want this page transition to be applied.
3. Enter the length of time that the effect should last (in seconds) in the Duration textbox.
4. Choose the page transition effect from the Transition Effect list box.
5. Click OK to close the dialog box and commit your changes.

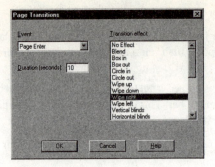

FIG. 13.12
The Page Transition dialog box lets you choose the transition effect for the current page. You can choose one of four events to trigger this transition.

To apply animation to your text, follow these steps in the FrontPage Editor:

1. Select the text in your Web page that will use this animation.
2. From the Format menu, choose the Animation sub-menu. This menu lists each animation effect you can use, as well as the default of "Off".
3. Choose the animation effect that you want to use for your selected text. If you want to disable animation for the selected text, choose "Off".

Dynamic HTML is a new and exciting way of authoring Web pages. Unfortunately, both Netscape and Microsoft offer differing "dynamic" HTML standards. FrontPage 98 supports Microsoft's own DHTML (as opposed to Netscape's dHTML). You can find out more information on both dynamic HTML standards at these addresses on the Web.

For Microsoft DHTML, visit Microsoft's own SiteBuilder network DHTML resources at **http://www.microsoft.com/workshop/author/dhtml/**.

Netscape's dHTML information is located at **http://developer.netscape.com/one/dynhtml/**, a part of their DevEdge Online site.

Finally, Macromedia has its own resource for budding DHTML and dHTML authors: **http://www.dhtmlzone.com**.

Pushing Your Site with the Channel Definition Format

FrontPage 98 includes the Channel Definition Wizard to help you create a Channel Definition Format (CDF) file. The CDF file is used by a visitors Web browser to let them subscribe to your site as a channel or desktop component. When a visitor subscribes to your Web site as a channel, they can browse your site contents offline, display your Web as their screen saver, and download or receive notification when the Web site is updated. Subscription features are only available to Web browsers that support the Channel Definition Format, such as Microsoft Internet Explorer 4.0. CDF lets you publish your Web site in parts or as a whole for subscription, as well as use your own logo and icon as a channel identification. Your CDF file resides on your Web site with the rest of your content, but is only used by subscribers. This method of publishing is known as "push" publishing, as opposed to traditional "pull" publishing where your visitor has to manually connect to your Web site to view it and its updates.

To begin creating your CDF for push publishing, follow these instructions in the FrontPage Explorer:

1. From the Tools menu, choose Define Channel... to open the Channel Definition Wizard, as shown in Figure 13.13.

FIG. 13.13
The Channel Definition Wizard makes it easy for you to start push publishing. You can use this wizard to create a new CDF, or modify an existing one.

2. To create a new CDF file, select the Create a new Channel Definition Format file for the current FrontPage Web radio button and click the Next button.
3. The second page of the wizard, shown in Figure 13.14, lets you describe your new channel. Specify the Title and an Abstract description using the appropriate text boxes.

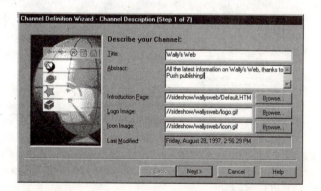

FIG. 13.14
The Channel Description page gives you the opportunity to describe your channel for visitors. You can also specify a channel logo and icon for their browser.

4. Enter the channel's introductory page (used for subscription) in the Introduction Page text box. You may optionally Browse for it in your Web site.
5. Each channel needs a logo and an icon that act as a graphic representation for the channel in the visitor's browser. Specify the logo in the Logo image text box, and the icon in the Icon image text box. You may Browse your Web site for these items.

6. Click the Next button to advance to the third page of the wizard, shown in Figure 13.15.

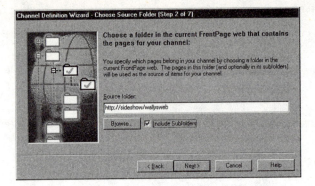

FIG. 13.15
The Choose Source Folder page lets you choose what the source directory is for your channel. You may optionally include subfolders of this directory.

7. Choose the folder in your Web site that contains the content you want to publish in your channel. You can Browse for the Source folder, and optionally Include subfolders. Click the Next button to proceed.

8. The next page, shown in Figure 13.16, lets you choose what pages of your Web site are included in the channel. Each page in the content directory (selected in step 7) is listed in the list box. To remove pages, select them from the list and click the Exclude button. To restore the excluded pages, click the Restore button.

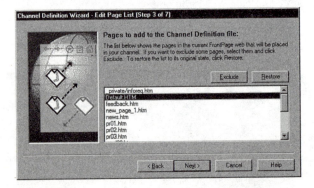

FIG. 13.16
Your channel contents can be refined in the Edit Page List page of the wizard. You can exclude certain Web pages from your channel if you want.

9. Click the Next button to open the fifth page of the wizard, shown in Figure 13.17. This page, Channel Item Properties, lets you define the properties for each page you have included in the channel.

10. Select each page from the Channel Items list and provide its properties. You can define an Abstract description, control how the page is cached in the Page cache drop box, and how the item is used in the channel.

Pushing your Site with the Channel Definition Format | 239

FIG. 13.17
Channel Item Properties can be set in this page. You can choose how your pages are described and used in your channel, and whether or not they are cached.

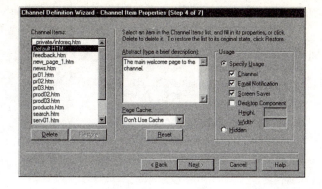

> **NOTE** Each item can be used in several different ways:
>
> - *Channel*—The item is used as part of the channel contents.
> - *E-mail Notification*—When the page is updated or modified, the subscribers will receive an e-mail notification.
> - *Screen Saver*—The selected item can be used as a screen saver on the visitor's computer.
> - *Des*k*top Component*—The item is used as a small region on the user's desktop. You can specify the height and the width of the component in pixels.
> - *Hidden*—The item is invisible in the channel but is downloaded for offline viewing. This is used if you do not want an item to appear as a channel item, but is hyperlinked to another channel item. ■

11. Click the Ne*x*t button to open the sixth page, Channel Scheduling. This page is used to control when the visitor's browser should check for updates to your site.

12. Define the *s*tart and *e*nd date by entering a date in the form of dd/mm/yy. If you want this channel to be checked indefinitely, use the values of {now} for the start and (for-ever) for the end.

13. Specify how often the visitor's browser should check for updates using the *C*heck every drop box and text box. You can enter a value set to days, hours, and minutes.

14. If you want to delay scheduled checks to minimize the load on your Web server, select the *D*elay checks check box and specify random delay values.

15. Click the Ne*x*t button to advance to the seventh page, shown in Figure 13.18. This page lets you define an optional URL for logging the channel usage.

16. Optionally enter an URL for the *L*og Target URL text box, or click the B*r*owse button to locate it. Click the Ne*x*t button to advance.

17. The final page of the wizard, shown in Figure 13.19, lets you specify an URL and file name for your CDF file, as well as set two additional options.

FIG. 13.18
Logging the usage of your channel is an optional feature. You can set the URL for your log or choose to leave it blank.

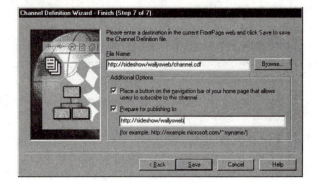

FIG. 13.19
The final page of the Channel Definition Wizard gives you the URL for your new channel file, as well as two options for publishing.

18. Confirm the URL for the CDF file in the File Name text box. You can click the Browse button to locate the URL.
19. If you want to add a button for your channel to your Web site's navigation bar, select the Place a button on the navigation checkbox.
20. If you want to prepare your channel for publication, select the Prepare for publishing to checkbox and enter the URL in the text box. If you do not want to publish your channel at this time and merely want to test it, do not select this. You can re-run the wizard and open your CDF file to change this in the future.
21. Click the Save button to store your CDF file.

To publish your channel to your Web server, click the Publish button in the FrontPage Explorer toolbar. You must have the Prepare for publishing checkbox selected in the Channel Definition Wizard for this to function. ●

PART V

Creating and Adapting Graphics with Image Explorer

- **14** Getting Started with Image Composer 243
- **15** Working with Sprites 261
- **16** Using Effects for Maximum Impact 279
- **17** Tailoring Your Images for FrontPage Documents 295

CHAPTER 14

Getting Started with Image Composer

■ **Linking image to executable**
You can save yourself a lot of work by associating your image files with Image Composer.

■ **Integration**
Learn how to use Image Composer with its sibling software, FrontPage Editor and FrontPage Explorer.

■ **Functionality**
Read this breakdown on the major tools to be found within Image Composer to learn some basic operating procedures.

■ **Anatomy of a Sprite**
Find out how to create and modify sprites within Image Composer.

Image Composer is a simple program, with a lot of complex applications. Much like any program, you need to learn the basic concepts before you can advance to complicated procedures. This is especially true in Image Composer, because it is in no way a traditional "drawing program" in the sense you are used to. In this chapter you'll learn the underlying concepts behind Image Composer and its various tools. You'll also learn why Image Composer is different from most of the other programs you'll encounter. ■

What Does Image Composer Offer?

Microsoft Image Composer 1.5 is a graphic manipulation program geared specifically towards developing images for use on the World Wide Web and other electronic formats. It's meant to be integrated with Microsoft's powerful FrontPage Web development suite, allowing for a seamless bond between author and graphic artist. The program's scope is specialized, allowing for a smaller footprint and more efficient processor use than other, general purpose programs.

What sets Image Composer apart from other programs is its philosophy of design. Image Composer can work with a variety of graphical formats, as well as other specialized items such as OLE objects. There are many preset tools included in the package, including warping, neo-impressionism, and other filtered effects. Not only that, but you can also take advantage of several automated processes such as the Button Wizard and the Save for the Web Wizard.

Image Composer works within its confines quite well. The interface is easy to use, the structure of the program is flexible and lends itself to expansion, and the filter format is powerful.

Associating Your Images with Image Composer

One of the most important aspects of any program is how easy it is to use. Image Composer has some esoteric concepts behind its design, but the interface and general use are pure Windows 95. The obvious advantage of this is that you know generally what to expect within the program, a file menu, an edit menu, view, insert, and so on. The other advantage to using Windows 95-isms is that you can associate all of your image files with Image Composer.

When you install Image Composer, it automatically associates itself with the file types with which it can work. However, if you have existing software that is already associated with a particular file type, that association will remain. For example, Microsoft Internet Explorer is associated with the .GIF file format, even though Image Composer works with that format. Assuming you want to change this, the steps for associating a file are listed as follows:

1. Open a File Explorer window within your operating system.
2. Go to the View menu, and choose the Options... item.
3. From there, select the File Types tab to view the listing of existing file types and their associations, as shown in Figure 14.1.
4. Choose the file's association that you wish to change and click Edit.... In this example, use the .GIF type currently associated with Internet Explorer (if you have Internet Explorer installed).
5. Under the Actions pane, select the Open command and click the Edit... button, as shown in Figure 14.2.
6. Click Use DDE off and enter the *exact* path to the Image Composer executable within the Application used to perform action: field. If you want, you can Browse to the file's location. Make sure you append a "%1" on the end of the path; that inserts the name of the file you're trying to open using that association. An example is shown in Figure 14.3.

Associating Your Images with Image Composer | 245

FIG. 14.1
You can control all of your file associations from the File Types tab. You can even change their icons.

FIG. 14.2
From the Edit File Type window you can add, remove, and edit various file type associations.

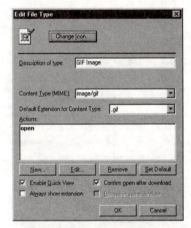

FIG. 14.3
It's very important to get the executable location right or else Windows won't know where to look for the program.

7. Finally, close the Editing Action window by clicking OK.

   N O T E An associated file's icon changes to illustrate that association. A file that has no associations simply has a small Windows 95 logo on it. ■

Using Image Composer with FrontPage

The FrontPage suite is powerful for many reasons, but one of the most obvious is the integration between programs. You can easily work within the FrontPage Explorer, make modification with the FrontPage Editor or Image Composer, and then continue within the Explorer. While all three are separate programs, they can spawn each other with specific criterion.

The biggest annoyance when working on the same files over three programs is opening a copy of each program, and then accessing the file you want to work on three times. Thanks to the integration between the FrontPage clients and Image Composer, you don't have to worry. Both the FrontPage Explorer and Editor have the means to link up to Image Composer. To edit an image file while in FrontPage Explorer you must:

1. Within FrontPage Explorer make sure that you're using either the All Files, Folders, or Navigation View, as shown in Figure 14.4.

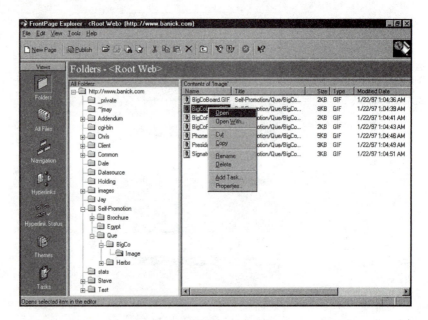

FIG. 14.4
The FrontPage Explorer can be used to access and organize your image content. All of your graphic files should have Image Composer icons.

2. Select the image file you wish to open in Image Composer by :

   Double Clicking or,

   Right-Clicking and choosing to Open or,

   Right-Clicking and choosing to Open With..., and then choosing Image Composer.

The FrontPage Explorer is meant more as an organizational tool than a front-end graphic editor. However, with its powerful preview capability, the FrontPage Editor can be an invaluable tool in determining what graphics need editing and which need discarding. To create an Image Composer session from within the FrontPage Editor you must:

1. Open an HTML document that contains graphics of some kind within the FrontPage Editor.
2. While in the Normal view, select the graphic you wish to edit by right-clicking it and selecting Image Properties.
3. When the Image Properties window appears (as shown in Figure 14.5), click the E<u>d</u>it button, which will bring up Image Composer with that picture loaded.

FIG. 14.5
The FrontPage Editor fulfills a valuable preview function for your graphics as well as providing a powerful editing environment.

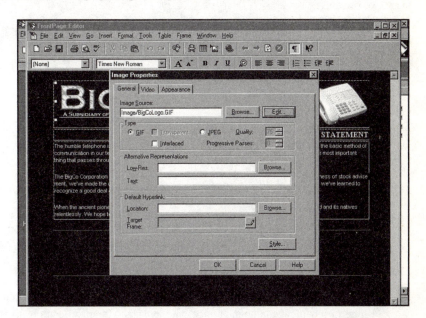

> **CAUTION**
> All of the previous methods will spawn a copy of Image Composer. That's the problem, each one creates a new session. If you are editing more than one document at a time, be careful to watch your resources, as each iteration of Image Composer adds to your processor load. The best way to manage this is to simply work on one document at a time, closing extraneous Image Composer windows and launching new ones as the situation warrants.

Using Tools, Toolbars & Palettes

Image Composer's Interface is much like any other Windows-oriented program, with the unique twists needed for a graphic manipulation utility. What makes Image Composer shine is its selection of tools and utilities, all available in easily accessible forms such as Toolbars and Palettes.

The place you'll be spending most of your time is in the primary toolbar, running along the left side of the screen. These 12 options encapsulate Image Composer's functions almost entirely, and are displayed in Figure 14.6.

FIG. 14.6
By using the primary toolbar you can create effective graphics within Image Composer.

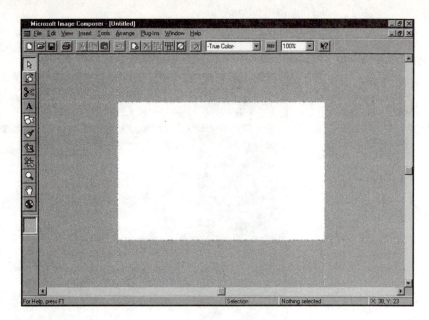

Most of the tools in the left tool bar will spawn a palette of their own if you click them. This way the Image Composer interface never gets too cluttered, since you can never have more than one variety of palette open at once. The tools, and the palettes they spawn are listed as follows, from the top of the left-hand toolbar to the bottom.

- The *Selection* arrow turns Image Composer into selection mode. It's from here that you can select and de-select a variety of objects, all to be manipulated later. If the selection controls seem a bit too simple, that's because Image Composer is a sprite-based system; sprites remain separate until combined. Since each sprite is usually a discrete object, all you really need to select one is a simple arrow pointer.

- The *Arrange* button brings up the Arrange palette, as shown in Figure 14.7. From here you can engage in a variety of activities, including warping, aligning, flipping, scaling, and cropping. The align tools especially are quite flexible, with 12 different options such as Align Centers, Lower Left Corner, Horizontal Centers, or Touch Edges. The Arrange tool is essentially a macro-manipulator; it operates on a sprite-wide scale to create larger changes within a picture.

- The *Cutout* button spawns the Cutout palette, as shown in Figure 14.8. The Cutout tool is actually more powerful than the button-image of a pair of scissors implies. It's here that you'll find the complex selection tools allowing you to work on a pixel-by-pixel basis, or select parts of objects based on color.

Using Tools, Toolbars & Palettes | 249

FIG. 14.7
The Arrange tool lets you coordinate gross scalar changes to an image, as well as control facing and alignment.

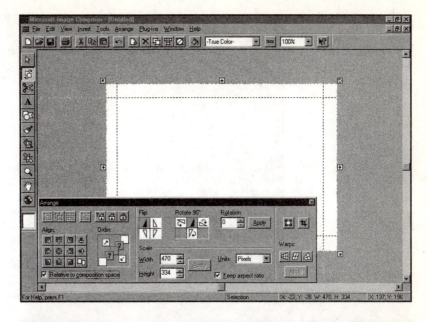

FIG. 14.8
Image Composer's selection tools are divided into two different categories: those that select sprites, and those that select specific pixels within those sprites.

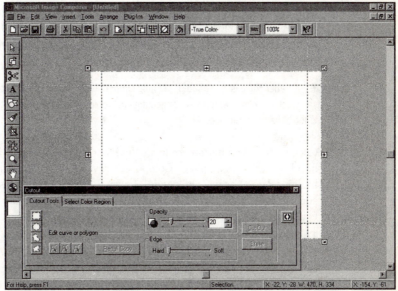

- The *Text* button generates the Text control palette, shown in Figure 14.9. It's from here that you create text objects to make up your headlines, articles, and menus. You can control all of the important attributes such as text alignment, font size, style, and color. It's also important to note that you can go back and edit the text after it's been placed, as opposed to bit-map programs such as Photoshop or Fractal Paint.

FIG. 14.9
Image Composer's text is truly object-based, and not just rendered and forgotten.

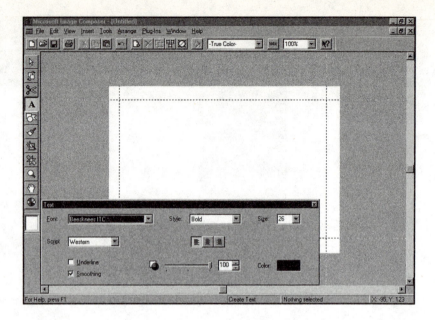

- Next comes the *Shapes* button, spawning the Shapes palette shown in Figure 14.10. The Shapes palette generates and edits basic geometric forms. From here you can create and control several shapes using bezier curves. You can also set options such as the shape's color, opacity, line weight, and so on.

> **N O T E** A bezier curve is a method of defining simple object-based shapes. The curve is created by placing "points," with a line connecting each point. By moving one of the points you can influence the behavior of the line.

- Clicking the *Paint* button produces the Paint palette, as shown in Figure 14.11. From here you can manage Image Composer's several painting tools, such as an airbrush, traditional paint brush, and pencil. However, you can also access several other tools, such as the Dodge/Burn tool and the Contrast and Tint controls. Lastly, you can define brush sizes and attributes.

- The *Effects* button brings up the powerful Effects palette, as shown in Figure 14.12. The Effects palette is the "gizmo-laden" segment of Image Composer. It's from here that you can apply effects to your sprites such as Charcoal, Colored Pencil, Vortex, and a host of others. You can also control the behaviors of these various effects by clicking over to the Details tab and changing any of the values found therein.

- Selecting the *Texture Transfer* button brings up the Texture Transfer palette, displayed in Figure 14 13. This powerful feature lets you combine two different sprites in a variety of ways. The Texture Transfer palette lets you control how the sprites will merge. Possible merge types include Glue, Snip, Tile, and many more.

Using Tools, Toolbars & Palettes 251

FIG. 14.10
Because of Image Composer's sprite based system, primitive shapes are infinitely resizable and scalable.

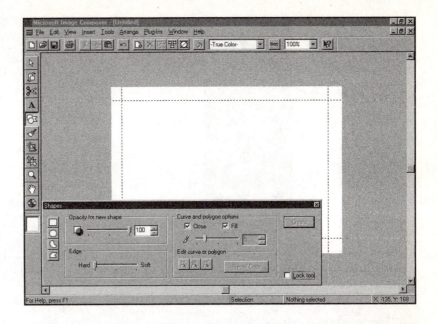

FIG. 14.11
You have total control over brushes and painting styles from the Paint palette.

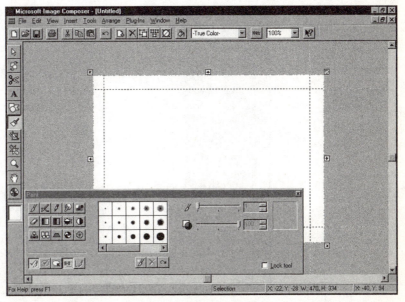

- Next comes the *Zoom* tool, which doesn't actually have an associated palette. However, it's just as valuable a tool as any of the others. Simply select the Zoom tool and click a desired area to zoom in on it. Hold down the Control key and click to zoom out.

FIG. 14.12
The Effects palette can change the tenor of an image almost instantly.

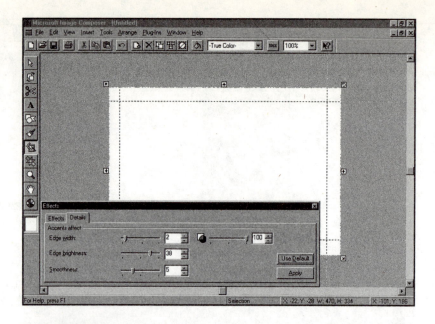

FIG. 14.13
The Texture Transfer palette is a simple yet powerful merging tool.

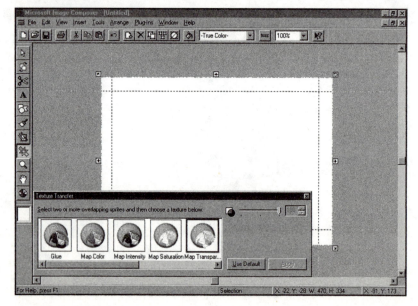

- Like the Zoom tool, the *Pan* button doesn't summon a new palette. Instead, it lets you position your viewpoint. This is especially handy when you're zoomed in and need to move the picture around, so certain parts of it are visible.

- The Color Tuning palette (Figure 14.14) is brought to the front by selecting the Color Tuning button, second from the bottom. These powerful tools let you control the color values for a particular sprite. You can also adjust the Highlight/Shadow depth, as well define the upper and lower ranges of intensity in the Dynamic Range tab.

FIG. 14.14
Because there's no preview on the color controls, you have to use the Apply button. Don't worry though, because if you get in trouble you can always hit the Reset button or choose to Undo from the Edit menu.

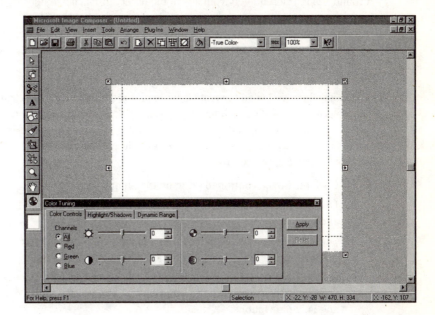

- Lastly comes the Color Selection square, firmly situated on the bottom of the toolbar. By clicking here you can change the current color to whatever you please. More importantly though, you can set and import color palettes, ensuring that your Web graphics share the same colors.

It's important to note that just about every single palette needs to have a sprite selected in order to be effective. You'll find that many of the options you wish to pursue are mysteriously grayed out until you actually make a selection. While you can select multiple sprites, not all of the above tools will work on them *en masse*. The tools that can influence multiple sprites at once are Effects, Texture Transfer, and Arrange. The rest either work on an individual basis, or simply create new sprites.

Creating and Editing Your First Sprites

As you may have guessed, sprites form the basis of Image Composer's design philosophy. It helps to simply think of sprites as an object within Image Composer, and that no image can exist without being composed of objects. If you just start up Image Composer and try to start painting, you'll find that you can't. Most of your available options are grayed out and are inaccessible. This is because you don't have a sprite to act upon, and in Image Composer even the background is a sprite.

Put another way, a new Image Composer document is an entirely clean slate. Traditionally in graphics programs you have a default blank "page" to start with, and you can then set up the page attributes as you wish. Image Composer lets you create your own background, granting a degree of control not seen in many other programs. It's also important to note that the background is not differentiated from any of the other sprites, it's in no way special or unique.

NOTE Despite what you may think, a sprite in this context is *not* an animation term. While animators have (and still do) referred to sprites in their jargon, Microsoft has settled on a different definition. They also have nothing to do with mythology.

Obviously then, you need to create a sprite of some kind before you can proceed. Remember that a sprite is basically anything that appears in your document. A sprite is usually a geometric primitive that has been modified somehow, be it by a size change or something painted on it. Every sprite that you'll be making yourself will likely originate from the Shapes palette. In order to create a sprite you must:

1. Click the Shapes button to bring up the Shapes palette.
2. Decide what variety of shape you desire. You can choose from Rectangle, Oval, Curve and Polygon.
3. Draw the shape to a desired size on your screen. Note that you can change the attributes of the shape, and the figure you've just drawn isn't the "final" version.
4. Set the Opacity option to determine the shape's translucence. Set how hard or soft you want the edges to be with the Edge control. Change the spline options using the Curve and Polygon Options.
5. If you haven't already, choose a color from the color picker.
6. Finally, click the Create button to render your shape.

So now that you've got your sprite, you need to make some basic changes to it. This is where the rest of the tools come into play. If you want to change your sprite's facing, alignment, or scale, select it and click the Arrange button. However, if you're creating your sprite from scratch and not importing an existing image, you'll probably want to paint on it. To paint on a sprite you must:

1. Select the sprite in question by using the Selection arrow. You can click the button on top of the tool bar, or just click anywhere that isn't a sprite in the document window. The selection tool will be chosen by default.
2. Click the Paint button, bringing up the Paint palette.
3. Choose a color to use, and select the paintbrush, airbrush or pencil icon. Now select a brush size, preferably something smaller than your actual sprite.
4. Draw or paint whatever you please on the sprite.

If you make a mistake, you can always use the eraser tool to remove it. However, the eraser doesn't just erase whatever you've applied to the sprite—it erases the sprite itself. For example, if you created a solid black rectangle you could erase parts of it to create a transparency effect.

The problem with this is that you can't paint over the transparent areas, as they cease to exist as an active area within the sprite. If you want to restore the transparent area, you need to recreate the sprite or use the Undo option from the Edit menu. It's actually a better idea to simply use the Color Fill paint bucket icon to cover up painting mistakes, so you can start over.

Changing and Copying Sprites

You've learned how to create and change the appearance of a sprite. Now it's time to learn how to manipulate and change a sprite's attributes. Image Composer treats each sprite as a single discrete unit, and therefore you can make changes on the sprite level. For example, each sprite has a relative position to other sprites. Since this is a two-dimensional program, there is no actual depth, but sprites can be layered behind one another. Layered positioning is just one of the things you can change about a sprite.

Another aspect you can modify is the sprite's size. Note the handles around each sprite, illustrated in Figure 14.15. By clicking and dragging one of these handles you can elongate or shrink the selected sprite, and by clicking the upper right handle, you can rotate it. These handles may change the sprite's size, but what if you wanted to actually crop or expand the sprite's area without affecting the image? In order to do so you must:

FIG. 14.15
The handles on a sprite allow you to change the sprite's dimensions or rotate it on the x and y axis.

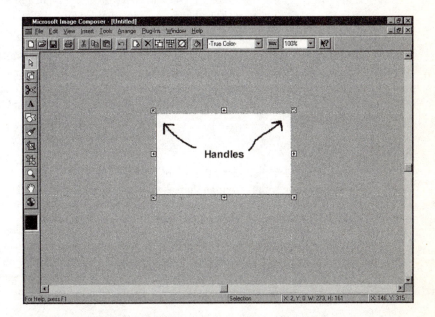

1. Right-click the sprite you wish to modify.
2. Choose Crop from the pop-up menu that results.
3. Either expand or shrink the sprite's display area as you please by dragging the cropping handles.

4. Make sure you get out of Cropping mode by clicking elsewhere in the document. You don't want to inadvertently crop the sprite twice.

Sprites are incredibly malleable objects. You can bend, pull, warp, and scale them all that you want. The important thing to remember when manipulating sprites is that they're objects; their attributes are not set in stone like a pure bitmap image. Once you start to take advantage of this flexibility you'll realize that there's little you cannot create within Image Composer's boundaries.

Using Composition Guides

If you look closely at a newly created document, you'll notice a white square bounded by four dotted lines. Those dotted lines are your Composition Guides. At first glance, they may appear to be nothing more than traditional rulers that help you position objects. However, Composition Guides actually control a great deal more.

The Composition Guide delineates your active space. You can change how much room you have to work with by dragging the guides around your document. In traditional desktop publishing programs, you set your space by an exact size because your work had to adhere to a standard size. In Image Composer, you don't have to. There's still a means for setting the exact size of your working space, but when preparing graphics for the Web there isn't as much emphasis on the precise area.

This too, may not seem important, but the Composition Guide determines what appears in the final graphic and what doesn't. When you're creating an image, you can draw sprites outside of the Composition Area. When you save the file into a non .MIC file, the material outside of the Composition Area is thrown out. This lets you create several fringe and bordering effects.

Using Clip Art

Sprites, as you've experienced them thus far, have been simple geometric primitives. However, you can do more with them than that, as you can import already existing graphics. This grants a particular degree of flexibility when creating new compositions, as it lets you use some of your already existing work.

All of the tools within image Composer work just as well with an imported image as they would on an existing object, since they are both classified as sprites. While you cannot stretch and warp a bitmap with the same impunity that you could a simple sprite, you *can* apply Effects to much greater effect. To import an existing graphic into Image Composer you must:

1. Go to Insert and select Clip Art....
2. The Microsoft Clip Gallery should appear, allowing you to choose from a variety of existing clip art.
3. After selecting an image, click the Insert button.
4. The image will be inserted into your document, size and modify as desired.

5. You can also just drag the clip art out of the gallery and into your document to add the image.

As a general note, the Insert menu can be used to add nearly any kind of image to your document. If you wanted to add an image from a Photo CD for example, you would follow roughly the same procedure as above, but would select From Photo CD... instead of Clip Art.... The ability to import and insert existing graphics into a document turns Image Composer from a glorified paint program into a powerful graphic utility.

There are six different formats to choose from when inserting objects. The first is the simple File... insertion. Basically all it does is let you insert any of the supported file graphics formats into your composition, essentially the equivalent of an import function. You can also import from a Kodak Photo CD directly using the From Photo CD... menu item. Thirdly you can insert a Button, bringing up the powerful Button Wizard. To create a button you must:

1. Select the Insert menu, and from there click Button.
2. Choose what style of button you wish to create (as shown in Figure 14.16) and click Next.

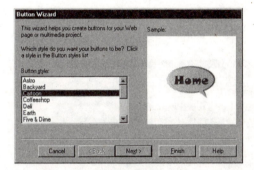

FIG. 14.16
You can create an amazing array of buttons with the Button wizard.

3. Choose how many buttons you wish to create and click Next.
4. Name your button, and if you want a graphic label instead of a textual one click the Image checkbox. Then select the graphic you want on the button by browsing (as shown in Figure 14.17).
5. Click on the size of button you wish. If you want the button to be the size of its label, click the Exact fit for each button radio button. If you want all the buttons to be the same size, click the Same size for all buttons radio button. The Same size button also lets you specify a size if you don't want to use the minimum fit size.
6. Click Finish to create your button(s), while keeping in mind that you can edit them from the Image Composer with as much control over the eventual result as you did when creating them.

Inserting and creating buttons can make your Web creation duties much easier, but the ability to influence and insert objects is an even more powerful function. The fourth option on the

Insert menu allows you to insert Objects, which at first glance seems to be the same thing as inserting a File, but with a different interface. What makes the Object insert function so powerful is that whatever you insert retains its original allegiance to the program which created it. The list of possible objects to insert is culled from your computer's existing application list. If you have Microsoft Excel you'll be able to insert a chart from that program. Not only that, but you'll be able to edit that chart within Image Composer. Using OLE technology Image Composer runs smaller versions of the object application within itself. From there you can edit or create an object as you wish. In order to insert a bitmap object you must:

1. Click on the Insert menu and select the Object item.
2. Select Bitmap image from the pick list. You can actually select whatever you want, but this example will be using a bitmap and the Paint program.
3. Make sure that the Create New radio button is selected. If it isn't, you'll just be able to browse to where the existing files are.
4. Click OK.
5. Create your bitmap image using the Paint tools. Note how Paint essentially runs within Image Composer, and that you can see the rest of your composition.
6. When finished, click outside of your Paint document window and Image Composer will automatically import the image into the existing composition.

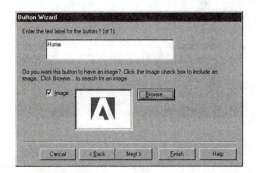

FIG. 14.17
By adding the ability to map graphical labels onto buttons the Button Wizard allows you to escape the traditional textual look and feel of a Web page.

Once the object has been created you can make changes to it using Image Composer's tools and palettes just as it were a normal sprite. You can also edit the object once more with the original program that created it, but at the expense of losing whatever changes you made with Image Composer. In order to edit an inserted object you must:

1. Right-click on the inserted object.
2. In the resulting pop-up menu choose the <object> object menu item. In the case of the previous example, the Bitmap object.
3. From there, choose to either Edit or Open the object. (In the case of non-visual and non-static mediums such as a .WAV file your options are Edit and Play).
4. If you choose Edit then the functionality of the program is inserted into Image Composer as you saw previously. If you Open the file it gets opened by a separate copy of

the application that created it instead of having the OLE version run within Image Composer (as shown in Figure 14.18).

FIG. 14.18
When you use Open over Edit the object is edited in its origin application. Note that the Paint window is separate from the Image Composer window this time.

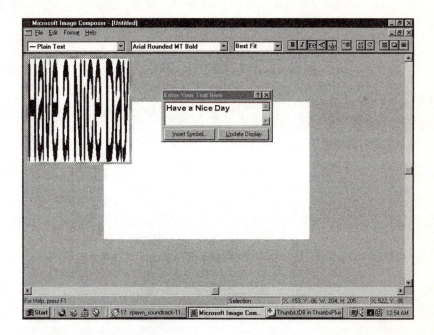

The next variety of item you can insert is Image Composer's WordArt. WordArt is essentially text that has been deformed and changed like a traditional bitmap. In order to insert WordArt you must:

1. Go to the Insert menu and choose the WordArt item.
2. Type the desired text into the entry box.
3. Distort and otherwise perturb the text by using the variety of buttons and commands.
4. When finished modifying the text, click anywhere outside the WordArt window and Image Composer will automatically import your new image.

Because you can insert nearly anything into a document, Image Composer becomes much more than just a simple Web graphics creation tool. By integrating the graphics from charts, word processing documents, and essentially any OLE compliant application you own, you can create images for presentations, Web pages, or any application you wish. ●

CHAPTER 15

Working with Sprites

Using Image Composer for text
Using Image Composer to create attractive and intricate graphical text for your Web page is a snap.

Creating geometric shapes
You can do amazing things with a rectangle. Turn geometry on its ear with Image Composer's toolkit.

Arranging your Sprites
Manipulating sprites doesn't have to be malicious when you're moving them for your composition.

The previous chapter introduced you to the basics on using Image Composer. This chapter focuses on the creation and manipulation of the fundamental elements of Image Composer graphics and sprites. An understanding of sprites is important if you plan to use Image Composer for more than an attractive doodling pad. Sprites are somewhat akin to single elements that you include in a collage. Tailoring the clipping or picture to your satisfaction, you insert the image into the collage to make a greater overall representation. Fortunately, to use sprites you aren't forced to work with sharp scissors or glue yourself to your canvas. ■

Composing Graphical Text

Likely the most common type of graphic on a Web site is graphical text. Using standard text layout within HTML usually doesn't let you get the exact effect you're looking for. Perhaps you are working on a logo, or a header for a new page. Either way, graphical text is an effective way to liven up your Web site. Using Image Composer, you can quickly create exciting logos and titles that will easily fit into your Web site. Image Composer has two methods for creating text:

- *The text tool*. Using the text tool, you can type any text you want into your composition and manipulate it. The text tool doesn't apply any special effects, but you can always do so later.
- *Word Art*. Image Composer's Word Art should be familiar to you if you've used Microsoft Word or Microsoft Publisher. Word Art lets you create text in a variety of shapes and styles.

These two different methods of graphical text are compared in Figure 15.1.

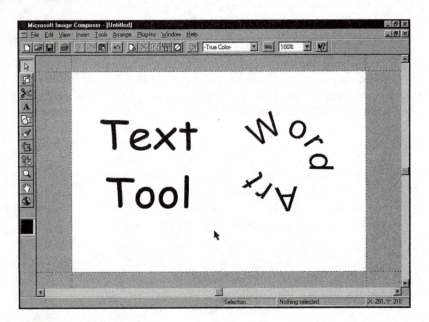

FIG. 15.1
Both methods for graphical text are useful. The text tool is best for buttons, while Word Art is best for titles and logos.

Creating text using either the Text Tool or Word Art is a simple process. Say that you need to create a title for your Web page. You are looking for something that is eye catching, but it also must compliment your entire Web site. Sitting down with Image Composer, you can easily get down to creating a striking title that will surely impress your visitors. First, let's create your title using the Text Tool. With Image Composer open to a new composition, follow these instructions:

1. Using your mouse, select the Text Tool icon from the toolbar. The Text palette appears, as shown in Figure 15.2.

Composing Graphical Text 263

FIG. 15.2
Once you select the Text Tool, the Text palette appears. Using this window you can change the font, font size, and color of your text.

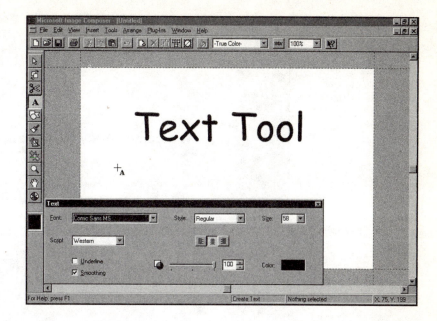

2. In the composition window, hold down the left mouse button and drag the bounding box to the size of the text area you want to create. Remember that you can always move and resize this box at any time.

3. In the Text palette, choose the font style you want your text to appear in from the Font drop box. Most fonts installed on your machine are listed alphabetically. Remember that you can always go back and change the font type at any time.

4. If you want your text to have a particular style (such as *italic* or **bold**), choose it from the Style drop box. Different fonts may not have every style available to them. Again, remember that you can always go back and change your font style at any time.

5. To determine the size of your text, choose the font size from the Size drop box. Remember that you can always go back and change this value, or manually resize your text.

6. Left click in the text region that you created in Step 2 to activate the text cursor. The blinking cursor indicates where you will be typing.

7. Enter your message into the text region. You can type as much information that you can fit into the text region. Remember that you can always go back and change what you typed. For example, Figure 15.3 shows a message entered in using the Comics Sans MS font at a 26pt size.

8. Use the text options window to change your font attributes (font face, style, size, color) until you are satisfied with your graphical text.

9. Left-click outside the text region that you drew to create your graphical text, as shown in Figure 15.4.

FIG. 15.3
Once you have entered your text, you can go back and change the font attributes to your satisfaction. You can even go back and change what you typed.

FIG. 15.4
Once your graphical text is created, you can manipulate it like you would any other sprite. You can always go back and change your text by double clicking it.

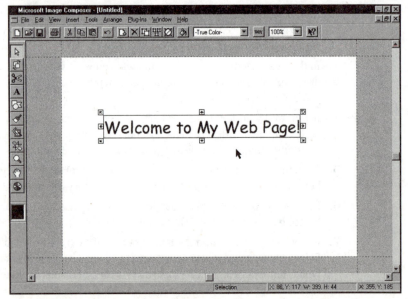

> **TIP** You can go back any time and change your text by double clicking it. This changes the graphical text back into editable text in a bounding box.

Composing Graphical Text

If you think that you want text that is a little more exciting, you can use Image Composer WordArt to create your message. To use Word Art, follow these instructions:

1. From the menu bar, choose Insert, Word Art. This opens the Word Art Editing Mode, as shown in Figure 15.5.

FIG. 15.5
Word Art Editing Mode lets you create your graphical text in a variety of shapes and styles. You also can always go back and change your text later if you change your mind.

2. In the Enter Your Text Here window, type your message. To update your display as you change your message, click the Update Display button.
3. With your text entered, move your mouse to the shape drop box on the left of the toolbar and select a shape for your text. The default shape is "plain text." This step is illustrated in Figure 15.6.
4. From the font face drop box (to the right of the shapes drop box), select the font to use for your text.
5. Beside the font face drop box is the font size drop box. Select the size you want your text to appear, or use the default of "Best Fit."
6. Use the icon buttons in the toolbar to select a style and color for your Word Art text. You can also apply shadows and borders for your Word Art.
7. Click the Update Display button in the text entry window. This updates your changes on the screen.
8. Left click outside of the bounding box for the Word Art. Your Word Art text is then created and can be freely manipulated and moved, as shown in Figure 15.7.

FIG. 15.6
The Word Art shapes drop box lets you choose a variety of shapes and styles for your text. You can choose something traditional, or something wild!

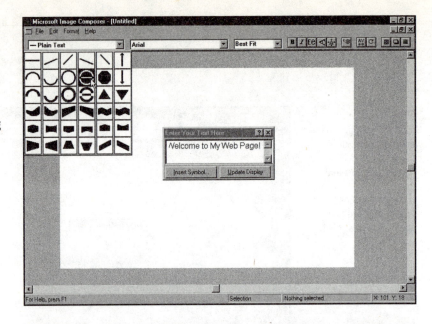

FIG. 15.7
Once your Word Art text is created, you can use it like any other sprite. You can always go back and change your Word Art by double clicking it.

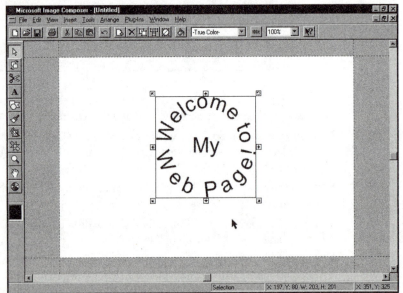

 T I P Just like text you created with the Text Tool, you can go back any time and change your Word Art text by double clicking it. This opens the Word Art Editing Mode so that you can make your changes. Keep in mind that in order to undo some Word Art editing mode changes, you may need to return to Image Composer, carry out the undo, and then return to Word Art mode.

Sizing and Rotating Your Graphical Text

Not all graphics are created equal: at least with regard to their size and style. Although creating graphical text in Image Composer is an easy effort, you may find that it doesn't always come out exactly how you want it. Thankfully, Image Composer's innate abilities for sprite manipulation come into play with your text too. If you want your text to be a different size than what you created, perhaps even skewed, you can alter your text in seconds. In addition, if you're looking to have your text appear at an angle for emphasis, Image Composer lets you do so without pause.

To resize your text, perform these few simple steps:

1. With your graphical text already prepared, left click the text to select it. A bounding box appears around your text, as shown in Figure 15.8. Each corner and side of the bounding box has an arrow to represent manipulation points.

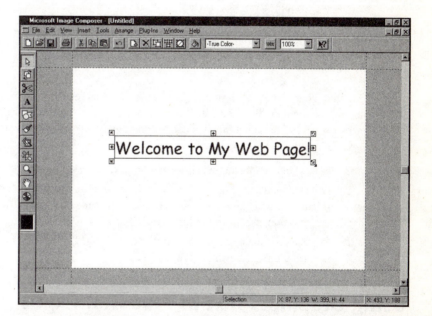

FIG. 15.8
The Bounding Box around your text tells you that it is selected. Each of the arrows around the box is a manipulation point you can use for resizing.

2. Left-button drag a manipulation point in the direction that you want to resize your text. If you move the point closer to the others, you are shrinking the text. If you move the point farther away, you are enlarging the text. You can also use these points to distort your text. As you move these points, a box is drawn to represent your text's change in position.

3. Release your mouse button from the manipulation point to confirm your changes. Your graphical text is redrawn to reflect your manipulation, as shown in Figure 15.9.

FIG. 15.9
Your text can be enlarged, shrunk, or even distorted. When you move the manipulation points, you can skew the perspective of the text. This doesn't necessarily improve readability though.

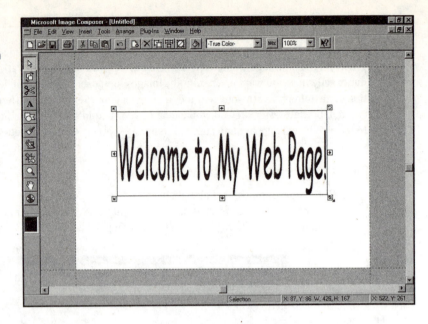

Rotating your text to a different angle is just as easy as resizing. You may have noticed the arrows on the bounding box are all the same except for one, the top right arrow. The top right arrow is curved to reflect that it is used for manipulating your text's rotation. To rotate your text, follow these steps:

1. Select your graphical text sprite with your mouse, so that the bounding box appears.
2. Left-button drag the top right arrow of the bounding box in the direction that you want to rotate your text. As you rotate your text, an outline box appears to represent the text's new position, as shown in Figure 15.10.
3. Release the mouse button to commit your changes. Your text is redrawn to reflect its new rotation, as shown in Figure 15.11.

Using Graphical Text in Your Web Pages

Using your graphical text in a Web page is identical to placing any graphic into a page. Before you can use your graphical text in the FrontPage Editor, you must save the graphic in a suitable format, such as a GIF or JPEG image. Once the graphic has been saved, you can easily place your text into a page. To use your text inside of a page, first save your text using these steps:

1. Select your text sprite so that the bounding box appears.
2. From the menu bar, choose File, Save for the Web. This opens the Save for the Web Wizard, shown in Figure 15.12. This wizard helps you prepare your graphic for use in a Web page.

Using Graphical Text in Your Web Pages | 269

FIG. 15.10
As you rotate your text, the outline box appears to show you its position. You can rotate to any angle you want, all by moving your mouse in a direction.

FIG. 15.11
Rotated text can be useful for emphasizing information or complimenting existing graphics. Make sure to use a readable font at a readable angle.

Part V
Ch 15

3. Select whether you want to save All sprites inside the composition area, or the Selected sprite or group. With your selected sprite ready, you most likely will want to save only the selected sprite. Click the Next button to proceed.

FIG. 15.12
The Save for the Web Wizard is useful for optimizing your graphic for the Web. You can easily create images for colored or tiled backgrounds too.

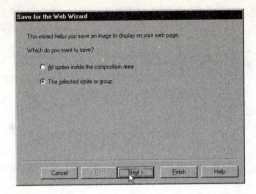

4. If your sprite has transparent areas (and it most likely does), you need to choose how Image Composer should deal with them. You can choose to Let the Web Page Background Show Through the Transparent Areas, or Fill Them With the Background Color.

5. If you specified to have the transparent areas show through, you are asked to specify whether the Web page has a solid background color (My Web Page's Background is the Following Solid Color…), or that is uses a tiled background image (My Web Page's Background is a Tiled Image). If your page uses a solid color, you can use the Color button to specify the precise color.

6. If you chose to fill the transparent areas of the image with a solid color, you are asked to choose the color by pressing the Color button.

7. Click the Next button to proceed. The next page of the Wizard differs depending on which option you chose in Step 4.

8. If you chose to leave transparent areas in your image, Image Composer automatically chooses to save your file as a GIF. The file information is summarized, as shown in Figure 15.13. By clicking the Save button you can save your graphical text for use in your Web site, and finish the wizard.

FIG. 15.13
The Save for the Web Wizard handles the complication of creating your transparent GIF. You are given a summary of the file information before saving.

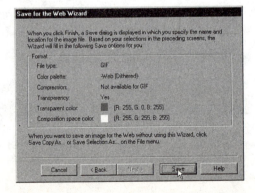

9. If you chose to use a solid color background, you are given an option screen to choose the format for your graphic, as shown in Figure 15.14. Using this screen, you can select the format for your saved image (GIF or JPEG), and the quality level. Select the format that you want to use and click the Ne<u>x</u>t button.

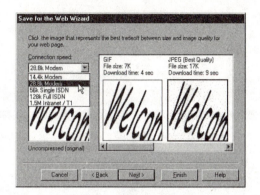

FIG. 15.14
You are given a sample of your image at different qualities and formats. You can use the <u>C</u>onnection speed drop box to determine the time required downloading the image.

10. The summary information screen appears. Click the <u>S</u>ave button to save your image.

Once you have saved your image, you can freely import your graphical text image for your Web site.

▶ For more information about importing an image into your web site and using it in the FrontPage Editor, **see** Chapter 8, "Enhancing Pages with Graphics and Multimedia," on **p. 123**.

Working with Rectangles and Ovals

Geometric shapes are an important part of graphics. You can use these shapes to create images of all sorts for your Web site. Image Composer gives you easy access to geometric shapes, such as rectangles and circles. Using the Shapes tool, you can create nearly any shape you would ever want. To use the shapes tool to create rectangles or circles, follow these steps:

1. Click the Shapes button on the toolbar to open the Shapes palette, shown in Figure 15.15.
2. Click either the rectangle or oval button, depending on which you want to create.
3. Use the Shapes palette to choose the opacity for your new shape. The higher the value (with a maximum of 100), the more opaque the shape. As a shape is more opaque, the color becomes less transparent.
4. If you want a soft, diffused edge for your shape, use the Edge slider to move closer to the Soft side. The softer the edge, the more diffuse your shape will be. This is very similar to *feathering* your image in other image manipulation programs.
5. Choose your shape's color by clicking the color box in the toolbar.
6. With your shape's attributes set to your satisfaction, drag your left button in the composition area to draw your shape. You can hold down the CTRL or the SHIFT button to constrain your shape's aspect ratio. When you are satisfied with your shape, release your mouse button.

FIG. 15.15
The Shapes palette lets you choose the type of shape you want to create. You can also control the fill color, the line width, and the opacity.

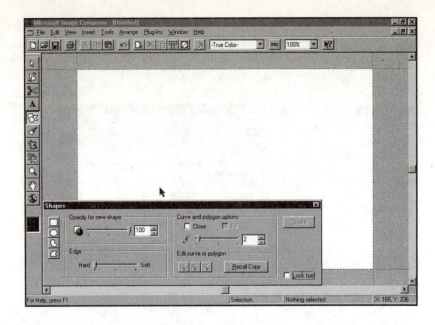

7. Click the Create button in the Shapes palette to render your shape sprite in your composition, as shown in Figure 15.16.

FIG. 15.16
Once you hit the Create button, Image Composer renders your shape in your composition. The shape then becomes a sprite that you can freely manipulate.

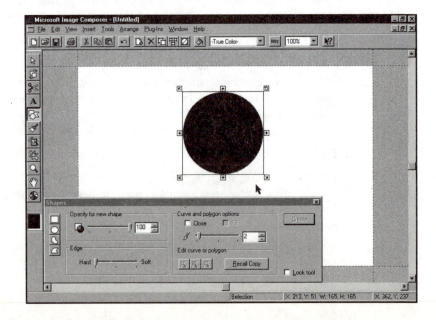

Using Curves in Images

A curve is a line... and more. Curves, also called splines, can include sprites with wavy or rounded edges. Image Composer's curves are a flexible and utilitarian tool for creating all kinds of shapes. You can set the width of a curve, edit nodal points within it, and elect to fill the curve or leave it open. Figure 15.17 shows one type of curve—a wavy line.

FIG. 15.17
Curves can be used to create nearly any shape. You'll most likely use them for straight and irregular lines, or odd shapes.

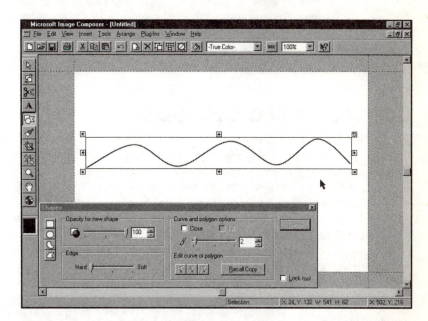

To create a curve in your image, follow these simple steps:

1. Click the Shapes button on the toolbar to open the Shapes palette.
2. Click the Curve button on the Shapes palette to activate it.
3. If you want to create an open curve, make sure that the Close checkbox is not selected. If you do want the curve to be closed (creating a solid shape), select the checkbox.
4. Use the Line Width slider (or spin control) to select the width of your curve's lines. The lower the number that you enter, the thinner your curve's lines will be.
5. Use the Shapes palette to choose the opacity for your new curved shape. The higher the value (with a maximum of 100), the more opaque the shape. As a shape is more opaque, the color becomes less transparent.
6. If you want a soft, diffused edge for your curve, use the Edge slider to move closer to the Soft side. The softer the edge, the more diffuse your curve's lines will be. This is very similar to *feathering* your image in other image manipulation programs.
7. Choose your curve's color by clicking the color box in the toolbar.

8. With your curve's attributes set to your satisfaction, begin creating your curve by clicking in the composition area where you want your spline to begin.
9. Continue to create your curve by clicking in the composition area in the path you want your curve to follow. Each point that you click becomes a *node* in your spline's path.
10. You can modify your curve's points by clicking the Move points button in the Shapes palette. By doing so, you can select points in your curve and drag them to a different position. You can also use the Add points and Delete points buttons to alter your curve's shape before you are done.
11. When you are satisfied with your shape, click the Create button in the Shapes palette to render your curve.

Odd Shapes and Zigzag Lines

The Polygon tool can be used to create odd shapes and zigzag lines through the same process as the Curve tool for splines. In fact, the Polygon tool and the Curve tool are identical in usage. The main difference between the Polygon tool and the Curve tool is how Image Composer handles the nodal points. For curves, Image Composer rounds each line and links the points together to create a smooth flowing curve (a spline). For polygons, Image Composer takes a different approach. Image Composer treats a polygon's nodal points as absolute points for connecting lines, much like a connect-the-dots game. Each point has a line connecting it to one another, without any curves or smoothness to the lines. A sample polygon that makes up a zigzag line is shown in Figure 15.18.

FIG. 15.18
Polygons can be used to create peculiar shapes or zigzag lines. Notice how polygons don't have the smooth curvature to lines that curves and splines do.

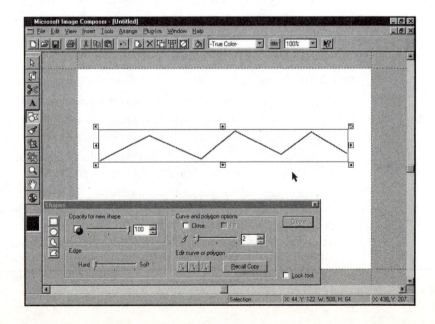

Moving Sprites Forward and Back

Once you have your sprites created to your satisfaction, you undoubtedly will need to move them into a pleasing arrangement. Sprites can not only be moved horizontally and vertically on your screen, but also forward and backward. Sprites can be layered on top of one another, like sheets of paper, to create the image that you want. Overlapping sprites can prevent sections from being visible in the composition. Moving your sprites forward and back is a simple effort of right-clicking the sprite and choosing how you want to move it. There are four options:

- *Bring to Front*. This moves the selected sprite to the very top of the composition, in front of all other sprites.
- *Send to Back*. When you want to move a sprite to the very bottom of the composition, behind all other sprites, choose this option.
- *Bring Forward*. If you only need to move your sprite up once in the composition, above one other sprite, this option is what you should choose.
- *Send Backward*. When you want to move the sprite down once in the composition, behind another sprite, this option is the appropriate choice.

TIP You can freely move your sprites forward and backward as much as you need. Coupled with a sprite's opacity, you can use the forward and backward movement to create interesting arrangements and effects.

Aligning Sprites

There are times that you may need to align sprites together. Perhaps you have two sprites that need to have their left edges aligned the same, or you want the two sprites centered together. Image Composer makes alignment of sprites easy with the Arrange palette. To align your sprites, first click the Arrange button in the toolbar. This opens the Arrange palette, shown in Figure 15.19.

To begin aligning your sprites, select the appropriate sprites. The Arrange palette gives you a series of buttons that you can use to align your sprites. You may choose to align the tops or bottoms of sprites (even by the left or right corner), the sides of the sprites, or the centering of the selected sprites. Figure 15.20 shows the use of alignment to perfectly center two sprites.

Grouping Sprites Together

Often you will have a number of sprites that make up one element in your composition. When you need to move or manipulate these sprites independently, it can grow tiresome and frustrating. Thankfully, Image Composer lets you "glue" sprites together and manipulate them as a whole. Alternatively, you can also "unglue" grouped sprites at any time in the future. To group a series of sprites, select them by holding down the SHIFT key and clicking each sprite. Right click over the top of the selected sprites and choose Group. This binds the sprites together into one bounding box that you can use for manipulation. To break up a group of sprites, select the grouped sprites bounding box and right-click, then choose Ungroup.

FIG. 15.19
The Arrange palette is used to manipulate your sprite's position. You can align sprites and group them. You can even use the palette for moving them forward and backward.

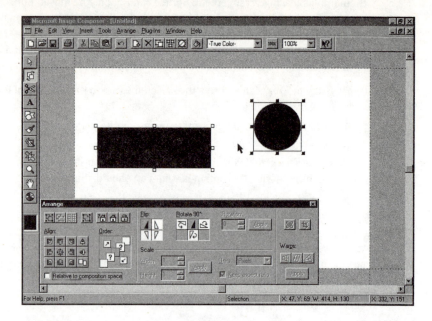

FIG. 15.20
Alignment is a powerful tool for creating graphics. In this example, two sprites have been centered horizontally. You can even center the sprites vertically, if you needed.

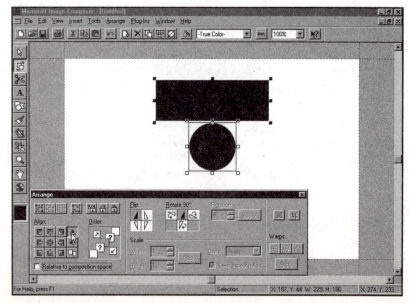

TIP You can also use the Arrange palette to group and ungroup sprites.

Flattening Sprites

After you have spent some time arranging and grouping sprites, you may want to permanently group them together. Image Composer lets you *flatten* grouped sprites together to create one sprite. Once you flatten grouped sprites together, they cannot be ungrouped. To flatten grouped sprites, right-click the group and choose Flatten Selection.

> **CAUTION**
> Remember! Once grouped or selected sprites have been flattened, you can't go back! Always leave flattening to the last step of creating your image.

Cropping, Resizing, and Rotating Sprites

There comes a time in every sprite's life when cropping, resizing, and rotating is needed. When you have created a sprite that needs a few changes to its size or position, you can use Image Composer's Arrange palette to do the job. The Arrange palette has controls and tools for controlling the size and rotation of your sprite. You can also resize or rotate your sprite by manipulating the sprite's bounding box. Cropping, resizing, and rotating all require that you have a selected sprite ready. Not all of these tools work on grouped sprites (you'll need to flatten them first).

If you have regions of a selected sprite that you want to "cut out," you can crop them by following these steps:

1. If the Arrange palette is not already open, click the Arrange button in the toolbar to open it. Select the Crop/Extend button.
2. Grab a manipulation handle on the sprite's bounding box and resize the box to display only the areas of the sprite that you want to keep. Any areas outside of the box will be cropped off.
3. Click the sprite once to confirm your changes. The display is updated to reflect your newly cropped sprite.

> **CAUTION**
> Any cropping you do on a sprite is permanent. You cannot bring back regions of your sprite that you have had cropped off unless you *immediately* choose the Edit | Undo (CTRL+Z) option.

You can also use the Crop/Extend tool to extend the space that your sprite takes up. Anything you have already cropped will not return, but you can use it to create more white space for your sprite.

To resize your sprite, select the sprite in the composition area. Using your mouse, drag a manipulation point (or handle) in the direction that you want to resize your sprite. You can hold down the SHIFT key to resize the sprite while retaining its aspect ratio. If you want to rotate your sprite, drag the top left manipulation point on the bounding box in the direction that you want to rotate. More information on resizing and rotating your sprites is given earlier in this chapter, in the "Sizing and Rotating Your Graphical Text" section.

Setting a Sprite's Home Position

If you wish to fix a set location in the composition area for a sprite, select the sprite and click the Home button—the one that looks like a house in the Arrange palette. Once you set a home location for your sprite, then wherever you have moved it, you can click the Return to Home Position button on the Arrange palette to zip the sprite back to its home. If you don't want the sprite moved once you have set its home position, you can click the Lock Position button on the Arrange palette. This button acts as a toggle, so clicking it again unlocks the sprite and lets you move it freely.

CHAPTER 16

Using Effects for Maximum Impact

Patterns and fills
If you've got a lot of screen real estate to fill, one of the better ways to do so is using Image Composer's Pattern features.

Modifying Sprites
Sprites on their own can be boring; luckily, you have several tools at your disposal to liven them up.

Basic tools
If you've mastered the traditional tools of paintbrush, pencil and airbrush, you'll be pleased to find out that Image Composer includes computer analogs of these tools that improve upon the originals.

The first thing most people notice about graphics programs isn't an easy interface or powerful basic functions, but rather what sort of gadgets they can use. Usually this involves warping an image, turning it inside out, or making it into a bas relief. Unfortunately, this tendency all too often leads to effects-driven graphics, with no real thought to what might be the best effects to use. Usually, everything but the kitchen sink is thrown into generating a new graphic, as people play with various filters and effects.

Microsoft Image Composer has its share of bells and whistles, and they're very powerful ones. From various fill types to sketch effects, you can spice up your graphics with an impressive array of effects.

Using Special Patterns

Almost all of the techniques you'll learn in this chapter will use the Effects tool. If you click the Effects button to bring up the related palette, you'll be presented with a bewildering array of choices. In order to narrow the field of choices, click the Category list selection box and choose "Patterns." This will display the effects related to patterns, as shown in Figure 16.1.

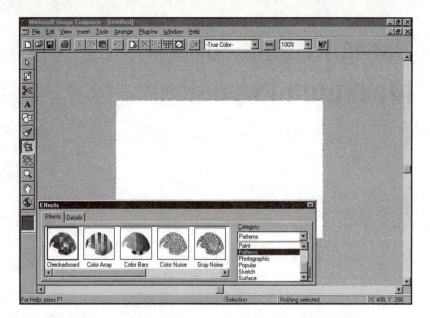

FIG. 16.1
By using the Category selection box, you can narrow your choice of Effects filters into easily understood sections.

Note the friendly parrot above each effect title. This is an indicator of what that effect will do for you. For example, the Stripes effect shows the parrot with a series of horizontal bars across the image. These previews are by no means absolute, but they can be useful in judging which effects you want to use on your masterpiece.

When you get right down to it, a pattern effect is simply a graphic that's applied to your existing sprite. In the case of the Color Bars effect, it's a television test pattern. The effect is laid on top of whatever background you may have for the sprite. The reason you'd want this is to fill in areas in your composition that would otherwise be "dead." While a television test pattern may be a little extreme, a soothing grayscale could easily become your next background. In order to apply a patterned fill, you must:

1. Select the sprite you want to fill.
2. Click the Effects button on the left-hand toolbar.
3. From the Category pick list, select the Pattern option.
4. In the resulting palette, click the effect you desire.
5. Click the Apply button in the Effects palette.
6. If you're unhappy with the results, hit Ctrl+Z to undo and start all over again.

These fill types aren't absolute; you have some control over them. The most important aspect you can modify is the opacity of the pattern effect; in other words, how transparent your fill is over your existing sprite. If you choose an opacity of 100 percent for a certain effect, your background sprite won't show through at all except in transparent areas (in the case of a checkerboard, the "white" squares). If you choose an opacity of 0 percent, you won't see the applied effect at all. This control is important because it lets you control the intensity of the effect. A glaring, 100 percent-opacity checkerboard might be considered garish by some, but a subtle, 40 percent checkerboard might be something else entirely.

In order to change the opacity, you need to use the Details tab of any of the Pattern effects. You can get there by tabbing your way through the palette or simply clicking the tab itself. The opacity is regulated by a slider control marked by a white square with a blue circle in its lower-right corner. You can drag the control, use the up and down arrows, or simply type in the new value to set the opacity of that effect.

On some Pattern effects, there are other controls available from the Details tab. These effects are invariably the ones that use generated patterns, as opposed to premade ones. An example of a generated pattern is the checkerboard, since you can control the size and distribution of the spaces. In the checkerboard's Detail pane, you can set the size of each square in the pattern, and you can even create rectangular checks. An example of a premade effect is the Color Bars; the graphic itself is an existing image that is applied to your sprite. The only thing you can control about the effect is the opacity.

Changing Colors in Patterns and Fills

There's more to Pattern effects than just that, of course. You can also control which colors are used by certain effects. Since most of the pattern effects are color gradients in the first place, there's no point in trying to set which colors they use. However, the simpler, "constructed" effects are a different matter. There are only two Pattern effects for which you can control the color directly: the checkerboard and stripes effects. However, there is another command you can influence the same way.

If you want to simply fill a sprite with a single color, you can choose the Fill function. Its operation is quite simple; you select a sprite and click the Fill icon (the paint bucket) on the top toolbar. This fills in the selected sprite with whatever color you've chosen. The checkerboard and stripes effects work similarly. All that remains is for you to choose the color:

1. Click the Color Swatch button, found at the very bottom of the left-hand toolbar, to bring up the Color Picker.
2. From the Color Picker, select the color you want to use in your effect or fill.
3. Execute your effect or fill as normal, and note how your new color is used.

The Color Picker is shown in Figure 16.2. The Fill tool itself is quite important, since it allows you to color an entire sprite quickly and efficiently. When you combine it with the transparency control available to the various Pattern effects, you can create quite a few interesting backgrounds and source images.

FIG. 16.2
The Color Picker is a powerful tool that lets you select colors quickly and precisely. If you want, you can input specific RGB/HSV values, or simply use the Eyedropper to pick up an existing color.

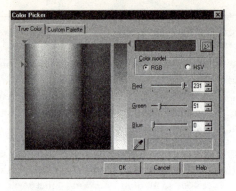

Applying Gradient Fills

Another important method of filling in blank space is using a gradient fill. This is not the same as the traditional Color Array or Hue effects found in the Patterns slot, but rather an effect that grants you more control over the actual colors used. To display the gradient effects, you need to use the Category pick list found in the Effects palette, and from there choose the Gradient option. You might feel cheated when only one effect appears in the palette, but the Square Gradient effect is a powerful one.

In order to observe the true power of the Square Gradient, you need to click the Details pane to get at the inner workings of the effect. When you do, you should see a display similar to Figure 16.3. From the Details tab, you can control the composition of your gradient fill: the colors, direction, and general shape.

FIG. 16.3
It's surprisingly easy to control gradients with Image Composer's Square Gradient effect, and in many ways it's more art than craft. If you create an especially good gradient, you can save it for later retrieval.

The gradiated square is the preview of what your gradient fill will look like. At each corner you should see a small box with a single color in it. It's from these four colors that your gradient is constructed. The default configuration, in counterclockwise order, is Red, Black, Blue, and Green. This creates a gradient that encompasses all of the traditional colors in the visible spectrum. However, you can do more with the gradient tool.

> **CAUTION**
> Gradients are certainly nice to look at, and are an invaluable tool to graphic designers everywhere. You should be wary, though, because they rarely work that well on the World Wide Web, especially the all-encompassing gradients that incorporate most of the visible spectrum. Because the majority of computers browsing the World Wide Web only display 256 colors simultaneously, your gradient-based picture may end up looking very poor indeed. You should always preview your images in the various Web palettes before deciding to use a gradient fill on them.

The four squares of color are an ingenious and intuitive means of constructing a gradient. They give you near-total control over what eventually appears on the screen. If you have four different colors at each corner, your gradient will look a bit confused, especially within a rectangular space. However, if the top two squares are the same color, and the bottom two squares are also identical to each other, then you have a gradient that flows from top to bottom, running smoothly from one color to the other. You can achieve a similar effect by having two of one color on the left side and two of another color on the right. By extension, you can create spotlight effects by having a single square of white in one corner, with the rest black. The possibilities are many and varied, and entirely up to you.

If you find that you're stumped creatively, you can draw upon the many gradients already in place by clicking the pick list next to the disk icon. With these you can load, save, and delete gradients, including the ones you make on your own. When creating your own vistas, the gradient can be useful for defining the sunset tones of the sky, or the gray shades of a rocky beach, whatever you decide.

Applying a Texture Transfer

There are many ways of applying one sprite's attributes to another, and all of them fall under the Texture Transfer tool. Despite its name, the Texture Transfer tool is not solely responsible for texture effects; in fact, it has very little to do with them. Instead, its specialty is in sharing effects between sprites, taking one sprite's appearance and applying it to another, in several specialized ways.

In the previous version of Image Composer, most of the effects you would find within the Texture Transfer tool could be found within the Effects palette. Now, however, effects such as Sprite to Sprite Fill and various others have been encapsulated within Texture Transfer.

There are nine different ways to influence one sprite's behavior upon another, and each and every one of them has a different net result. However, their method of application is usually identical. In order to effect a texture transfer you must:

1. Select the sprite you want to be your source.
2. Multiple-select a destination sprite by Shift-clicking it. This keeps the two sprites selected simultaneously.

3. Click the Texture Transfer button to bring up the appropriate palette.
4. Choose a Texture Transfer option, and configure it depending on what options appear in the palette.
5. Click Apply.

> **CAUTION**
>
> It's extremely important that you get your source and destination sprites sorted before you apply the effect. The source sprite is always the first you select, and the destination is always the second. You can differentiate them by the fact that your source sprite will have opaque handles on its corners, and your destination sprite will have transparent ones.

The effects of the various Texture Transfers are many, but each of them has an important function to fulfill, as outlined in Table 16.1.

Table 16.1. Texture Transfer Effects

Title	Effect
Glue	Will map all of the opaque pixels from the source sprite onto the destination sprite where the two overlap.
Map Color	Will map the opaque color values of the source sprite onto the destination sprite where the two overlap.
Map Intensity	Will map the color intensity of the source sprite onto the destination sprite where the two overlap. The actual colors of the destination sprite will not change, just their intensity level.
Map Saturation	Will map the intensity levels of the source sprite onto the destination sprite's saturation levels where the two overlap.
Map Transparency	Will map the intensity levels of the source sprite onto the destination sprite's transparency levels where the two overlap.
Snip	Cuts the shape of the source sprite out of the destination sprite where the two overlap, regardless of the source's color or intensity.
Tile	Copies multiple editions of the source sprite onto the destination sprite.
Transfer Full	Copies the entire source sprite over the destination sprite, where the two overlap. Transparent space in the source sprite is rendered as white upon the destination.
Transfer Shape	Copies the opaque pixels of the source sprite over the destination sprite's where the two overlap. The transparent pixels in the destination sprite are not affected.

Knowing all that may do you some good, but how do you know when to use certain transfer effects over others? It depends wholly on the effect you're seeking. If you want to repeat a sprite a number of times over another sprite, then you'd obviously want to use the Tile effect. If you wanted to copy the outline of one sprite over another, you'd use the Snip effect. Lastly, if you wanted to use a certain sprite but were dissatisfied with the intensity or saturation of the colors, you could use Map Intensity or Map Saturation to transfer the sprite to a different one with a more compatible color scheme. The limitations are left entirely up to you. The texture transfer tool is especially valuable for creating images that may eventually have to be sectioned up for use on the World Wide Web, as it grants you a degree of control over sprite interaction that you wouldn't have in a traditional bitmap-based program.

Outlining Sprites

You are working within an obviously two-dimensional space within Image Composer, but that doesn't have to limit you to a dimensional look. You can use the various tools within the program to help you differentiate one object's perspective from another, or, you can use the Outlining effects to do it for you. Once again you'll be returning to the familiar Effects palette, however this time you'll want to choose Outline from the Category pick list.

The advantages of outlining sprites are obvious; it makes them stand out where they might normally be lost in the clutter of other objects. An outline adds emphasis to one particular item, and with the Outlining effects you have lots of choice about how your outlining is accomplished.

The Drop Shadow effect is the most powerful and complex of them all, seeing as it in many mimics the effect of light striking your sprite. The Drop Shadow creates a shadow behind your sprite, granting it and its surroundings an illusion of depth. Drop shadows are especially useful on text areas and menu buttons, as they create a much more distinct "real world" effect, especially when used for Web graphics.

The strength of the Drop Shadow effect lay in its flexibility. You can define a shadow from any angle, of any strength, of any color. This powerful functionality is controlled from the Drop Shadow Details tab, displayed in Figure 16.4.

FIG. 16.4
The Drop Shadow Details tab controls every aspect you would want or need when defining the scope of the effect.

The Angle control determines what angle the shadow falls from the sprite. It can be set by either clicking one of the eight cardinal directions or by entering your own value into the entry box. The Distance slider control determines how long the shadow is by setting how far away from the sprite the light source lay. The Color box lets you decide which color the shadow should be, although default black is usually the safest choice. The familiar opacity control can also be found on the Details tab, which determines how distinct or subtle the shadow itself is in terms of its intensity. Lastly, comes the Softness control, which determines how "fuzzy" the edge of the shadow is. A hard edge will be obviously sharper than a soft edge, which is somewhat feathered. All of these controls can give your potential drop shadow several different possibilities, all of them effective.

After the Drop Shadow comes the Edge effect, which is not nearly so complex. The Edge effect simply draws a line of variable width and color around the opaque edges of the selected sprite. You can control the thickness, color, and opacity of the line from the Details tab. The Edge Only effect operates on a similar principle with the same controls, only in this case it eradicates everything *but* the edge of a particular sprite. This preserves the overall shape of the sprite, but leaves the inside blank, outlined by a line whose width, color, and opacity can be controlled by you.

The Recess and Relief effects don't have any configurable options, since their operation is so straightforward. The Recess effect creates the illusion that the sprite has been inset into some other material, like a wax seal. The Relief effect is quite the opposite, creating the illusion that the sprite is slightly raised from whatever surface it lay upon, like raised lettering. Both of these are potent pseudo-3D effects that give your images a subtle flair.

Filtering Sprites

As you may have noticed, there are far more effects contained within the Effects palette than can be classified within the simple categories of Patterns, Gradients, and Outlines. Most of these effects are intended for no specific use beyond enhancing your images as you desire, and because of this, they have been created to be as flexible as possible.

Image Composer 1.5 has many more effects options than its predecessor did, so many that it's impossible to cover them all in a book meant primarily for FrontPage 98. However, these effects have been efficiently grouped into several sub-categories, which all have similar attributes, and can be used in the same ways. All of these sections are accessible via the Categories pick list on the Effects palette.

The Arts and Crafts effects are composed of some of the less subtle changes, those that rely on different media. For example, the Stained Glass effect attempts to emulate an image in a cathedral as opposed to on your computer screen. The Sandpaper effect creates the illusion of a harsh background material, as do the Mosaic and Cutout effects. The important thing to remember with all of the Arts and Crafts effects, and indeed, all the effects, is what your current color is. The Flocking effect, for example, will make the chosen sprite look like it's been upholstered in flocked velvet, but in the color currently selected in the Color Picker. The controls within the Details tab are important here too, as they determine the attributes of the various media the Arts and Crafts effects emulate.

Next come the Color Enhancement effects. These are your rough and ready color adjustment tools, when you don't feel like fooling around with the Color Tuner. There are five different Color Enhancement effects, but the most important one is the Transparency effect. With this you can control the overall transparency of a sprite, instead of just one effect you're about to apply to it. You can also add overtones of a certain color to the entire sprite with the Dye effect, change the whole thing with the Tint function, or make it all gray with the Grayscale effect. Lastly, you can fill the entire bounding box one color with the Color Bounding Box effect.

After that come the more interesting effects, those that seriously warp and perturb the image. These are grouped under the Distort category, and all of them operate under simple mathematical procedures of rearranging the pixels within a sprite based on a formula. For those not familiar with filtering terminology, the preview parrot is invaluable. Here the little fellow gets Bulged, Fisheyed, Mesad, Radial Swept, and much more, all in the name of previews. The distort functions all operate along the same lines, and the Details tab is once more home to the all-important controls which determine the amplitude of the distortion.

Passing over the Gradient and Outlines effects next come the Paint effects. These were all designed to emulate the look of a particular type of brush, and are labeled to match. The Details tab in these cases allow you to control how detailed or coarse an emulation the program carries out. Of particular use in image manipulation are the Watercolor and Drybrush effects, since both are a particularly faithful emulation. However, the use of Paint effects is not for every picture. Many people think that they can simply slap an effect on top of an existing picture and that this changes it considerably. Most effects are meant to be used subtly, and not as the mainstays of a particular picture's impact.

Skipping over the Patterns effect, next on the list comes the Photographic effects. These all concern themselves with effects that you would normally associate with a camera, such as Blur, Sharpen, and Negative. However, you can also apply a Halftone Screen effect, or a Neon Glow. Mostly, the Photographic effects exist either to help you edit actual photographs, or create photographic situations in your compositions. For example, if you have some edges that look too blurry you can Sharpen them, or, if they are too sharp, you can Blur them. Most of these effects are designed to add realism to your photo-realistic images, but you can also use them to add artful effects of your own to an existing piece. The judicious application of the Film Grain effect can age a photo, and the Diffuse Glow effect can give compositions a bit of eerie backlighting. Once again, the Transparency effect in included, but is no different from the effect found in the Color Enhancement effects.

Next come the Popular effects. All of these effects exist in other categories, but are grouped together here for convenience's sake. They include Blur, Drop Shadow, Emboss, Rough Textures, and Sharpen. This is essentially a mini-toolkit of the various effects, gathered together for quick and dirty access.

After the Popular effects come the Sketch effects, dealing entirely with the artistic world. Like the Paint effects, these effects deal with traditional art forms, but instead focus on pencil, pen, charcoal, and other tools. There are 11 different effects, ranging in diversity from Pencil Crayon to Chalk and Charcoal to Technical Pen. Like the Paint effects, the Details tab lets you control the precision or coarseness of the particular tool's emulation. Also like the Paint effects, what color you have selected is of paramount importance. For example in the Chalk and Charcoal effect, the "chalk" is whatever color you have selected in the Color Picker. This isn't to say that whatever colors contained within the sprite are academic, but most of the effects will use your selected color as the primary color when rendering the new sprite.

Lastly come the Surface effects. These are like the Arts and Crafts effects in that they change the appearance of the sprite's underlying media. However, the Surface effects differ in the fact that they represent non-traditional mediums. The Broken Tile, Chrome, Cracked Varnish and Plastic Wrap effects all fall under the purview of Surface effects. The primary focus behind Surface effects is to change the entire appearance of the sprite, instead of merely modify it as other effects do. You can think of the Surface effects as a sort of powerful extension of the Pattern and Gradient Fill effects, as they are all three suitable for filling large areas with subtle textures.

> **CAUTION**
>
> All of these effects can have a beneficial effect on your composition. However, you should be careful not to overuse them, especially in conjunction with one another. Effects can make an image that much more powerful and effective, but they can also make that same image blurry and impossible to discern. The boundary is obviously a fluid one, but your primary concern should always be coherence and readability (especially with graphical text).

Table 16.2 Basic Summary of Filter Groups

Group Name	Design Philosophy	Example Filters
Arts and Crafts	Home-made graphics	Stained Glass, Sandpaper, Mosaic, Cutout, Flocking
Color Enhancement	All the color you need	Transparency, Dye, Tint, Grayscale, Color Bounding Box
Distortion	Like putting a magnet on your screen	Bulge, Mesa, Fisheye, Radial Sweep
Paint Effects	A Great Master in every computer	Watercolor, Drybrush, Sumi-e
Photographic	Your own home dark room	Blur, Sharpen, Negative, Halftone Screen, Neon Glow, Film Grain, Diffuse Glow
Popular Effects	All your favorites from the other palettes	Blur, Drop Shadow, Emboss, Rough Texture, Sharpen
Sketch Effects	Pen and paper, and more...	Pencil Crayon, Chalk and Charcoal, Technical Pen

Group Name	Design Philosophy	Example Filters
Surface Effects	Fun with textures	Broken Tile, Chrome, Cracked Varnish, Plastic Wrap

Using Color Tuning to Enhance Your Sprites

When dealing with photographs, the situation is rarely ideal. There are still several obstacles to overcome with transferring the image from camera to computer, and none of them guarantee that the photographer actually took a good picture. Luckily, you can Color Tuning to help you adjust and balance photos that have gone awry. It can also help you get just the right colors out of your latest composition.

The Color Tuner, pictured in Figure 16.5, is a powerful tool that lets you adjust the very basis of color within the sprite. Normally, you probably won't need the Color Tuner if you're creating your own images from scratch. However, if you need to deal with photos from external sources, it can be an invaluable tool.

FIG. 16.5
You can use the Color Tuner to do more than just brighten and darken a picture; you can control nearly every aspect of a sprite's color disbursement.

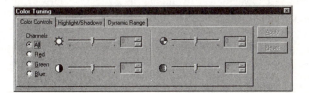

The Color Tuner is composed of three primary tabs, each with a different responsibility. The first, pictured above in Figure 16.5, controls the general color information for the sprite. If you want to adjust the colors one way or another, you drag the sliders around. If you want to adjust only one aspect of the sprite's color (Red, Green, or Blue) then you click one of the radio buttons under the Channels label. The first slider deals with the sprite's brightness level, essentially how much light is in the picture. The second slider deals with contrast, how white the whites and black the blacks. The third control determines the Hue within the image. The last slider control determines the Intensity, or how bright a particular color is within its range.

The second tab controls the depths of the shadows and brightness of the highlights. This is essentially a specialized contrast control, that lets you determine how certain colors appear within very specific ranges. This is especially useful if you want a particular range of intensity to stand more than another.

The third tab controls the range of color, from lightest to darkest. From here you can set what color is the darkest within your image, and which is the lightest. This is especially useful for black and white images that you are trying to apply a median "black" to. Anything that falls below the minimum darkness for that sprite is changed to the darkest intensity you have set. The same is true in reverse for the lightest colors.

Using Warp Transformations to Enhance Your Sprites

There apparently is no end to the ways you can transfigure your sprites with, and Warps are just another method to be put into your Image Composer tool box. Warps essentially let you change the geometric dimensions of your sprite in odd and interesting ways, to create illusions of perspective, and to just stretch them out. In order to do any warping you have to do the following:

1. Select the sprite to be warped.
2. Click the Arrange button to bring up the Arrange palette.
3. On the Arrange palette click one of the three Warp types.
4. Drag and stretch the sprite to your satisfaction, changing Warp types if need be.
5. Click Apply to enact the change on your sprite.

The Warp tool is a powerful way to change the size and shape of your sprite quickly and intuitively, as opposed to cropping and scaling. Plus, several of the Warp effects can't be achieved any other way since they work on the actual sprite's borders, and not just the pixels within. You can emulate the look Warps can achieve by using some of the Distortion effects, but you wouldn't be able to actually change the sprite the way a true Warp can.

There are three different Warp types to choose from on the Arrange palette, pictured in Figure 16.6. Each has a particular specialty of use.

FIG. 16.6
Warps can be invaluable for creating images quickly, when you need them to fit into a particular space.

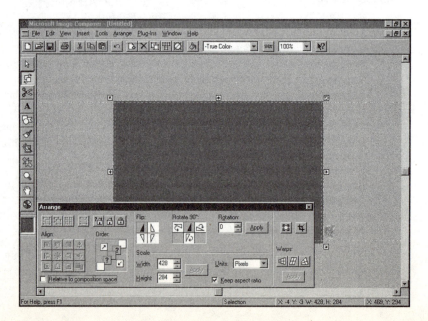

The first Warp type available to you is the Perspective Warp. This allows you to mimic the effects of perspective and the illusion of distance. If have a sprite of a building, and want it to loom tall, use the Perspective Warp to shrink the top and make it look far away. The use of exaggerated perspective can be quite useful in distinguishing certain objects, especially if you can get away with things being ridiculously out of perspective.

The second Warp type is the Skew Warp. This lets "lean" on a particular sprite, until it looks as if it had been blown around by an exacting wind storm. This also lets you stretch the borders along their axes, resulting in a particularly elongated look. This Warp is invaluable if you're trying to get a squarish image to map to a 3-D object such as a cube. Using the Skew Warp, you can stretch each object to reflect exactly each face of the cube.

The Bilinear Warp is similar to the Skew Warp, except that it's more flexible. In the Skew Warp you were forced to adhere to the one to one relationship of the distortion—for every pixel you stretched one side, the other side would go one pixel in the opposite direction. The Bilinear Warp lets you stretch and mangle corners of a sprite independently of each other. This is an incredible degree of control, but it comes at a price; most of the things stretched and mauled out of shape by the Bilinear Warp look pretty ugly. The main role the Bilinear Warp plays is as a step in a process; first Warp, *then* apply a Surface effect, or something similar.

Using the Paintbrush, Airbrush, and Pencil

Image Composer's paintbrush is an incredibly flexible tool, and is in no way limited to the same roles that traditional sticks of wood with hair on them are. The paintbrush itself is controlled by the Paint palette, from which you can control a brush's size, stroke density, hardness, and opacity. By the judicious application of these controls you can create an incredible variety of brush strokes and compositions, all within one tool.

> **NOTE** It's important to remember with any of the tools on the Paint palette that none of them can create independently. If you were to select the Paint palette and try to start painting, you would be unable to, because there's no sprite for you to paint *on*. There is no default background or "paper" within Image Composer; you need to create it all from scratch in the form of a new sprite.

The power of the paintbrush is increased by the fact that you can load and save your own brush creations, letting you keep the equivalent of your favorite #2 Sable on hand at all times. The important thing to remember when using the paintbrush is how configurable it is. If you find something that you dislike or is wrong for your composition, odds are you can change it.

The airbrush and pencil tools react much the same way, with the same degree of flexibility. However, the airbrush's scope is much larger, and thanks to the configurability of brush heads, can almost be used interchangeably with the paintbrush. You can apply diffuse, large area brushes to the paintbrush just as easily as you can apply concentrated, smaller brushes to the airbrush. This is also true of the Pencil tool, which is primarily intended for creating anti-aliased lines. If you have a series of lines, use the pencil. If you have large areas of color, or subtle highlights, use the airbrush. If you have detail work, use the paintbrush.

Using the Smear and Impression tools

The other tools in the Paint palette are just as powerful as the paintbrush, but far more varied in their use. However, the rest all deal with modifying an existing patch of image, instead of creating or painting over like the paintbrush and its associated ilk. The Smear tool replicates the effect of a finger being dragged over wet paint; the size and nature of the finger are controlled by you within the Paint palette. Smudging can create some interesting effects, especially if you want to imply motion or lack of focus within a specialized area.

The Impression tool duplicates the effects of the great Impressionist painters, by effectively blurring sections of the background while still maintaining the same level of color intensity. You can use this effect to great use in your images, especially if you have an artistic bent or want to "Impressionize" some photos.

Using the Eraser and Tinting Effects

The Eraser obviously lets you erase portions of a sprite, but what makes it a cunning tool is how much control you have over that erasing. You can set the Eraser's opacity to whatever level you please, which can lead to some very artful effects in translucency and layering. The Eraser also serves as a rough and ready transparency tool, since everything it erases then becomes transparent. The Eraser can be configured to the same extent that the paintbrush can, allowing for some very subtle transparency effects as well.

The Color Tuner is certainly very powerful, and allows you to set just about every color control possible for a sprite. However, it is somewhat intrusive and theory-heavy. If you have simpler demands, or simply want to affect one part of a sprite, then there are four tools in the Paint palette for you.

The strength of these tools over the traditional Color Tuner is the fact that their use is relative—you can Colorize a certain segment of an image using the paintbrush interface, and then decide it needs a bit more. It also prevents you from doing mathematics trying to get color values to add up exactly, and lets you eyeball everything as you do it.

The first tool is the Colorize tool. It essentially adds whatever color you have selected to whatever you paint over. It's different from the paintbrush tool in that it doesn't actually change the intensity of the pixels, only their hue. If you want to make your red car blue, or change a night sky from blue to green, then the Colorize tool is the way to go.

The second utility is the Burn/Dodge tool. Basically, this tool acts under the photographic principle that more light equals darker pictures. If you are "burning" an image, it slowly becomes darker, and if you are "dodging" it, it slowly becomes lighter. This can be particularly handy for emphasizing certain areas of a sprite, or correcting exposure problems in a poorly-taken photo.

The third color correction tool deals with Contrast. The Contrast tool lets you adjust the contrast of an area within the confines of a brush, much as the contrast options within the Color Tuner work on an entire sprite. The Contrast tool can be especially handy in creating fading effects and bringing up obscure details such as faded letters. Mostly though, you would use it where the Color Tuner would be too much of a brute force approach, changing the contrast on too much of the sprite at once.

Lastly comes the Tint tool, which operates by applying a layer of whatever color is selected to the sprite. It's function is comparable to the Colorize tool, but in a much more subtle fashion. With Tint you can lightly apply the color of your choice, and layer it to make the color more apparent. Colorize simply converts the hue of the areas you paint over to whatever color you have selected. Both apply color without really affecting intensity, but the Tint tool can be used for finer detail work such as reflections and highlighting.

Transferring and Using the Rubber Stamp

The Rubber Stamp tool lets you clone parts of the sprite by painting them. When you first select the Rubber Stamp tool, the icon is enclosed in a box. By clicking the sprite, you've set the position of the rubber stamp, and every move you make with the tool after that is relative to that first click. So if you click in the lower left hand corner of a sprite, and then go to paint in the upper right, the contents of the lower left would be painted in the upper right as if you were copying it across directly. Since you can apply any brush to the Rubber Stamp tool that you normally could the paintbrush, this lets you create some interesting tiling effects that aren't just another sprite endlessly repeated, such as the Texture Transfer Tile effect.

The Transfer tool is very similar to the Rubber Stamp except for the fact that its reference point can be within another sprite entirely. This lets you export certain parts of a sprite quite easily, without having to rely on the Texture Transfer effects. Essentially the Transfer tool is a hands-on equivalent to Texture Transfer palette just as the Tinting Effects complement the Color Tuner.

Creating Warp Effects

There are more Warps in Image Composer than just in the Arrange palette. In fact, some of the more interesting effects can be found within the confines of the Paint palette. There are three paint-oriented Warp effects that you can use, and each can take the form of a loose, airbrush-like stream, or a dense pencil line, like any tool in the Paint palette.

The first Warp effect is the Mesa tool, which creates the illusion of a slightly raised surface on objects within its path. Repeated use can give a sprite a slightly bumpy, or "corrugated" look that isn't easily duplicated within the Effects palette. The second Warp is the Vortex tool, which creates the impression that the surrounding pixels are being sucked toward a central point along a circular path, much like water going down a drain. The third Warp is the Spoke Inversion, which mimics the Spoke Inversion effect on a brush-scale. Basically it takes the pixels within its brush effect radius and inverts their position, with pixels near the middle going out to the edge and vice versa. The Spoke Inversion can be useful in creating several effects depending on the size of the brush and its opacity.

NOTE You can apply brush size, opacity, density, and hardness to *any* of the tools found within the Paint palette. This means that you can adjust contrast with the Contrast tool with an airbrush brush head if you so desire. ■

CHAPTER 17

Tailoring Your Images for FrontPage Documents

Image Composer makes it easy to create attractive graphics. Using its myriad of features and tools, you can make Image Composer part of your regular toolbox. Unfortunately, Image Composer's ease of use does not necessarily translate into graphics that are perfectly suited for the Web. Graphics for the Web have to face a number of hurdles, most important of which is size and functionality. In the previous chapters, you have explored a variety of tools and effects available in Image Composer. In many cases, all that will be required to place your graphic creations in a FrontPage Web site is to copy selected sprites to the FrontPage Editor. This chapter takes the knowledge you learned from the previous chapters and applies it to creating graphics that ideally suit your Web site and FrontPage. ■

Using a background

Web sites before backgrounds were dry and formulaic. Now they can be rich and vibrant using background fills that are easily made in Image Composer.

Understanding compression for images

Anyone who has surfed the Web using an old modem is painfully aware of how slow many Web sites can be. A firm understanding of compression and image formats can help you create a site that quickly loads for almost everybody.

Animation and transparency

The GIF file format lets you do amazing things, including transparent images that display the page background, or animations comprised of many different images. So how do you use them?

Using the Sprite catalog

The Sample Sprite Catalog gives you a variety of sprites that you can incorporate into your compositions, all without needing to be an artist.

Designing a Background Image

Your Web page backgrounds are a crucial part of setting the tone for your site. They exude an atmosphere like the paint on your living room walls or the music in the air when someone visits your home. Background images, as distinct from background colors, are actual graphics that sit behind your text and your foreground images. You use them to add texture, color, site identification, or other visual effects to your pages. Aesthetics and legibility are important here; remember, a background is just that. You shouldn't let it get above itself and have ambitions of becoming the foreground. If it distracts from your content or diffuses the impact of your foreground images, it's trying too hard.

Creating your background in Image Composer is a simple effort. What you are looking to do is to create a small, attractive graphic that will tile well. Effective backgrounds have a few traits in common:

- *Small size*. Good backgrounds are small and load quickly. Trying to tile large graphics takes considerable time for a browser to download and display. Small graphics can be downloaded quickly, making the background appear in an instant.
- *Simple subject matter*. Whether your graphic is a logo, texture, or cartoon, the best-tiled images aren't complex. Detailed graphics make awkward backgrounds and interfere with the foreground.
- *Complimentary colors*. Good background graphics are made of colors that compliment the foreground. Bad background images force the eye to fight with the foreground for focus. Using complimentary colors makes the reading experience easier.

Using a small composition space, you can edit your background using any of the techniques you have learned in the previous chapters. A good technique is to combine one fill—gradient ramps often work well—with one effect. There is no substitute for trial and error when creating backgrounds. See how the image looks behind your FrontPage Web page. You may want to test your background using a Web browser, to see how long it takes to load the background image. If you don't like the image, you can reopen the file in Image Composer and edit it to your satisfaction.

When creating your background, you may want to open an existing background (perhaps one of the ones provided with FrontPage) and edit it to suit your needs. Using this technique, you can make sure that your graphic is a small size.

Using Custom Background Fills

The FrontPage Editor lets you use any graphics file as a background. If you don't want to use one of your own images, a few banks of appropriate images are available on the Web, and you can download them for your own use. If you have MS Office installed on your system, you can use its clip art, and there's also the clip art that ships with FrontPage 98.

Using Custom Background Fills

 One such background resource on the Web is Randy's Icon and Image Bazaar. You can find it at **http://www.iconbazaar.com/backgr/**.

> **CAUTION**
>
> If you draw on a Web or Internet resource (other than simply linking to it), find out whether the site wants an acknowledgment that it supplied the resource. Copyright laws apply on the Internet, just as they do elsewhere. Besides, acknowledging someone else's contribution to your work is good manners. Incidentally, be very wary of using obviously copyrighted images, such as cartoon figures.

Once you've obtained the image, you can make it into your background. FrontPage Editor does this by treating the image like a tile and laying enough identical tiles to cover everything in sight. To put in the image, use the following steps:

1. Choose File, Page Properties to open the Page Properties dialog box. Click the Background sheet tab and mark the Background Image check box.
2. Click the Browse button. The Select Background Image dialog box appears.
3. Select the name of the background file, and return to the Background sheet by choosing OK or Open, depending on context.
4. The image is tiled across the page to produce your background (Figure 17.1).

FIG. 17.1
A successful background image compliments the site, without compromising readability.

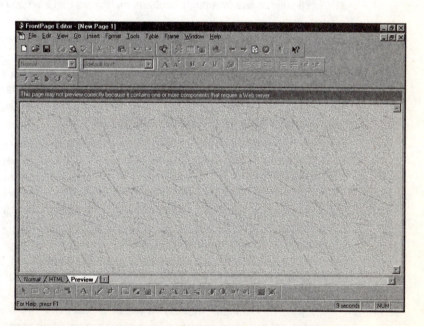

 TIP A real time-saver is using the Get Background and Colors from Page check box in the Background sheet of the Page Properties dialog box. This copies all the color choices and the background image from another page into the current one. It's very handy for keeping your pages' appearance consistent.

Remember that using a background image from another site puts your page's appearance at someone else's mercy. If the site's URL changes or its Webmaster deletes the image file, you'll lose your background. You're better off downloading the image and storing it locally.

 When you use a background image, also set the page's background color so that it's close to the predominant hue of the image. Why—so that a browser running with images turned off (which will include background images) displays your page with something like its intended appearance.

You can also use Image Composer to create truly unique, fully customized backgrounds and fills for your Web pages. All of the fills and effects that are explored in the previous chapters can be combined to create background fills. It is important to avoid the temptation to make your page background so flashy or distracting that it overshadows your Web site content—you may have noticed a site or two with this problem in your travels.

The following is a list of five things to avoid in backgrounds:

- Dark colors combined with dark text fonts
- Distracting images that overshadow the site contents
- Image files so large that visitors wait too long for the page background to resolve
- Backgrounds that clash with your images
- And finally, always avoid ugly background images (get a second opinion when in doubt).

What File Type Should I Use?

After working a while with graphics for your Web page, you may be a little confused on when to use certain file types for your images. There are two standard formats for images on the World Wide Web, JPEG and GIF. Each format has its own unique benefits (and negatives) that makes it best in certain situations. The two formats are described below:

- *JPEG*. The JPEG format was created by the Joint Photographic Experts Group as a means for compressing digital images. It uses a method for *compression* based on averaging what the eye can naturally see. This scheme is known as a *lossy compression* because it removes information from the picture. JPEG is intended for the compression of photographs, preferably natural scenery, and performs best when using images of this type. Images using intricate detail or flat color do not survive JPEG compression well. Solid colors tend to mottle and artifact.

- *GIF*. The Graphics Interchange Format is another compressed, lossy format. The main differences between GIF and JPEG is the limited color palette that GIF uses. GIF images only use an 8-bit color palette, for a maximum of 256 colors (JPEG can handle 24-bit color images). This limitation of the color palette means that GIF is less ideally suited for photographs and is of more use for detailed images (such as diagrams), or images that use flat color (text, for example). New extensions to the GIF format also support transparent backgrounds and animation.

What Are Compression Levels?

As was mentioned above, both JPEG and GIF use compression to shrink the size of the file for transmission. Compression can be achieved through a number of different means. The first, and most common method for compression is to strip repeated information in the image. Consider that each of your pictures is made up of a series of *pixels* (picture elements) that are displayed in a particular color. If the first line of pixels for your image is made up of three black pixels followed by four red pixels, traditionally the file is stored as saying "black pixel, black pixel, black pixel, red pixel, red pixel, red pixel, red pixel." Compression schemes may choose to save your image in a more efficient manner by stripping the repetition, such as "three black pixels, four red pixels." GIF and JPEG both use this method for minimizing the file size. Another form of compression, used in both formats, is to average information. This simply means that the image has some of its detail stripped from it to save space. Your eye is only able to discern so much information from a picture, so this method relies on choosing to average information that your eye does not see. JPEG works on this premise.

Using these two schemes, file sizes for your Web graphics can be reduced drastically over the alternative image formats (such as Windows BMP bitmap files). However, because the files are compressed, they do lose some quality. Compression can be controlled by adjusting the *compression level*. Available only to JPEG graphics, the compression level lets you determine just how much information is stripped from your graphic to save space. The less information you choose to sacrifice the greater the size of your graphic.

Why Should I Change Compression?

With more and more Web pages relying on intricate and overwhelming graphics, the need to minimize the size per graphic is growing. You may be looking to trim down the amount of time that it takes to download your Web page, due to a few sizeable web graphics. There is no such thing as "too small of a graphic" in terms of file size, so any extra speed that you can squeeze out of your Web page is a good thing. Unfortunately, the more you try to shrink graphics, the more you lose quality in your image. Figure 17.2 and Figure 17.3 compare the same image at different compression levels. The first screenshot shows a JPEG image at minimal compression, the second at maximum. Notice the artifacting and loss of quality around the edges of the image.

Artifacts are a common problem in computer graphics. The tiny stray pixels that appear in an image due to compression are called artifacts, because they are the remnants of the image before compression. As compression levels increase, so do artifacts.

Adjusting JPEG Compression

Image Composer makes it easy to adjust the compression for your JPEG images. You even have the option of using the Save for the Web Wizard, which provides you with a preview of your compression choices. When you have your image ready to save in Image Composer, follow these steps to adjust the compression using the standard Save As dialog box:

FIG. 17.2
This first image is a JPEG saved with minimal compression, resulting in a cleaner and crisper picture.

FIG. 17.3
The second image was saved with maximum compression, with a noticeable loss in quality. Although it is unlikely you would ever want to compress your image this much, it illustrates how quality is affected.

1. From the menu, choose File, Save As to open the Save As dialog box, shown in Figure 17.4.

FIG. 17.4
The Save As dialog box lets you choose the attributes for your saved image. For JPEGs, you can adjust the compression level using the Amount slider at the bottom.

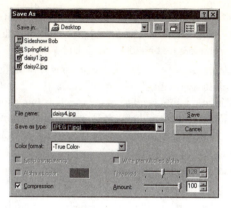

2. From the Save as Type drop box, choose JPEG (*.jpg) to save your image as a JPEG file.
3. Make sure that the Compression checkbox is selected. Control the compression level by moving the Amount slider. Moving it to the left lowers the compression level, while moving it to the right increases the compression level. You may optionally use the spin wheel control to directly control the compression level, with a higher value meaning more compression.
4. Enter a name for your image in the File Name text box. Be sure to include the .JPG suffix.
5. Click the Save button.

> **CAUTION**
> Because JPEG is a lossy format, each time you save your JPEG, the quality of the image suffers. Each subsequent save applies the compression to the already compressed image. Instead, when you are working with your graphic files, make sure to do your changes in the Image Composer .MIC file and then save the final result as a JPEG for the Web.
>
> ▶ If you would prefer to use the Save for the Web Wizard, **see** Chapter 15, "Working with Sprites" on **p. 261**

Why Use GIFs?

As mentioned earlier in the "What File Type Should I Use?," the GIF file format is ideal for detailed images or pictures that use a lot of flat color. The GIF format works best when it isn't used for photographic material, where its 8-bit color palette limitation becomes painfully obvious. Some perfect examples on when to use GIF images are:

- *Text.* Graphical text is almost always best saved as a GIF. All but the lowest compression levels for JPEG cause artifacting and noticeable loss in the quality of graphical text. GIF's treatment of flat color makes text an ideal candidate.
- *Charts, graphs, and diagrams.* Most charts and graphs rely on flat color (a lot of a few solid colors). Flat colors mottle badly using JPEG, making it a poor choice for these types of graphics. Diagrams that require detail (such as line comments) artifact badly using JPEG, but GIF can cleanly and clearly display the diagram without a loss of detail.
- *Images requiring transparency.* There comes a time when you need to have an image that shows through the background of the Web page. It may be text, it may be an icon. Because JPEG does not support transparency, you are forced to try to duplicate the background colors or image. This technique almost never works successfully.
- *Animation.* If you are looking to incorporate a lively animated image into your Web site without relying on third-party plug-ins, animated GIFs may be your best choice. These animations can be small and quick load, using frames made up of different GIF images.

Creating Transparent GIFs

When you are looking to have your Web page background appear through sections of graphic, you need transparency. Transparent GIFs let you create graphics that have clear sections, without needing to match the background. You can use this for titles and floating images, rather than having a distinct "frame" around your pictures. Figure 17.5 demonstrates a traditional image and a transparent GIF.

FIG. 17.5
On the left is a traditional picture, with a noticeable frame around the image. On the right is a transparent GIF, creating a "floating" effect.

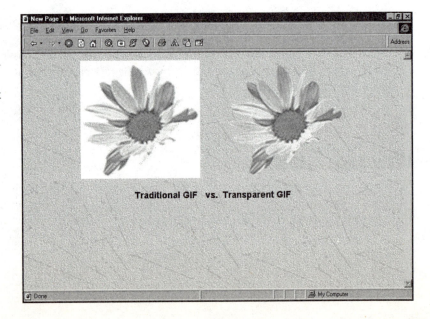

To create a transparent GIF, you can use the Save for the Web Wizard, or the following steps:

1. Select the sprite that you want to save as a transparent GIF.
2. Choose File, Save As from the menu bar to open the Save As dialog box, shown in Figure 17.6.

FIG. 17.6
The Save As Dialog box gives you options dependent on the file type. When you choose to save a GIF image, you can set the transparency color.

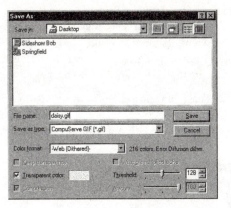

3. From the Save as Type drop box, choose CompuServe GIF (*.gif).
4. Select the Transparent color checkbox. This color will be used to reflect transparent regions in your image. Any transparent areas in your sprite will be filled with this color, and then interpreted as transparent by a Web browser. You can change the color by clicking the color box.

  N O T E The transparency Threshold slider lets you control the transparency level. The threshold is used to decide how transparency relates to colors next to the transparency color. Experiment with the threshold to decide on the best settings for your picture. ■

 Make sure that the transparent color isn't used in your image. Any areas of your image that use the transparent color will display the background of your Web page.

5. Enter a name for your new transparent GIF in the File Name text box.
6. Click the Save button.

▶ If you would prefer to use the Save for the Web Wizard, **see** Chapter 15, "Working with Sprites," on **p. 261**

Creating Animated GIFs

Maybe it's a flashing "New!" sign, or maybe it's a moving envelope for e-mail. Regardless of what it may be, you doubtlessly have been tempted to include an animated GIF into your Web page. Animated GIFs let you add some excitement to your Web page without relying on complicated plug-ins or programming efforts. You can use animated GIFs to reinforce a message on your page, demonstrate information, or even just add some flair to normally static pictures. FrontPage 98 includes a new Microsoft GIF Animator that is closely tied into Image Composer.

Animated GIFs are very easy to create, but they require some dedicated time. For each frame of your animation, you must create a GIF file. Each successive frame is a separate GIF file that is played in order by the visitor's browser. Using Image Composer, you must create each frame for your animation using the same standard size and GIF settings (dithered palette, for example). Once you have your frames created, you can use the GIF Animator to put it all together. To create your first animated GIF, follow these steps:

1. After you have created each of your frames for the animation, open the Microsoft GIF Animator. You can launch it from the Start menu, or by choosing Tools, Microsoft GIF Animator from the menu bar. The GIF Animator screen is shown in Figure 17.7.

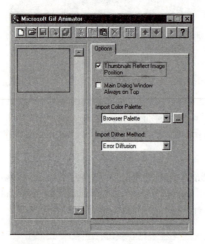

FIG. 17.7
The Microsoft GIF Animator is a very simple tool for creating animations. You can even use the GIF Animator to convert an existing Video for Windows (.AVI) file.

2. Click the Open button, or press CTRL+O. The Open dialog box appears. You can open an existing animated GIF or an AVI file. To begin your animated GIF, open the file that represents the last frame for your animation. For the GIF Animator, you'll create your animation in reverse order, starting with the last frame first.

3. Your frame appears in the thumbnail preview. To continue, add the next frame, click the Insert button (pr press CTRL+I). This displays the Open dialog box and lets you choose another frame.

4. Continue Step 3 for each successive frame in your animation. Note that each new frame is inserted before the previous one.

5. If you need to change the order of any frames, select the frame from the thumbnail previews, click the arrow buttons for Move Up and Move Down. This shifts the position of the frame in your animation.

6. To control aspects of your animation, such as looping, click the Animation tab. This tab, shown in Figure 17.8, lets you control your animation size and looping attributes.

FIG. 17.8
The Animation tab lets you control your animation's looping and size. You can set your animated GIF to play once, loop a number of times, or repeat forever.

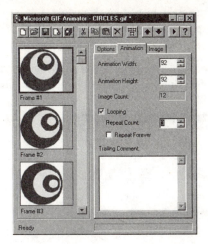

7. When you are satisfied with your animation, test it out by clicking the Preview button (or press CTRL+R). This opens the Preview window to play back your animation, as shown in Figure 17.9.

FIG. 17.9
Previewing your animated GIF is the best way to make sure that you've got it the way you want. You should also preview it inside a web browser to confirm the timing.

8. With your animation complete, click the Save As button (CTRL+A) to save your newly created animated GIF.

> **NOTE** The GIF Animator lets you control basic aspects of your frames, such as dithering and palette limitations. However, the Microsoft GIF Animator is a very simple tool for animation. For more complex control over an animated GIF, you may want to look into other programs such as the GIF Construction Set for Windows from Alchemy Mindworks. You can find this software at **http://www.mindworkshop.com/alchemy/gifcon.html**. ∎

Using the Sample Sprite Catalog

Once you know how to create your own sprites, you can appreciate and take advantage of the sample sprite photos and other sample image files that come with Image Composer. You can view thumbnail images of the sprites on the Image Composer CD-ROM by selecting Help, Sample Sprites Catalog.

The Index tab in the Sample Sprites Catalog dialog box shows an alphabetical list of sample sprites. Looking for a picture of an almond? Scroll down the list and find one. See Figure 17.10.

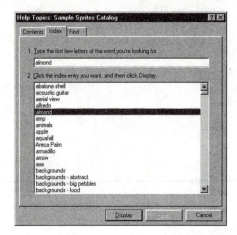

FIG. 17.10
Looking for an almond? Using the Index tab, you can search the Sample Sprites Catalog for whatever you want.

To view a sample Sprite, click the Display button in the Sample Sprites Catalog dialog box (see Figure 17.11).

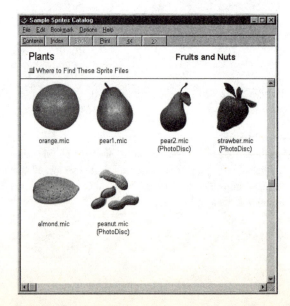

FIG. 17.11
Now that's an almond! Once you have found the sprite you are looking for, you can use the display preview to make sure it will work well for what you need.

You can also look for sample sprites by category. You do this from the Contents tab of the Sample Sprites dialog box. Then select either photos or Web images by double-clicking one of those two icons. See Figure 17.12.

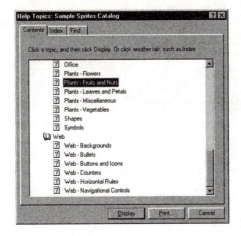

FIG. 17.12
Using categories to search for sprites is often easier when you don't know exactly what you're looking for.

The Web images include:

- Backgrounds
- Bullets
- Buttons
- Counters
- Horizontal Rules
- Navigational Controls

From these categories, you'll find hundreds of images to spruce up your site. You may even find some that are as good as ones you make yourself!

Once you find an image you like, click the Where to Find These Sprite Files button of the Catalog. This opens a second window (shown in Figure 17.13) that gives you the location of these sprite files on the FrontPage CD-ROM. Using this map, you can open the sprite files inside Image Composer. Of course, you can edit these images and resave them to create custom tools, buttons, and backgrounds.

N O T E In version 1.0 of Image Composer, you could double-click a sprite in the Sprite Catalog to have it automatically loaded into Image Composer. This functionality was not present in the beta versions of Image Composer 1.5, but may very well be present in the release version.

FIG. 17.13
You can use this map to find the sprite files on your CD-ROM.

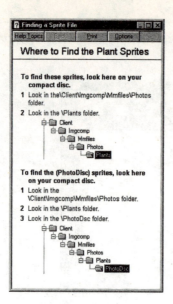

PART VI

Appendix

A FrontPage and Other Web Servers 311

APPENDIX

FrontPage and Other Web Servers

This appendix has been written for readers who are using FrontPage 98 with a Web server other than the Microsoft Personal Web Server included with the FrontPage 98 package. Whether you are using a Web server on a Windows 95 box or a UNIX station, the FrontPage Server extensions can help you make better use of FrontPage. If you are looking to use the extensions with a different Web server, read the material in this appendix closely. Information on the supported platforms and servers, as well as installation and administration tips are provided here.

Web server basics

The power of FrontPage 98 as a complete authoring environment is its tight integration with your Web server. Before you can take advantage of these features, you should brush up on your server basics.

Introducing FrontPage server extensions

The clever FrontPage server extensions make possible the communication between FrontPage 98 and your Web server. This solution makes your server and FrontPage an idiosyncratic couple that can accomplish great things.

Installing FrontPage server extensions

Installing and administering the FrontPage server extensions doesn't have to be a complex job, provided you're aware of what you're getting yourself into.

Getting help with server extensions

If you're encountering problems with the FrontPage server extensions and your Web server, it may be time to ignore your pride and get a little help.

Server Basics

Web servers come in many different sizes and varieties, namely for various platforms with a certain scope in mind. Regardless of the vendor or platform, all Web servers share a fundamental similarity in how they operate—HTTP, the *HyperText Transfer Protocol*, the transport level that the Web operates at between the client and the server. For all Web servers HTTP acts as the natural language that is used for communication between the client and the server. The Web browser (client) connects to the server and (via HTTP) requests a resource, such as a page or a graphic. The Web server then returns the requested resource to the client using HTTP. Figure A.1 illustrates communication between the server and the client using HTTP.

FIG. A.1
At its heart, nearly all communication on the World Wide Web uses HTTP. It doesn't matter what Web server you connect to, or which Web browser you use.

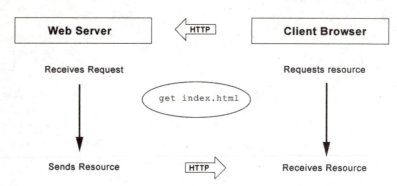

Regardless of what type of Web server you are connecting to, and what Web browser you are using, the HTTP protocol is there. The Web server uses the HTTP protocol to receive the requests that it in turn uses to send out resources. All Web servers manage resources in a similar manner. Although the physical location and storage of resources may differ, all Web servers use conventional *Universal Resource Locators* (URLs) for resource reference. A Web client requests a resource (such as a specific Web page), the Web server then takes the URL it was given and reverse engineers it to find out what specific resource is being requested. The Web server then locates the appropriate resource locally and transmits it to the client. Figure A.2 demonstrates how a Web server views a URL in comparison to how a client views it.

FrontPage Server Extensions: What Are They?

Without FrontPage server extensions, FrontPage would be no more than a glorified Web-authoring environment. Instead, with them, FrontPage becomes a powerful Web development and management tool. The server extensions act as an add-on to the Web server, allowing FrontPage to communicate directly with the Web server to manage the Web content. Without server extensions, the FrontPage Explorer and Editor have no means of communicating with the server for content management. The FrontPage server extensions act as an intermediary between the FrontPage environment and the Web server. FrontPage itself does not control or have any effect on the Web server, instead, FrontPage communicates with the server extensions that do.

FrontPage Server Extensions: What Are They? 313

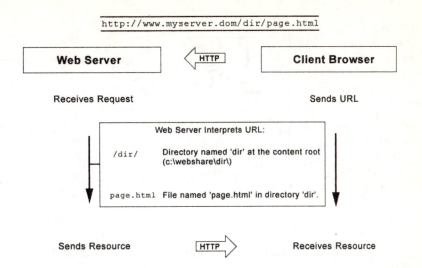

FIG. A.2
All requests to a Web server are carried out through URLs. A URL tells the Web server what resource the client wants. The server then reverse engineers the URL to find the resource locally.

The FrontPage Server extensions are a set of programs that sit on the Web server and extend FrontPage functionality. The server extensions support:

- *Web site management and authoring.* When you are looking to update or modify the contents of your Web site, the server extensions manage the server-side tasks for you. For example, if you need to move a file into a different fold and create a new one to take its place, the server extensions handle the job based on instructions from the FrontPage Explorer. The server extensions can also manage the updates for each hyperlink that is involved in a file being moved.

- *Web site administration.* Using the server extensions, you can control who can modify the contents of your Web site, who can browse it, and who else can administer it. You can also create new Web sites and delete existing ones (based on permissions).

- *Server side activation and enhanced Web pages.* The FrontPage server extensions not only assist in the creation and management of your Web site, they also can enhance your Web site with new features. Server side extensions give you powerful features such as rotating banners, discussion forums, and forms handling that you can incorporate into your site.

Using FrontPage with the server extensions minimizes the need for file transfers to and from the server. The server extensions only transfer information that is needed for editing, rather than transferring every resource for your Web site. Simply put, the server extensions make Web development easier and more powerful while simplifying the steps involved. Beyond the server extensions, no additional programs are needed, nor is special access or file sharing involved. A Microsoft diagram, Figure A.3, illustrates the communication process involved with the server extensions.

The FrontPage server extensions are available for a variety of Web servers on the Windows platform (Windows 95 and Windows NT), as well as several UNIX platforms. The supported Web servers and platforms are shown in Table A.1.

FIG. A.3
FrontPage server extensions use the standard HTTP protocol for communication. All communication between the client (such as FrontPage Explorer) and the server is handled in this manner.

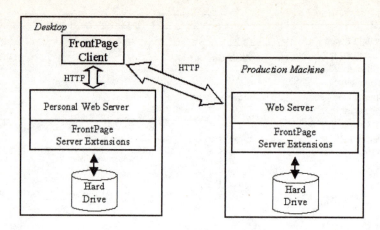

Table A.1. FrontPage server extensions: Supported Platforms.	
On the following operating systems:	**The FrontPage Server Extensions are available for the following Web servers:**
Windows NT Server, Windows NT Workstation, and Windows 95	
Intel x86 Win 32	Microsoft Internet Information Server (IIS) 2.0 or higher
	Microsoft Peer Web Services 2.0 or higher
	Microsoft Personal Web Server
	FrontPage Personal Web Server
	Netscape Commerce Server 1.12
	Netscape Communications Server 1.12
	Netscape Enterprise Server 2.0 and 3.0
	Netscape FastTrack Server 2.0
	O'Reilly WebSite and WebSite Pro
Alpha (WinNT 4.0)	Microsoft Internet Information Server (IIS) 2.0 or higher
	Microsoft Peer Web Services 2.0 or higher
UNIX	
Digital UNIX 3.2c, 4.0 (Alpha)	Apache 1.1.3, 2.0
BSD/OS 2.1 (Intel x86)	CERN 3.0
BSD/OS 3.0 (Intel x86)	NCSA 1.5.2

On the following operating systems:	The FrontPage Server Extensions are available for the following Web servers:
Linux 3.03	Netscape Commerce Server 1.12 (RedHat Software) (Intel x86)
HP/UX 9.03, 10.01 (PA-RISC)	Netscape Communications Server 1.12
IRIX 5.3, 6.2 (Silicon Graphics)	Netscape Enterprise Server 2.0 and 3.0
Solaris 2.4, 2.5 (SPARC)	Netscape FastTrack 2.0
SunOS 4.1.3, 4.1.4 (SPARC)	

For the most recent information on the FrontPage server extensions, including platform availability, visit the FrontPage Web Presence Provider's site at **http://www.microsoft.com/frontpage/wpp**.

If you do not have the server extensions on CD-ROM, or are looking for more recent versions, visit **http://www.microsoft.com/frontpage/wpp/exts.htm**. You can download the complete server extensions setup archive for your computer platform.

Using FrontPage with Windows 95 and Windows NT Web Servers

The installation process for the server extensions on a Windows machine is relatively painless. Several files are copied to your local hard drive. Once the files are copied, the FrontPage Server Administrator installs the server extensions into your Web server and updates your site for its use. The larger your site, the longer this process will take. To install the server extensions on your windows machine, follow these steps:

1. To start the installation, run the server extensions Setup program. Be sure to use the setup program for your language and processor type (for example, English x86 for an Intel based PC using English). Your Web server is stopped to make sure that files are not locked by the Web server. The server extensions are then copied to your local hard drive, and the Web server is restarted upon completion.

2. If your server hosts more than one Web site, the Multi-hosted Server dialog box asks you to select the virtual servers on which the FrontPage server extensions should be installed. On single-hosted servers, the extensions are automatically installed on the content root of the server without a dialog box.

3. You are prompted for the name of a new FrontPage Administrator account. Under Windows NT, this must be an existing account. You can add additional administrators in the FrontPage Explorer after installing the extensions.

4. The installation of the server extensions on each Web site may take several minutes and increase the load on your CPU. Once this process is complete, you are done with the server extensions installation.

The FrontPage server extensions installation process modifies the security on files under Windows NT. The Access Control Lists (ACL) for files are modified to ensure that the correct permissions and security are present for FrontPage operation. For complete information on the ACLs set on FrontPage files, along with a list of the entire contents of the FrontPage installation, see **http://www.microsoft.com/frontpage/wpp/SERK/a_iisprm.htm** on the World Wide Web.

Using FrontPage with UNIX Web Servers

Installation of the server extensions under UNIX involves three files: the installation script file (fp_install.sh), the server extensions .TAR file for your platform (fp30.*platform*.tar.gz for example), and an Apache server upgrade script (change_server.sh) if you are using the Apache Web server. The actual installation process requires careful attention to insure a proper installation. All installations require superuser (root) permissions. To install the server extensions on a supported UNIX platform, follow these steps:

1. As root, run the fp_install.sh script to begin the installation. This script steps you through the installation and configuration process.

2. If you have backed up your Web server configuration and content files, answer yes to the backup prompt. If you have not already done so, be sure to backup all of your server configuration files, your Web content files, and your FrontPage installation directory.

3. Provide the destination directory for the server extensions. By default this directory is /usr/local/frontpage. If you select a different location, a symbolic link will be created from the default directory to the directory you specified.

4. If the FrontPage server extensions tar file is not in the default directory, enter the path to the tar file. Answer yes to the prompt to extract the archive.

5. If your Web server does not have existing FrontPage server extensions, the extensions are installed at the content root. If you do have existing extensions, they are interactively upgraded to the FrontPage 98 extensions.

6. After installing the stub server extensions on the root Web site, you are prompted for the name of each sub-Web to install the extensions to. For each sub-Web that you choose to install the extensions on, you are prompted for any missing information (such as port number and owner) and then the stub extensions are installed for each Web.

7. After installing the extensions on the root Web and any sub-Webs, you are prompted if you want to install the server extensions on any virtual servers. If you indicate that you do have virtual Webs to install, you are prompted with a list of the virtual servers to interactively upgrade.

8. Once the installation is complete, the script then completes the installation process by indexing the Web sites. If you are prompted to supply any missing information, be careful to note which Web it is prompting you for.

9. If you are using the Apache Web server, consider running the `change_server.sh` script to update your Apache executable with an update one that has been tailored for FrontPage support and security.

FrontPage server extension installation and security is considerably more complex and involved than that of Windows platform installations. For information on the file permissions for the server extension files, visit **http://www.microsoft.com/frontpage/wpp/SERK/security.htm#UNIX MAIN** on the World Wide Web.

Getting Help

Installation and maintenance of the FrontPage server extensions can be a bit troublesome and complex. Thankfully, Microsoft has provided an incredibly useful resource for the server extensions in the form of the server extensions Resource Kit (SERK). The SERK is available both on the World Wide Web and as part of the server extensions distribution. The document completely details the installation of the server extensions for both Windows and UNIX platforms, as well as security information and troubleshooting resources. You should have this document in hand when installing or configuring the server extensions on your machine.

The SERK is found on the World Wide Web at **http://www.microsoft.com/wpp/SERK**. It is also installed as part of the server extensions distribution. Do not overlook this invaluable resource!

In addition to the SERK, Microsoft has a few other resources for help with the server extensions. Microsoft's own public newsgroups on the Internet (**msnews.microsoft.com**) are a peer-to-peer resource for assistance. You can find helpful users and Microsoft staffers that can likely answer any question you may have about the extensions. The Microsoft newsgroups that pertain to FrontPage are:

- microsoft.public.frontpage.extensions.windowsnt
- microsoft.public.frontpage.extensions.unix
- microsoft.public.frontpage.client

> **NOTE** You'll need an NNTP newsgroup reader to access these newsgroups. These three newsgroups (as well as many others for Microsoft products) are found on the **msnews.microsoft.com** news server, and not on your Internet Service Provider's normal news server.

For additional help with the UNIX server extensions, you can also visit their developers at Ready to Run Software. Ready to Run Software's Web site lists helpful information on the server extensions, as well as an open Web discussion group that can be used to ask questions.

Ready to Run Software can be found on the Web at **http://www.rtr.com**.

As a final resort, you can also consult the Microsoft Knowledge Base, part of Microsoft's online support site. The Knowledge Base is a searchable database of articles relating to all

Microsoft products. Any problems and answers encountered by Microsoft's technical support department (such as via their telephone lines) are available here.

 The Microsoft Knowledge Base can be found at **http://www.microsoft.com/support**. You can select any Microsoft Product for a list of Frequently Asked Questions (FAQs), troubleshooting wizards, help files and updates, and the searchable Knowledge Base.

Index

A

ActiveX, 17
    controls, inserting, 157-161
ActiveX Control Properties dialog box, 158
airbrush tool (Image Composer), 291
alignment (images), 130
All Files View command (View menu), 85
All Hyperlinks pane (Hyperlinks view), 87-88
alternative text, 132
animated GIFs, 303-305
animation
    Image Composer (GIF Animator), 28
    text (dynamic HTML), 235-236
Appearance Sheet, resizing images, 130-131
applets (Java), 161-163
Arrange palette (Image Composer), 248
artifacts (image compression), 299
.asp file extension, 14
Assigned To column (Task view), 207

AU files, adding to Web pages, 143
audio, adding to Web pages, 142-144
    AU files, 143
    backgound music, 143-144
    linking to audio files, 144
    MIDI files, 142
    RealAudio, 143
    WAV files, 143
.avi file extension, 14
AVI files (video), 144-145

B

background images, 120, 132-133, 296
    compression levels, 299
        JPEGs, 299-301
    custom fills, 296-298
    GIFs, 298, 301-302
        animated GIFs, 303-305
        transparent, 302-303
    JPEGs, 298
        compression levels, 299
    music, adding, 143-144
    Sample Sprites Catalog, 306-307
    watermarked, 133
Bilinear Warps (sprites), 291
bitmaps (Windows Bitmaps), 14

blank Web pages
    adding from within Explorer, 68
    creating with Editor, 69
Blink character style, 112
.bmp file extension, 14
BMP files (images), 124
borders
    adding to images, 132
    shared (Web site navigation structure), 219-222
braces (JavaScript syntax), 150
browsers, 102
building Web sites
    from scratch, 66
    importing existing sites, 59-62
    wizards and templates, 62-65
bulleted lists, 72
Burn/Dodge tool Image Composer), 292

C

Cascading Style Sheets, 224-225
    styles
        CDF files (Channel Definition Format), 236-240
        creating, 225-229
        defined, 231
        dynamic HTML, 231-236

external style sheets,
  linking to, 229-231
  inline, 231
**case-sensitivity
  (JavaScript syntax), 150**
**CDF files (Channel Definition
  Format), 236-240**
**Cell Properties dialog
  box, 116**
**cells, table, properties,
  116-117**
**CGI (Common Gateway
  Interface), 45**
**Channel Definition Format,
  see CDF, 236-240**
Citation character style, 112
**Clear command
  (Edit menu), 142**
**client-side tools
  (Explorer), 14**
clip art, 26
  Image Composer, 256-259
  inserting into Web pages, 127
Code character style, 112
**collapsible outlines
  (dynamic HTML), 233-234**
color
  Color Tuning palette (Image
    Composer), 253
  Colorize tool (Image
    Composer), 292
  HTML text, 120
  Pattern effects, 281
  sprites (color tuning), 289-290
**columns (Task view),
  206-207**
commands
  Edit menu
    Clear, 142
    Copy, 71
    Cut, 72
    Horizontal Line
      Properties, 113
    Hyperlink, 134
    Link, 141
    Paste, 71
  File menu
    Import, 189
    New, 166
    Open FrontPage Web,
      82, 189

Page Properties, 106, 297
Preview in Browser, 80
Print Navigation View, 195
Publish FrontPage Web,
  97, 191
Save, 80
Save As, 172
Format menu
  Font, 111
  Paragraph, 106
  Stylesheet, 225
Insert menu, Hyperlink, 76
JavaScript syntax, 150
Table menu
  Draw Table, 74
  Insert Table, 74
Tools menu
  Define Channel, 237
  Options, 201
  Recalculate Hyperlinks,
    95, 213
  Spelling, 210
  Verify Hyperlinks, 94, 216
View menu
  All Files View, 85
  Expand All, 219
  Folders View, 83
  Format Marks, 152
  Hyperlink View, 195
  Hyperlinks, 87, 214
  Image Toolbar, 141
  Navigation View, 86
  Options, 244
  Show All Hyperlinks, 216
  Size to Fit, 219
  Task History, 209
  Tasks, 96, 207, 208
**Comment component, 176,
  179-180**
**comments (JavaScript
  syntax), 151**
**Common Gateway Interface,
  see CGI**
**compact installations
  (Image Composer), 27**
components, 176-183
  Comment, 179-180
  Confirmation Field, 180
  Editor, 17, 40-44
    interface, 42-43
    SDK (Software
      Development Kit), 18
  Explorer, 38-39
    interface, 39

Hit Counter, 180
Image Composer, 46-49
  interface, 47-48
Include Page, 181
Insert HTML, 181
installing
  default, 24-27
  Image Composer, 27-29
  Personal Web Server,
    29-35
  Server Extensions, 34
  Web server
    connections, 29
  WWW Administration
    pages, 30-34
Navigation Bar, 179
Page Banner, 181-182
Personal Web Server, 44-45
  interface, 45
proofing tools and
  converters, 26
Scheduled Image, 182
Scheduled Include, 182
Server Extension
  Administration Forms, 26
Server Extension Resource
  Kit, 26
Substitution, 183
Table of Contents, 178
Timestamp, 177-178
Web Publishing Wizard, 49-51
  interface, 50
Web site themes, 26
**Composition Guide
  (Image Composer), 256**
**compression (background
  images) 299-301**
**Confirmation Field
  component, 176, 180**
**connections
  Web page administration
  limitations), 31**
content
  dividing into Webs, 13-14
  planning Web sites, 56-57
**Contrast tool (Image
  Composer), 292**
controls, 42
  ActiveX, inserting, 157-161
  navigational (images as
    controls), 134
converters, 26
  image file formats, 137-138

Copy command
(Edit menu), 71
copying sprites (Image
Composer), 255-256
Corporate Presence
Wizard, 62
Create Hyperlink dialog
box, 76
Create Link dialog box, 141
cropping sprites, 277
curves (graphical text),
273-274
see also, splines
custom fills (background
images), 296-298
Cut command
(Edit menu), 72
Cutout palette
(Image Composer), 248
cutting text (creating Web
pages), 71-72

D

default
components, installing, 24-27
documents (Web page
startup), 33
Define Channel command
(Tools menu), 237
defined styles, 231
Definition character
style, 112
definition lists, 72
deleting
headings
(from Web pages), 107
hotspots (imagemaps), 142
images
(from Web pages), 125
text (from Web pages), 71-72
virtual directories, 33
Web pages (with Explorer),
91-92
Description column (Task
view), 207
design (creating Web pages),
102-105
layout, 104-113

DHTML, *see* dynamic HTML
dialog boxes
ActiveX Control
Properties, 158
Cell Properties, 116
Create Hyperlink, 76
Create Link, 141
Edit Hyperlink, 216
File Open, 71
Format Stylesheet, 225, 230
FrontPage Web, 125
Hit Counter Properties, 180
Image, 124-125, 132
Image Properties, 132, 138
Include Page Component
Properties, 181
Insert FrontPage Component,
180-181
Insert Image, 77
Insert Java Applet, 162
Insert Plug-In, 156
Insert Table, 74
List Item Properties, 118
List Properties, 118, 233
Navigation Bar
Properties, 179
New, 166
New File, 69
New FrontPage Web, 172
New Task, 96, 208
Object Parameters, 159
Open FrontPage Web, 83
Open Web, 82
Open with, 200
Options, 202
Page Banner Properties, 181
Page Properties, 106, 120,
132, 144, 297
Page Transition, 235
Paragraph Properties,
106, 231
Preview In Browser, 80
Publish FrontPage Web, 191
Save As Template, 172
Scheduled Image
Properties, 182
Script, 149, 152, 154
Select Background Image,
132, 297
Shared Borders, 220
Style, 226
Substitution Component
Properties, 183
Table of Contents
Properties, 178

Table Properties, 114
Task Details, 96, 209
Text Box Properties, 234
Timestamp Properties, 177
Web Theme, 64
Windows File Open, 70
directories
browsing, 34
Directories page (Web page
administration), 33
lists, 72
virtual, 33
Discussion Web Wizard,
172-173
documents, 14-15
default (Web page startup), 33
Editor, 15
graphic formats, 14
HTML pages, 14
importing (Editor), 42
multimedia files, 14
downloading images (from the
Internet), 126-127
Draw Table command
(Table menu), 74
dynamic HTML (Cascading
Style Sheets), 231-233
collapsible outlines, creating,
233-234
form field extensions, 234-235
page transitions, 235-236
text animations, 235-236

E

ECMA (European Computer
Manufacturers Association),
148
Edit Hyperlink dialog
box, 216
Edit menu commands
Clear, 142
Copy, 71
Cut, 72
Horizontal Line Properties,
113
Hyperlink, 134
Link, 141
Paste, 71

editing
  sprites (Image Composer), 253-255
  text (creating Web pages), 71-72
  virtual directories, 33
Editor (FrontPage), 15-18, 40-44
  components, 17
    SDK (Software Development Kit), 18
  HTML views, 17
  Image Composer, integrating, 246-247
  Image Manipulation Toolbar, 128
  images (custom background fills), 296-298
  interface, 42-43
  JavaScripts, adding to Web pages, 149
  Normal views, 17
  Preview views, 17
  Script Wizard, 154-155
  utilities, 18
    Image Composer, 18-19
    Personal Web Server, 19-20
    Web Publishing Wizard, 20
  Web pages, creating, 102-113
    backgrounds, 120
    blank pages, creating, 69
    fonts, 119
    headings, adding (Format menu), 106-108
    horizontal rules, 112-113
    justifying text, 111
    layout, 104-113
    lists, 117-118
    logical text styles, 111-112
    paragraphs, adding, 108-109
    resizing text, 110-111
    tables, 113-117
    text color, 120
    titles, adding, 105-106
effects
  Pattern, 280-281
    airbrush tool, 291
    color tuning sprites, 289-290
    colors, changing, 281
    filtering sprites, 286-289
    gradient fills, 282-283
  Impression tool, 292
  outlining sprites, 285-286
  paintbrush tool, 291
  pencil tool, 291
  Rubber Stamp tool, 293
  Smear tool, 292
  texture transfer effects, 283-285
  Transfer tool, 293
tinting
  Burn/Dodge tool, 292
  Colorize tool, 292
  Contrast tool, 292
  Eraser tool, 292
  Tint tool, 293
warp, 290-291
  Mesa tool, 293
  Spoke Inversion, 293
  Vortex tool, 293
  transformations (sprites), 290-291
Effects palette (Image Composer), 250
Emphasis character style, 112
enlarging HTML text, 110-111
Eraser tool (Image Composer), 292
European Computer Manufacturers Association, *see* **ECMA**
existing Web pages, opening, 70-71
Expand All command (View menu), 219
Explorer (FrontPage), 15-16, 38-39
  client-side tools, 14
  Image Composer, integrating, 246-247
  interface, 39
  reconfiguring, 201-202
  views, 83-89, 191-200
    All Files, 85
    Folder, 191
    Folders, 83-84
    Hyperlink Status, 195
    Hyperlinks, 86-89, 195
    Navigation, 86, 192
    Tasks, 200
    Themes view, 198
  Web pages, creating (adding blank pages), 68

Web sites, creating
  adding pages, 89-91
  deleting pages, 91-92
  loading sites, 82-83, 188-190
  publishing your site, 97-98
  recalculating hyperlinks, 94-95
  reorganizing, 92-93
  spell checking, 95
  Task lists, 96-97
  verifying hyperlinks, 94-95
extensions
  server, 14, 312-315
    installing, 34
    SERK (Server Extensions Resource Kit), 26, 317
    suggested platforms, 314-315
  Server Extension Administration Forms, 26
external links (Hyperlink Status view), 215-217
external style sheets, linking to, 229-231

F

File menu commands
  Import, 189
  New, 166
  Open FrontPage Web, 82, 189
  Page Properties, 106, 297
  Preview in Browser, 80
  Print Navigation View, 195
  Publish FrontPage Web, 97, 191
  Save, 80
  Save As, 172
File Open dialog box, 71
File Transfer Protocol, *see* **FTP**
fills
  custom (background images), 296-298
  Pattern effects
    changing colors, 281
    gradient fills, 282-283
filtering sprites, 286-289
  group summary, 288
Folders view, 83-84, 191
  command (View menu), 83

Font command (Format menu), 111

fonts (Web page design), 119

form field extensions (dynamic HTML), 234-235

Form Page Wizard, 174-175

Format Marks command (View menu), 152

Format menu commands
  Font, 111
  Paragraph, 106
  Stylesheet, 225

Format Stylesheet dialog box, 225, 230

formats (graphic), 14

forms, 42

frames, 42
  templates, 168-171

FrontPage 98, installing, 24
  default components, 24-27
  Image Composer, 27-29
  Personal Web Server, 29-35
  Server Extensions, 34
  Web server connections, 29
  WWW Administration pages, 30-34

FrontPage Editor, *see* **Editor**

FrontPage Explorer, *see* **Explorer**

FrontPage Web dialog box, 125

FTP (File Transfer Protocol), 12

functions (JavaScript), 150

G

GIFs (Graphics Interchange Format), 14, 47, 124, 135-139
  background images, 298, 301-302
    animated, 303-305
    transparent, 302-303
  file formats, converting, 137-138
  GIF87 files, 136
  GIF89a files, 136
  Image Composer (GIF Animator), 28
  interlaced, 138
  Low Res option, 138
  transparent images, 138-139

Glue effect (texture transfers), 284

gradient fills (Pattern effects), 282-283

graphical text, 262-266, 268-271
  curves, 273-274
    see also, splines
  polygons, 274
  rectangles and ovals, 271-272
  sizing and rotating, 267-268
  sprites
    aligning, 275
    cropping, 277-278
    flattening, 277
    grouping, 275-277
    home positions, 278
    moving forward and back, 275
    resizing, 277-278
    rotating, 277-278
  Word Art (Image Composer), 262
  zigzag lines, 274

graphics, 124-134
  clip art, 26
  formats, 14
  GIFs (Graphics Interchange Format), 135-139
    file formats, converting, 137-138
    interlaced, 138
    Low Res option, 138
    transparent images, 138-139
  Image Composer, 18-19, 46-49, 244
    clip art, 256-259
    Composition Guide, 256
    FrontPage client integration, 246-247
    GIF Animator, 28
    Impressionist plug-ins, 28
    installing, 27-29
    interface, 47-48, 244-245
    online help, 28
    palettes, 247-253
    sprites, 253-256
    tools, 247-253
    tutorial samples, 28
    Word Art, 28
  imagemaps, 140-142
    creating, 140-141
    hotspots, deleting, 142
  importing (Editor), 42
  JPEGs, 135-139
    file formats, converting, 137-138
    Low Res option, 138
    transparent images, 138-139
  PNGs, 135-139
    file formats, converting, 137-138
    Low Res option, 138
    transparent images, 138-139
  Web pages
    alignment choices, 130
    alternative text, 132
    Appearance Sheet size adjustments, 130-131
    as hyperlinks, 133-134
    background images, 132-133
    borders, adding, 132
    clip art, 127
    deleting from, 125
    inserting into, 124-127
    modifying, 127-129
    navigational controls, 134
    placing text around, 129-130
    scanning, 127
    spacing between text and images, 130
    thumbnails, 134
    watermarked backgrounds, 133
  Web Publishing Wizard, 49-51
    interface, 50

H

hard drives, inserting images from, 125-126

hardware (installation requirements)
  minimum, 20-21
  recommendations, 21

headings (Format menu)
  adding to Web pages, 106-108
  deleting, 107

help, online (Image
  Composer), 28
Hit Counter component,
  176, 180
Hit Counter Properties dialog
  box, 181
Horizontal Line Properties
  command (Edit menu), 113
horizontal rules (HTML text),
  112-113
hotspots, deleting
  (imagesmaps), 142
.htm file extension, 14
.html file extension, 14
HTML (HyperText Markup
  Language), 13, 102
    dynamic (Cascading Style
      Sheets), 231-236
    hyperlinks (creating Web
      pages), 74-77
    tags (<SCRIPT>), 148
    text
      horizontal rules, 112-113
      justification, 111
      logical styles, 111-112
      resizing, 110-111
    Web pages, 14
      views (Editor), 17
HTTP (Hypertext Transfer
  Protocol), 12
Hyperlink command
  Edit menu, 134
  Insert menu, 76
Hyperlink Status view, 195
  external links, 215-217
Hyperlink view
  command (View menu),
    195-197
  internal links, 213-215
    All Hyperlinks pane, 87-88
    Individual Hyperlinks pane,
      88-89
hyperlinks, 74-77
  external (Hyperlink Status
    view), 215-217
  images as hyperlinks, 133-134
  internal (Hyperlink view),
    213-215
  recalculating, 94-95, 213
  verifying, 94-95
Hyperlinks command
  (View menu), 87, 214

HyperText Markup Language,
  see HTML
Hypertext Transfer Protocol,
  see HTTP, 12

I

Image Bazaar Web site, 297
Image Composer, 46-49
  FrontPage Editor, 18-19
  GIF Animator, 28
  Impressionist plug-ins, 28
  interface, 47-48
  online help, 28
  Pattern effects, 280-281
    airbrush tool, 291
    color tuning sprites,
      289-290
    colors, changing, 281
    filtering sprites, 286-289
    gradient fills, 282-283
    Impression tool, 292
    outlining sprites, 285-286
    paintbrush tool, 291
    pencil tool, 291
    Rubber Stamp tool, 293
    Smear tool, 292
    texture transfer effects,
      283-285
    Transfer tool, 293
  tinting effects
    Burn/Dodge tool, 292
    Colorize tool, 292
    Contrast tool, 292
    Eraser tool, 292
    Tint tool, 293
  tutorial samples, 28
  warp effects
    Mesa tool, 293
    Spoke Inversion, 293
    transformations (sprites),
      290-291
    Vortex tool, 293
  Word Art, 28, 262
Image dialog box, 124,
  125, 132
Image Manipulation Toolbar
  (Editor), 128
Image Properties dialog box,
  132, 138
Image Toolbar command
  (View menu), 141

images, 124-134
  background, 296
    animated GIFs, 303-305
    compression levels,
      299-301
    custom fills, 296-298
    GIFs, 298, 301-302
    JPEGs, 298
    Sample Sprites Catalog,
      306-307
    transparent GIFs, 302-303
  formats, 14
  GIFs, 135-139
    background images, 298,
      301-305
    file formats, converting,
      137-138
    interlaced, 138
    Low Res option, 138
    transparent images,
      138-139
  Image Composer, 244
    clip art, 256-259
    Composition Guide, 256
    FrontPage client
      integration, 246-247
    interface, 244-245
    palettes, 247-253
    sprites, 253-256
    tools, 247-253
  imagemaps, 140-142
    creating, 140-141
    hotspots, deleting, 142
  JPEGs, 135-139
    background images, 298
    file formats, converting,
      137-138
    Low Res option, 138
    transparent images,
      138-139
  PNGs, 135-139
    file formats, converting,
      137-138
    Low Res option, 138
    transparent images,
      138-139
  Web pages
    alignment choices, 130
    alternative text, 132
    Appearance Sheet size
      adjustments, 130-131
    as hyperlinks, 133-134
    background images,
      132-133
    borders, adding, 132

clip art, 127
deleting from, 125
inserting into, 124-127
modifying, 127-129
navigational controls, 134
placing text around, 129-130
scanning, 127
spacing between text and images, 130
thumbnails, 134
watermarked backgrounds, 133

Import command (File menu), 189

Import Web Wizard, 190

Import Wizard, 60

importing
documents (Editor), 42
graphics (Editor), 42
Web sites, 59-62

Impression tool (Image Composer), 292

Impressionist plug-ins (Image Composer), 28

Include Page component, 176, 181

Individual Hyperlinks pane (Hyperlinks view), 88-89

inline styles, 231

Insert FrontPage Component dialog box, 180-181

Insert HTML component, 176, 181

Insert Image dialog box, 77

Insert Java Applet dialog box, 162

Insert menu commands, Hyperlink, 76

Insert Plug-In dialog box, 156

Insert Table command (Table menu), 74

inserting
ActiveX controls, 157-161
images (into Web pages), 124-134
plug-ins, 156-157

Install Wizard, 24

installing FrontPage 98, 24
default components, 24-27
hardware requirements, 20, 21
Image Composer, 27-29
Personal Web Server, 29-35
Server Extensions, 34
Web server connections, 29
WWW Administration pages, 30-34

integrating Image Composer (with FrontPage clients), 246-247

interfaces
Editor, 42-44
Explorer, 39
Image Composer, 244-245
Personal Web Server, 45
Web Publishing Wizard, 50

interlaced GIFs, 138

internal links (Hyperlink view), 213-215

Internet image access, 126-127

ISAPI (Internet Server Application Programming Interface), 44

J

Java applets, 161-163

JavaScript, 148-152
scripts
adding with Editor, 149
executing, 152
syntax, 150-151
braces, 150
case-sensitivity, 150
comments, 151
functions and commands, 150
properties, 150
VBScript, 152-154

JavaScript Authoring Guide Web site, 151

JPEGs (Joint Photographic Experts Group), 14, 47, 124, 135-139
background images, 298
compression, 299-301
file formats, converting, 137-138

Low Res option, 138
transparent images, 138-139

JScript, 148

justification (HTML text), 111

L

layout
planning Web sites, 59
Web page design, 104-113
backgrounds, 120
fonts, 119
headings, adding (Format menu), 106-108
horizontal rules, 112-113
justifying text, 111
lists, 117-118
logical text styles, 111-112
paragraphs, adding, 108-109
resizing text, 110-111
tables, 113-117
text color, 120
titles, adding, 105-106

Link command (Edit menu), 141

Linked To column (Task view), 207

links, 74-77
external (Hyperlink Status view), 215-217
images as hyperlinks, 133-134
internal (Hyperlink view), 213-215
recalculating, 94-95, 213
verifying, 94-95

List Item Properties dialog box, 118

List Properties dialog box, 118, 233

lists, 72-73
bulleted, 72
definition, 72
directory, 72
menu, 72
numbered, 72
Web page design, 117-118

LiveScript, 148

loading Web sites, 188-190

local-side, *see* client-side
Logging page (Web page administration), 34
logical styles (HTML text), 111-112
Low Res option (image files), 138

M

Map Color effect (texture transfers), 284
Map Intensity effect (texture transfers), 284
Map Saturation effect (texture transfers), 284
Map Transparency effect (texture transfers), 284
Menu Bar system (reorganizing Web sites), 92-93
menu lists, 72
Mesa tool (Image Composer), 293
Meshmart VRML Page Web site, 164
Microsoft
    ActiveX Web site, 161
    Clip Gallery, 256
    Image Composer, 18-19
    Knowledge Base Web site, 318
    Paintbrush, 46
    Personal Web Server, 19-20
    Web Publishing Wizard, 20
MIDI files, adding to Web pages, 142
minimum hardware requirements (installing FrontPage 98), 20-21
Modified Date column (Task view), 207
MPEG video, 145
MPWS, *see* Personal Web Server
multimedia
    Image Composer, 18-19, 46-49
        GIF Animator, 28
        Impressionist plug-ins, 28

installing, 27-29
interface, 47-48
online help, 28
tutorial samples, 28
Word Art, 28
Web Publishing Wizard, 49-51
    interface, 50

N

navigating Web sites
    image controls, 134
    Navigation view, 218-219
    shared borders, 219-222
Navigation Bar component, 176, 179
    dialog box, 179
Navigation view, 86, 192-195
    command (View menu), 86
    Web site navigation structure, 218-219
New dialog box, 166
New File dialog box, 69
New FrontPage Web dialog box, 172
New Task dialog box, 96, 208
Normal views (Editor), 17
numbered lists, 72

O

Object Parameters dialog box, 159
online help (Image Composer), 28
Open FrontPage Web command (File menu), 82, 189
Open FrontPage Web dialog box, 83
Open Web dialog box, 82
Open With dialog box, 200
opening existing Web pages, 70-71
Options command
    Tools menu, 201
    View menu, 244
Options dialog box, 202

outlining sprites, 285-286
ovals (graphical text), 271-272

P

Page Banner component, 181-182
    Properties dialog box, 181
Page Properties command (File menu), 106, 297
Page Properties dialog box, 106, 120, 132, 144, 297
Page Transition dialog box, 235
page transitions (dynamic HTML), 235-236
Paint palette, 254
    Image Composer, 250
paintbrush tool, 46
    Image Composer, 291
palettes (Image Composer), 247-253
Paragraph command (Format menu), 106
Paragraph Properties dialog box, 106, 231
paragraphs, adding to Web pages, 108-109
    horizontal rules, 112-113
    logical text styles, 111-112
    resizing HTML text, 110-111
    text, justifying, 111
passwords, authenticating (Web page administration), 31
Paste command (Edit menu), 71
Pattern effects, 280-281
    colors, changing, 281
    gradient fills, 282-283
    sprites
        color tuning, 289-290
        filtering, 286-289
        outlining, 285-286
        warp transformations, 290-291
    texture transfer effects, 283-285

tools
　airbrush, 291
　Impression, 292
　paintbrush, 291
　pencil, 291
　Rubber Stamp, 293
　Smear, 292
　Transfer, 293

PCX image files, 124

pencil tool (Image Composer), 291

Personal Web Server, 44-45
　FrontPage Editor, 19-20
　installing, 29-35
　　WWW Administration pages, 30-34
　　interface, 45

Perspective Warps (sprites), 291

planning Web sites, 56-59
　change, incorporating, 58-59
　content, 56-57
　layout, 59
　style, 57-58

platforms (server extensions), 314-315
　UNIX, 316-317
　Windows 95, 315-316
　Windows NT, 315-316

plug-ins
　Image Composer, 47
　　Impressionist, 28
　inserting, 156-157
　ScriptActive, 153

PNGs, 47, 124, 135-139
　file formats, converting, 137-138
　Low Res option, 138
　transparent images, 138-139

polygons (graphical text), 274

Preview in Browser command (File menu), 80

Preview In Browser dialog box, 80

Preview views (Editor), 17

previewing Web pages, 77

Print Navigation View command (File menu), 195

Priority column (Task view), 207

Progressive Networks Web site, 143

proofing tools, 26

properties
　JavaScript, 150
　table
　　adjusting, 114-116
　　cell properties, 116-117

protocols
　FTP (File Transfer Protocol), 12
　HTTP (Hypertext Transfer Protocol), 12

Publish FrontPage Web command (File menu), 97, 191

Publish FrontPage Web dialog box, 191

publishing Web sites, 97-98, 190-191

Q-R

QuickTime video, 145

Ready to Run Software Web site, 317

RealAudio
　adding to Web pages, 143
　Web site, 143

RealVideo, 144-145

Recalculate Hyperlinks command (Tools menu), 95, 213

recommendations, hardware (installing FrontPage 98), 21

rectangles (graphical text), 271-272

remote-side, *see* **server-side**

resizing
　HTML text, 110-111
　images (Appearance Sheet), 130-131
　sprites, 277

rotating
　graphical text, 267-268
　sprites, 277

Rubber Stamp tool (Image Composer), 293

S

Sample character style, 112

Sample Sprites Catalog (background images), 306-307

Save As command (File menu), 172

Save As Template dialog box, 172

Save command (File menu), 77, 80

scanning images, 127

Scheduled Image component, 177, 182

Scheduled Image Properties dialog box, 182

Scheduled Include component, 182

Scheduled Include Page component, 177

<SCRIPT> HTML tag, 148

Script dialog box, 149, 152, 154

Script Wizard, 152, 154-155

ScriptActive plug-in, 153

scripting
　Web pages, 148-161
　　ActiveX controls, inserting, 157-161
　　Java applets, 161-163
　　JavaScript, 149-152
　　plug-ins, inserting, 156-157
　　Script Wizard, 154-155
　　VBScript, 152-154
　　VRML (Virtual Reality Modeling Language), 163-164

scripts, executing (JavaScript), 152

SDK (Software Development Kit), 18

Secure Sockets Layer, *see* **SSL**

security, passwords, authenticating, 31
Select Background Image dialog box, 132, 297
SERK (Server Extensions Resource Kit), 26, 317
servers, 312
    extensions, 14, 312-315
        SERK (Server Extensions Resource Kit), 317
        suggested platforms, 314-315
        UNIX platforms, 316-318
        Windows 95 platforms, 315-318
        Windows NT platforms, 315-318
    Server Extension Administration Forms, 26
    Server Extension Resource Kit, see SERK
    Web, 13
        connections, 29
        Personal Web Server, 19-20, 29-35, 44-45
        Server Extensions, 34
        WWW Administration pages, 30-34
Setup Wizard, 25
Shapes palette, 254, 273
    Image Composer, 250
shared borders (Web site navigation structure), 219-222
Shared Borders dialog box, 220
Show All Hyperlinks command (View menu), 216
shrinking HTML text, 110-111
.shtml file extension, 14
Silicon Graphics Web site, 164
sites (Web), 13-14
    Explorer, loading into, 82-83
    Image Bazaar, 297
    JavaScript Authoring Guide, 151
    Meshmart VRML Page, 164
    Microsoft
        ActiveX, 161
        Knowledge Base, 318
        Progressive Networks, 143
        Ready to Run Software, 317
        RealAudio, 143
        SERK (Server Extensions Resource Kit), 317
    server extensions, 14
    Silicon Graphics, 164
    themes, 26
    VRML Repository, 164
    Yahoo!, 58
Size to Fit command (View menu), 219
sizing graphical text, 267-268
Skew Warps (sprites), 291
Smear tool (Image Composer), 292
Snip effect (texture transfers), 284
Software Development Kit, see SDK
sound, adding to Web pages, 142-144
    AU files, 143
    backgound music, 143-144
    linking to audio files, 144
    MIDI files, 142
    RealAudio, 143
    WAV files, 143
spacing (between text and images), 130
spell checking (Web sites), 95, 209-213
Spelling command (Tools menu), 210
splines (graphical text), 273-274
Spoke Inversion effect (Image Composer), 293
sprites
    attributes (texture transfer effects), 283-285
    color tuning, 289-290
    filtering, 286-289
        group summary, 288
    graphical text
        aligning, 275
        cropping, 277-278
        flattening, 277
        grouping, 275-277
        home positions, 278
        moving forward and back, 275
        resizing, 277-278
        rotating, 277-278
    Image Composer, 46
        copying and changing, 255-256
        creating and editing, 253-255
    outlining, 285-286
    Sample Sprites Catalog, 306-307
    warp transformations, 290-291
SSL (Secure Sockets Layer), 83
Status column (Task view), 206
Strike-through character style, 112
Strong character style, 112
style (planning Web sites), 57-58
Style dialog box, 226
styles
    CDF files (Channel Definition Format), 236-240
    creating (Cascading Style Sheets), 225-229
    defined, 231
    dynamic HTML, 231-233
        collapsible outlines, creating, 233-234
        form field extensions, 234-235
        page transitions, 235-236
        text animations, 235-236
    external style sheets, linking to, 229-231
    HTML text (logical styles), 111-113
    inline, 231
Stylesheet command (Format menu), 225
Substitution component, 177, 183
syntax (JavaScript), 150-151
    braces, 150
    case-sensitivity, 150
    comments, 151
    functions and commands, 150
    properties, 150

T

Table menu commands
    Draw Table, 74
    Insert Table, 74

Table of Contents component, 176, 178
    Properties dialog box, 178

Table Properties dialog box, 114

tables, 42, 73-74
    Web page design, 113-117
        cell properties, 116-117
        properties, adjusting, 114-116

tags, HTML, <SCRIPT>, 148

Task column (Task view), 206

Task Details dialog box, 96, 209

Task History command (View menu), 209

task lists (creating Web sites), 96-97

Tasks command (View menu), 96, 207-208

Tasks view, 200, 206-209
    columns, 206-207

templates
    Three Column Layout, 70
    Web pages, 166-172
        creating, 69-71
        creating your own, 172
        frames, 168-171
    Web sites, building, 62-65

terminology, 12

text
    adding to Web pages, 108-109
    alternative, 132
    animating (dynamic HTML), 235-236
    deleting (creating Web pages), 71-72
    editing (creating Web pages), 71-72
    graphical, 262-266, 268-271
        aligning sprites, 275
        cropping sprites, 277-278
        curves, 273-274
        flattening sprites, 277
        grouping sprites, 275-277
        moving sprites (forward and back), 275
        polygons, 274
        rectangles and ovals, 271-272
        resizing sprites, 277-278
        rotating sprites, 277-278
        sizing and rotating, 267-268
        sprites, 278
        zigzag lines, 274
    HTML (HyperText Markup Language)
        enlarging and shrinking, 110-111
        horizontal rules, 112-113
        justification, 111
        logical styles, 111-112
    placing around images, 129-130
    spacing between images, 130
    Web page design (changing colors), 120

Text Box Properties dialog box, 234

Text control palette (Image Composer), 249

texture transfer effects (Pattern effects), 283-285
    palette (Image Composer), 250

themes, 26
    Web Theme dialog box, 64

Themes view, 198

Three Column Layout template, 70

thumbnails, 134

TIFFs, 47, 124

Tile effect (texture transfers), 284

Timestamp component, 176-178
    Properties dialog box, 177

Tint tool (Image Composer), 293

tinting effects
    Burn/Dodge tool, 292
    Colorize tool, 292
    Contrast tool, 292
    Eraser tool, 292
    Tint tool, 293

titles, adding to Web pages, 105-106

To Do Lists, 16

tools (Image Composer), 247-253
    airbrush, 291
    Burn/Dodge, 292
    Colorize, 292
    Contrast, 292
    Eraser, 292
    Impression, 292
    Mesa, 293
    paintbrush, 291
    pencil, 291
    Rubber Stamp, 293
    Smear, 292
    Spoke Inversion, 293
    Tint, 293
    Transfer, 293
    Vortex, 293

Tools menu commands
    Define Channel, 237
    Options, 201
    Recalculate Hyperlinks, 95, 213
    Spelling, 210
    Verify Hyperlinks, 94, 216

Transfer Full effect (texture transfers), 284

Transfer Shape effect (texture transfers), 284

Transfer tool (Image Composer), 293

transparent images, 138-139
    GIFs, 302-303

tutorial samples (Image Composer), 28

U-V

UNIX (server extensions), 316-318

utilities (Editor), 18
    Image Composer, 18-19
    Personal Web Server, 19-20
    Web Publishing Wizard, 20

values (style), 226

Variable character style, 112

VBScript, 148, 152-154

VDOLive video, 145
Verify Hyperlinks command (Tools menu), 94, 216
video
   adding to Web pages, 144-145
      AVI file, 144-145
      RealVideo, 144-145
Video for Windows (.avi), 14
View menu commands
   All Files View, 85
   Expand All, 219
   Folders View, 83
   Format Marks, 152
   Hyperlink View, 195
   Hyperlinks, 87, 214
   Image Toolbar, 141
   Navigation View, 86
   Options, 244
   Show All Hyperlinks, 216
   Size to Fit, 219
   Task History, 209
   Tasks, 96, 207-208
views
   Explorer, 83-89, 191-200
      All Files, 85
      Folder, 191
      Folders, 83-84
      Hyperlink Status, 195
      Hyperlinks, 86-89, 195
      Navigation, 86, 192
      Tasks, 200
      Themes view, 198
   HTML (Editor), 17
   Hyperlink (internal links), 213-215
   Hyperlink Status (external links), 215-217
   Normal (Editor), 17
   Preview (Editor), 17
   Tasks, 206-209
      columns, 206-207
virtual directories, 33
   adding, 33
   deleting, 33
   editing, 33
Virtual Reality Modeling Language, *see* VRML
Vortex tool (Image Composer), 293
VRML (Virtual Reality Modeling Language), 150, 163-164
   Repository Web site, 164

W

warp effects
   Mesa tool, 293
   Spoke Inversion, 293
   transformations (sprites), 290-291
   Vortex tool, 293
WAV files, adding to Web pages, 14, 143
Web browsers, 102
Web pages, 13
   adding (with Explorer), 89-91
   audio, 142-144
      AU files, 143
      backgound music, 143-144
      linking to files, 144
      MIDI files, 142
      RealAudio, 143
      WAV files, 143
   Cascading Style Sheets, 224-225
      CDF files (Channel Definition Format), 236-240
      defined styles, 231
      dynamic HTML, 231-236
      external style sheets, linking to, 229-231
      inline styles, 231
      styles, creating, 225-229
   components, 176-183
      Comment, 179-180
      Confirmation Field, 180
      Hit Counter, 180
      Include Page, 181
      Insert HTML, 181
      Navigation Bar, 179
      Page Banner, 181-182
      Scheduled Image, 182
      Scheduled Include, 182
      Substitution, 183
      Table of Contents, 178
      Timestamp, 177-178
   creating, 68-70, 102-105
      adding blank pages (from within Explorer), 68
      adding text, 71-72
      blank pages, adding from within Explorer, 68
      creating blank pages (with Editor), 69
      cutting text, 71-72
      deleting text, 71-72
      editing text, 71-72
      existing pages, opening, 70-71
      hyperlinks, 74-77
      layout, 104-113
      lists, 72-73
      previewing and saving, 77
      tables, 73-74
      templates and wizards, 69-70
   default startup documents, 33
   deleting (with Explorer), 91-92
   graphical text, 262-266, 268-271
      aligning sprites, 275
      cropping sprites, 277-278
      curves, 273-274
      flattening sprites, 277
      grouping sprites, 275-277
      moving sprites (forward and back), 275
      polygons, 274
      rectangles and ovals, 271-272
      resizing sprites, 277-278
      rotating sprites, 277-278
      sizing and rotating, 267-268
      sprites, 278
      zigzag lines, 274
   images, 124-134
      alignment choices, 130
      alternative text, 132
      animated GIFs, 303-305
      Appearance Sheet size adjustments, 130-131
      as hyperlinks, 133-134
      background, 132-133, 296-298
      borders, adding, 132
      clip art, 127
      compression levels, 299-301
      deleting from, 125
      GIFs, 135-139, 298, 301-302
      imagemaps, 140-142
      inserting, 124-127
      JPEGs, 135-139, 298
      modifying, 127-129
      navigational controls, 134
      placing text around, 129-130
      PNGs, 135-139

Sample Sprites Catalog, 306-307
scanning, 127
spacing between text and images, 130
thumbnails, 134
transparent GIFs, 302-303
watermarked backgrounds, 133
scripting, 148-161
    ActiveX controls, inserting, 157-161
    Java applets, 161-163
    JavaScript, 149-152
    plug-ins, inserting, 156-157
    Script Wizard, 154-155
    VBScript, 152-154
    VRML (Virtual Reality Modeling Language), 163-164
templates, 166-172
    creating your own, 172
    frames, 168-171
video, 144, 145
    AVI files, 144-145
    RealVideo, 144-145
viewing (Editor), 17
views
    Browser Panel, 200-201
    View Panel, 191-200
wizards, 172-175
    Discussion Web, 172-173
    Form Page, 174-175

Web Publishing Wizard, 49-51
    FrontPage Editor, 20
    interface, 50

Web servers, 13
    connections, 29
    Personal Web Server, 19-20, 44-45
        installing, 29-35
        interface, 45
        Server Extensions, 34
        WWW Administration pages, 30-34

Web sites, 13-14
    building
        from scratch, 66
        importing existing sites, 59-62
        wizards and templates, 62-65

Cascading Style Sheets, 224-225
    CDF files (Channel Definition Format), 236-240
    defined styles, 231
    dynamic HTML, 231-236
    external style sheets, linking to, 229-231
    inline styles, 231
    styles, creating, 225-229
creating
    adding pages (with Explorer), 89-91
    deleting pages (with Explorer), 91-92
    recalculating hyperlinks, 94-95
    reorganizing, 92-93
    spell checking, 95
    Task lists, 96-97
    verifying hyperlinks, 94-95
Editor, 40-44
    interface, 42-43
existing, importing, 59-62
Explorer, loading into, 82-83
graphical text, 262-266, 268-271
    aligning sprites, 275
    cropping sprites, 277-278
    curves, 273-274
    flattening sprites, 277
    grouping sprites, 275-277
    moving sprites (forward and back), 275
    polygons, 274
    rectangles and ovals, 271-272
    resizing sprites, 277-278
    rotating sprites, 277-278
    sizing and rotating, 267-268
    sprites, 278
    zigzag lines, 274
hyperlinks
    Hyperlink Status view (external links), 215-217
    Hyperlink view (internal links), 213-215
    recalculating, 213
JavaScript Authoring Guide, 151
Image Bazaar, 297
loading, 188-190

Meshmart VRML Page, 164
Microsoft
    ActiveX, 161
    Knowledge Base Web site, 318
navigation structure
    Navigation view, 218-219
    shared borders, 219-222
planning, 56-59
    change, incorporating, 58-59
    content, 56-57
    layout, 59
    style, 57-58
Progressive Networks, 143
publishing, 97-98, 190-191
Ready to Run Software, 317
RealAudio, 143
SERK (Server Extensions Resource Kit), 317
server extensions, 14
Silicon Graphics, 164
spell checking, 209-213
themes, 26
views, 83-89
    All Files, 85
    Browser Panel, 200-201
    Folders, 83-84
    Hyperlinks, 86-89
    Navigation, 86
    View Panel, 191-200
VRML Repository, 164
Yahoo!, 58

Web Theme dialog box, 64

Windows 95 server extensions, 315-318

Windows Bitmaps, 14

Windows File Open dialog box, 70

Windows NT server extensions, 315-318

wizards
    Corporate Presence, 62
    Image Composer Setup, 27
    Import, 60, 190
    Install, 24
    Script, 152, 154-155
    Setup, 25
    Web pages, 172-175
        creating, 69-71
        Discussion Web, 172-173
        Form Page, 174-175

wizards
    Web Publishing Wizard, 20,
        49-51
    Web sites, building, 62-65
**Word Art (Image Composer),
    28, 262**
WWW (World Wide Web)
    Editor, 40-44
        interface, 42-43
    Image Composer, 46-49
        interface, 47-48
    Personal Web Server, 44-45
        interface, 45
    Web Publishing Wizard, 49-51
        interface, 50
**WYSIWYG (What-You-See-Is-
    What-You-Get), 13**

X-Y-Z

Xing StreamWorks video, 145

Yahoo! Web site, 58

zigzag lines
    (graphical text), 274

Complete and Return this Card for a *FREE* Computer Book Catalog

Thank you for purchasing this book! You have purchased a superior computer book written expressly for your needs. To continue to provide the kind of up-to-date, pertinent coverage you've come to expect from us, we need to hear from you. Please take a minute to complete and return this self-addressed, postage-paid form. In return, we'll send you a free catalog of all our computer books on topics ranging from word processing to programming and the internet.

Mr. ☐   Mrs. ☐   Ms. ☐   Dr. ☐

Name (first) ☐☐☐☐☐☐☐☐☐☐☐☐☐ (M.I.) ☐ (last) ☐☐☐☐☐☐☐☐☐☐☐☐☐☐☐☐☐☐

Address ☐☐☐☐☐☐☐☐☐☐☐☐☐☐☐☐☐☐☐☐☐☐☐☐☐☐☐☐☐☐☐☐☐☐☐☐

City ☐☐☐☐☐☐☐☐☐☐☐☐ State ☐☐ Zip ☐☐☐☐☐ ☐☐☐☐

Phone ☐☐☐ ☐☐☐ ☐☐☐☐ Fax ☐☐☐ ☐☐☐ ☐☐☐☐

Company Name ☐☐☐☐☐☐☐☐☐☐☐☐☐☐☐☐☐☐☐☐☐☐☐☐☐☐☐☐☐☐☐☐☐

E-mail address ☐☐☐☐☐☐☐☐☐☐☐☐☐☐☐☐☐☐☐☐☐☐☐☐☐☐☐☐☐☐☐☐☐

1. Please check at least (3) influencing factors for purchasing this book.

Front or back cover information on book .... ☐
Special approach to the content .... ☐
Completeness of content .... ☐
Author's reputation .... ☐
Publisher's reputation .... ☐
Book cover design or layout .... ☐
Index or table of contents of book .... ☐
Price of book .... ☐
Special effects, graphics, illustrations .... ☐
Other (Please specify): _____ ☐

2. How did you first learn about this book?

Saw in Macmillan Computer Publishing catalog .... ☐
Recommended by store personnel .... ☐
Saw the book on bookshelf at store .... ☐
Recommended by a friend .... ☐
Received advertisement in the mail .... ☐
Saw an advertisement in: _____ ☐
Read book review in: _____ ☐
Other (Please specify): _____ ☐

3. How many computer books have you purchased in the last six months?

This book only .... ☐   3 to 5 books .... ☐
2 books .... ☐   More than 5 .... ☐

4. Where did you purchase this book?

Bookstore .... ☐
Computer Store .... ☐
Consumer Electronics Store .... ☐
Department Store .... ☐
Office Club .... ☐
Warehouse Club .... ☐
Mail Order .... ☐
Direct from Publisher .... ☐
Internet site .... ☐
Other (Please specify): _____ ☐

5. How long have you been using a computer?

☐ Less than 6 months   ☐ 6 months to a year
☐ 1 to 3 years   ☐ More than 3 years

6. What is your level of experience with personal computers and with the subject of this book?

	With PCs	With subject of book
New	☐	☐
Casual	☐	☐
Accomplished	☐	☐
Expert	☐	☐

Source Code ISBN: 0-7897-1497-3

7. Which of the following best describes your job title?

- [ ] Administrative Assistant
- [ ] Coordinator
- [ ] Manager/Supervisor
- [ ] Director
- [ ] Vice President
- [ ] President/CEO/COO
- [ ] Lawyer/Doctor/Medical Professional
- [ ] Teacher/Educator/Trainer
- [ ] Engineer/Technician
- [ ] Consultant
- [ ] Not employed/Student/Retired
- [ ] Other (Please specify): _____

8. Which of the following best describes the area of the company your job title falls under?

- [ ] Accounting
- [ ] Engineering
- [ ] Manufacturing
- [ ] Operations
- [ ] Marketing
- [ ] Sales
- [ ] Other (Please specify): _____

9. What is your age?

- [ ] Under 20
- [ ] 21-29
- [ ] 30-39
- [ ] 40-49
- [ ] 50-59
- [ ] 60-over

10. Are you:

- [ ] Male
- [ ] Female

11. Which computer publications do you read regularly? (Please list)

_____
_____
_____
_____
_____
_____
_____
_____

Comments: _____

Fold here and scotch-tape to mail

BUSINESS REPLY MAIL
FIRST-CLASS MAIL PERMIT NO. 9918 INDIANAPOLIS IN

POSTAGE WILL BE PAID BY THE ADDRESSEE

ATTN MARKETING
MACMILLAN COMPUTER PUBLISHING
MACMILLAN PUBLISHING USA
201 W 103RD ST
INDIANAPOLIS IN 46290-9042

NO POSTAGE NECESSARY IF MAILED IN THE UNITED STATES